Young Masculinities

D0176966

Also by Stephen Frosh

* *The Politics of Psychoanalysis*
  For and Against Psychoanalysis
  Sexual Difference
* *Identity Crisis*
* *Psychoanalysis and Psychology*
  Psychoanalysis in Contexts (with A. Elliott)
* *Child Sexual Abuse* (with D. Glaser)
* *The Politics of Mental Health* (with R. Banton, P. Clifford,
  J. Lousada and J. Rosenthall)

Also by Ann Phoenix

Standpoints and Differences (with K. Henwood and C. Griffin)
Crossfires (with H. Lutz and N. Yuval-Davis)
Black, White or Mixed Race? (with B. Tizard)
Motherhood: Meanings, Practices and Ideologies (with A. Woollett
  and E. Lloyd)
Young Mothers?

* *From the same publishers*

Young Masculinities

Understanding Boys in Contemporary Society

Stephen Frosh, Ann Phoenix and Rob Pattman

WITHDRAWN

© Stephen Frosh, Ann Phoenix and Rob Pattman 2002

All rights reserved. No reproduction, copy or transmission
of this publication may be made without written permission.

No paragraph of this publication may be reproduced, copied or
transmitted save with written permission or in accordance with
the provisions of the Copyright, Designs and Patents Act 1988,
or under the terms of any licence permitting limited copying
issued by the Copyright Licensing Agency, 90 Tottenham Court
Road, London W1P OLP.

Any person who does any unauthorised act in relation to this
publication may be liable to criminal prosecution and civil
claims for damages.

The authors have asserted their rights to be identified
as the authors of this work in accordance with the
Copyright, Designs and Patents Act 1988.

First published 2002 by
PALGRAVE
Houndmills, Basingstoke, Hampshire RG21 6XS and
175 Fifth Avenue, New York, N. Y. 10010
Companies and representatives throughout the world

PALGRAVE is the new global academic imprint of
St. Martin's Press LLC Scholarly and Reference Division and
Palgrave Publishers Ltd (formerly Macmillan Press Ltd).

ISBN 0–333–77922–3 hardback
ISBN 0–333–77923–1 paperback

This book is printed on paper suitable for recycling and
made from fully managed and sustained forest sources.

A catalogue record for this book is available
from the British Library.

10   9   8   7   6   5   4   3
11   10   09   08   07   06   05   04

Printed in China

KEELE UNIVERSITY

− 6 FEB 2006

10125590

Contents

Acknowledgements

The research study which formed the basis for this book was funded by the Economic and Social Research Council (grant reference L/129/25/1015) as part of a programme of research entitled 'Children 5–16', directed by Alan Prout. We would like to express our thanks to the ESRC and to Alan Prout, not just for the funding, but for the encouragement and intellectual stimulation received from them over the course of the project. We also want to thank the members of the project Advisory Group (Debbie Epstein, Wendy Hollway, David Jackson, Gill Lenderyou, Michael Marland and Peter Redman), who offered considerable help to us in thinking through the planning and analysis of the research. The feedback received from anonymous referees of the project has been additionally helpful to us.

Additional funds were obtained from Birkbeck College, University of London, to support the interviews with girls, and we are grateful for this.

We wish particularly to thank, albeit anonymously, the schools which allowed us access to their students. We had enormous help from a range of headteachers, year heads and class teachers without which the research could not have proceeded. Most of all, of course, this project depended totally on the involvement and interest of the young people who we interviewed, in groups or individually, and we are immensely grateful to them for their goodwill, energy and thoughtfulness.

Finally, this book is dedicated to some specific young people: Aisha, Daniel, Joel and Arieh.

S.F.

A.P.

R.P.

Introduction

Many researchers in the area of gender and identity have drawn attention to an apparent 'crisis' in contemporary forms of masculinity, marked by uncertainties over social role and identity, sexuality, work and personal relationships – and often manifested in violence or abusive behaviours towards self and others (e.g. Frosh, 1994, 2000; Jukes, 1993; Seidler, 1989). If there is such a crisis, it presumably has roots in a range of social phenomena. These include the collapse of traditional men's work, the growth of a technological culture which cannot be 'passed on' in any recognisable way between the generations, the rise of feminist consciousness amongst women, and, more abstractly, challenges to the dominance of the forms of rationality with which masculinity has been identified, at least in the West (e.g. Connell, 1995; Seidler, 1994; Segal, 1990). It also both reflects and contributes to the production of a parallel developmental 'crisis' for boys, engaged in the process of identity construction in a context in which there are few clear models and in which the surrounding images of masculinity are complex and confused.

This situation is also reflected in the way masculinities, particularly those of young men, have been seen as problematic within British society. We have used the terms 'boys' and 'young men' fairly interchangeably in this book, reflecting a considerable amount of ambiguity in the literature. What we are referring to is a period mainly in the teenage years in which boys are becoming acculturated (or acculturating themselves) into increasingly salient masculine identities. Much of the social concern hinges around the control of young men's masculinities in the interest of maintaining social order, with particular reference to criminality and child abuse. Indices of gender-specific disturbance in adolescence, such as delinquency and sexual abuse perpetration, suggest that this is a particularly important period. Thus, delinquency rates in boys peak at age 17 (Farrington, 1995) and a substantial proportion of convicted or cautioned sex offenders are in the 10 to 16-year-old age group (Vizard *et al.*,

1995). More generally, changes in employment and in normative gender relations mean that boys and young men are having to forge new, more flexible masculine identities. Developing an understanding of the ways in which they manage this task is made especially complex by the fact that masculinities are racialised and expressed through social class positions (Back, 1994; Edley and Wetherell, 1995; Westwood, 1990). For example, in the social identities study of 14–18 year olds carried out by Ann Phoenix (Tizard and Phoenix, 1993), there were social class and racialised differences between boys in terms of their everyday experiences of masculinity. Generalisations about the experience and identities of boys and young men therefore require considerable qualification.

In response to concerns over this supposed crisis in masculinity, various researchers have addressed questions relevant to the understanding of how boys and men are dealing with social changes. The study of boys and masculinities is not new (although the ways in which boys in late-middle childhood and early adolescence construct their masculine identities have received little attention, an omission we set out to remedy in our own work). Indeed, Willis' (1977) study of white working-class young men making the transition from school to employment produced findings which fit with current claims that masculine cultures are violent, misogynist and anti-school. However, a decade or two ago it was more easily assumed that even if specific groups of boys and young men were considered problematic because of their poor educational performance and culture of toughness (e.g. working-class and/or black boys), this was not to be seen as a general problem with masculinities. More recent writers have been inclined to assume the existence of such a general problem and have suggested a variety of (sometimes contradictory) explanations, including the absence of adult male role models in the classroom (Pollack, 1998), boys' problematic behavioural styles (e.g. Jackson, 1998; Salmon, 1998) and the impact of feminism (Kryger, 1998).

Some researchers have pointed out, however, that the evidence on which notions of a 'crisis' in masculinity has been constructed is not as robust as might be expected. For example, they argue that the choices made of educational statistics for comparison are frequently selected in order to make specific political points; that there has been a neglect of the fact that working-class and black boys have always done badly, while the most privileged boys continue to do well; that much work romanticises boyhood; and that there is an implicit blaming of girls, women teachers and feminists and neglect of the fact that half of all girls in Britain do not gain five grades A–C at GCSE (the standard measure of academic success). These issues have all been identified as making simple explanations of the underachievement of boys in terms of some essential mismatch between school achievement and the masculine psyche, or masculine socialisation, less than helpful (Epstein *et al.*, 1998; Reed, 1999; Skelton, 1998; Yates, 1997). Instead, these researchers argue that the ways in which boys act as masculine, and their masculine identities, need to be seen as gendered practices which are relational, contradictory and multiple. In this respect, a gap in our current understanding of boys and masculinities is of complex notions of what it means to 'do boy' in specific contexts (Connell, 1996; Davies, 1997), that is, of the multifarious ways in which young masculinities are made.

For reasons such as these, we have come to view gender as performative and relational. Here we are drawing on work arguing that masculinity exists only in relation to femininity and is *constructed*, through everyday discourses, in various 'versions' or *masculinities* (e.g. Edley and Wetherell, 1997; Mac an Ghaill, 1994). This is not to say that boys and men create themselves out of nothing, in any way they wish. Rather, there are popular and culturally specific ways of positioning boys and men which, for example, emphasise their toughness and propensity for 'action', whether it be harmless, responsible or disruptive. In this regard, our work follows ethnographic and discursive studies that address boys' cultural practices (see Chapter 2). These studies converge on the idea (first developed by Connell, 1987, 1995) that it is possible to view constructions of masculinity as the products of interpersonal work, accomplished through the exploitation of available cultural resources such as the ideologies prevalent in particular societies. There are two especially key issues here: first, the everyday practices associated with what Connell (1995) theorises as 'hegemonic' masculinity (the ways in which 'approved' modes of being male are produced, supported, contested and resisted, discussed in Chapter 3) and, secondly, the commonalities and differences in gendered identities created by, for example, social class and 'race'. Few studies in this area have taken this theoretical perspective to identity and fewer still have included a mix of 'racialised' and social class groups as well as girls in order to get a broad understanding of gendered identities.

In the study described in this book, we aimed to enhance understanding of the ways in which the gendered subject positions that boys occupy arise, as well as of differences between boys in their 'performances' of masculinities. Such differences between boys potentially allow spaces for intervention and change through social policy, educational and youth-work practices. The research addresses boys and young men as people whose identities are continually reinvented in the accounts they produce as they construct and re-construct gender and sexuality. They are, thus, active participants in the research process, in that our core interest is in trying to understand what they say about themselves and their experiences from the boys' own points of view. However, being 'boy-centred' in our work does not imply uncritical acceptance of boys' versions of themselves; rather, it builds on the idea of masculinities as *achieved* – a set of practices (Wetherell and Edley, 1999), 'performative acts' (Butler, 1990; Nyak and Kehily, 1996) or ways of 'doing' gender (Bohan, 1997) related to the social contexts in which they are found. Boys' accounts and ethnographic descriptions of their activities give access to this performance, but still require interpretation.

Clearly, the choice of interpretive framework is a central issue for researchers engaged in work which focuses on accounts and, hence, language, yet does not take these as unproblematic or 'transparent'. In the recent literature on boys and young men, with its focus on the production of masculine subjectivities, a combination of psychoanalytic and social constructionist perspectives has become apparent. In an influential article, Hollway (1984: 238) argues that any description of the formation of subjectivities 'requires an account of the investment that a person has in taking up one position rather than another in a different discourse', and she looks to psychoanalytic theory for help in providing such an account. Similarly, researchers alert to the emotional and psychic investments of particular boys in the kinds of subject positions available to them in various contexts, have increasingly been drawing on psychoanalytic categories to flesh out their explanations (e.g. Nyak and Kehily, 1996; Redman and Mac an Ghaill, 1997). Contemporary research on masculinities is consequently in a stronger position to question different boys' psychic investments, as well as how subject positions are constructed and sustained by projecting anxieties and desires on to others – for example, girls in general, as well as particular girls and particular boys. It is upon this combination of social scientific theories of identities with psychoanalytic ideas that our study is based.

The general orienting perspective which we adopt is that a person's 'identity' is in fact something multiple and potentially fluid, constructed through experience and linguistically coded. In developing their identities, people draw on culturally available resources in their immediate social networks and in society as a whole. These 'resources' are, generally speaking, strongly gendered, with males and females receiving different messages, being constrained differently, and having access to different codes. Identity and gender consequently stand in a dynamic relationship to one another: 'gender identity' is a central component in identity construction as a whole; conversely, identities of various kinds (ethnic, class, geographical etc.) are deeply infiltrated by gender issues. For example, the experience of inhabiting the identity of 'black man (or boy)' is likely to be different from that of 'white man (or boy)', but also different from 'black woman (or girl)'. The process of identity-construction is therefore one upon which the contradictions and dispositions of the surrounding socio-cultural environment have a powerful impact. This is one reason why an individual may find it difficult to describe the sources and nature of her or his various identities. In line with many discursive psychologists who are looking for constructs and methods which will enable them to analyse the positions taken up by people in terms other than those employed by the 'subjects' themselves – for example, Hollway (1989), Billig (1992) – we suggest that attention to the gaps in discourse, the contradictions, silences and other absences, is an important strategy for conceptualising the limits of conscious articulation. Drawing on contemporary psychoanalytic theory, we argue that the structures of gendered identity are complex and 'over-determined' (Benjamin, 1995; Frosh, 1994) and that it is likely this will be revealed in indirect ways in the narratives and responses of interviewees. Our study therefore employs an analytic framework with a focus on emotionally laden material, on absences as well as presences in the 'texts', as a way of documenting both the conscious positions taken up by boys in the period of early adolescence, and their less clearly articulated wishes and anxieties.

The research: emergent identities, masculinities and 11–14-year-old boys

This book offers a description and exploration of emerging masculinities in the early teenage years. It arises out of a large research project on 11–14-year-old boys in London schools, carried out by the authors from 1997 onwards. It examines aspects of 'young masculinities' which have become central to contemporary social thought, paying attention both to psychological formulations and to social policy concerns. It also addresses research on young men (particularly ethnographic research in schools) before considering in detail the findings of our own research project. This entails in-depth exploration, through individual and group interviews, of the way boys in the early years of secondary schooling conceptualise and articulate their experience of themselves, their peers and the adult world. The research project investigates boys' aspirations and anxieties, their pride and loss. As such, it offers an unusually detailed set of insights into the experiential world inhabited by these boys – how they see themselves, what they wish for and fear, where they feel their accession to 'masculinity' to be advantageous and where it inhibits other potential experiences. In describing this material, we explore questions such as the place of violence in young people's lives, the functions of 'hardness', of homophobia and football, the discourse of boys' underachievement in school, and the pervasive racialisation of masculine identity construction. Our findings, we believe, will be of profound interest to researchers in psychology, sociology, gender and youth studies, as well as to those determining social policy on boys and young men.

A major concern in this research was to be able to accurately represent boys' thinking on their own emergent masculine identities. Our aim was to develop a methodology for interviewing and analysis in which boys would be encouraged to speak freely, allowing them space for reflection and revision of their views whilst also enabling the researchers to address issues of specific theoretical and practical concern. Our method built on recent innovative work in narrative and discourse analysis (e.g. Riessman, 1993) and on the 'clinical interviewing' technique described by Hollway and Jefferson (2000).

The sample

Our original plan was to run an intensive, 'qualitative' study based on in-depth interviews with 40 boys from London schools, seen twice each, plus 38 group interviews with boys and some girls. In the event, as we describe below, both of these numerical targets were exceeded. This was for two main reasons. First, we aimed to have a sample stratified by 'race' and social class in both the group and individual interviews so that we could make at least some statements about the influence these factors have on masculine identities. As is common in 'real-life research', this cannot neatly be organised. This factor, in conjunction with the second reason – that many boys were extremely eager to be interviewed and it was ethically desirable to disappoint as few as possible – led to more time being spent in the recruitment and interviewing process than we had orig-inally intended. The final sample is described below.

Our original proposal involved the interviewing of some mixed groups of girls and boys about masculinity. However, as the research developed, it became clear to us that the design could be improved by the addition of a sample of girls in order to avoid what some have called the 'over-gendering' of boys (e.g. Mac an Ghaill, 2000). We therefore appointed a female psychologist (Ruksana Patel) to interview girls individually about their views on boys, masculinity and gendered relations. These data allow us to compare girls' and boys' narratives on masculinities and to avoid erroneously thinking that issues that preoccupy both boys and girls are only of interest to boys. The interview material with girls is described in a separate chapter in the book (Chapter 5) as well as at various points throughout.

Participants

The boys were drawn from 12 secondary schools in London. These schools comprised four in the private ('independent') and eight in the state education sector, four of which are boys' schools and eight co-educational. In addition, 24 girls were interviewed; these girls were drawn from four of the same schools as the boys. We conducted 45 group interviews with groups usually of 4–6 young people (and a range from 4–8). Thirty-six of these group interviews were with boys in single-sex groups and nine interviews were with mixed groups of boys and girls about boys. This involved a sample of 245 boys and 27 girls.

Seventy-eight volunteers from the boys who had taken part in the group interviews were selected for individual interviews. The design of the study was for a follow-up to the individual interview approximately two weeks after the first interview and 71 boys were given a second interview. In seven cases, boys were either away from school when we returned or suspended. We also interviewed 24 girls, once each, with a focus on their thoughts about boys. Details of the participants, with the pseudonyms used for them, are given in Appendix 1, while characteristics of the sample (such as ethnicity, family situation and social class) are given in the tables in Appendix 2. Throughout the book, we refer to boys by their pseudonyms; where relevant, we give important identifying features of them in the text (for example, ethnicity or family structure), but generally we have tried to keep the text reasonably uncluttered and refer the reader to Appendix 1 for details on individuals.

The interviews

All the interviews took place in school rooms allocated for the purpose by the teaching staff. With the constraints of taking time from the school timetable in mind, interviews were designed to last about an hour. As mentioned above, there were two types of interview involved: group 'discussions' and individual in-depth interviews:

1. *Group discussions.* Discussions on the topic of 'growing up as a man' were held with 45 groups of youngsters in the selected schools. Thirty-six of these were single-sex and nine mixed-sex groups. The discussions were unstructured but facilitated by Rob Pattman, who had an aide memoire with topic headings in case issues we had identified as important did not spontaneously arise in the discussion. Appendix 3 contains an outline of the procedure employed.
2. *Two individual interviews* of approximately one hour duration were given to each of the 78 boys in the main sample. The interviews were 'interviewee centred' with the interviewer taking a facilitative role, picking up on issues the interviewees raised and encouraging them to develop and reflect upon these and to provide illustrative narrative accounts. These interviews were also all carried out by Rob Pattman and were conducted in what Hollway and Jefferson (1995) have referred to as a 'clinical style' to address issues of self-definition as male/masculine, identificatory models (also studied via a photo exercise with 54 of the boys), relationships with boys and with girls, intimacy and friendship, attitude towards social and media representations of masculinity, and so on. The second interview explored repetitions, contradictions and gaps in the material from the first interview, allowed more focused investigation of specific points relating to the research questions and offered the respondent the opportunity to reflect and comment on the process of the interview itself. The protocol guiding the interview is contained in Appendix 4. In addition, 24 girls were interviewed once each by a female psychologist employed specifically for this purpose; the protocol guiding this interview, which focused on girls' thoughts about boys their age, is included as Appendix 5.

Analysing the material

The huge amount of interview material generated by this study, amounting to over 4000 pages of transcribed text, has meant that we have had to adopt a number of strategies for analysis – and that we have not come anywhere near exhausting the richness of the data. All of our strategies reflect the research philosophy of attending closely to the form and content of young people's descriptions of their experiences.

1. *Summaries and transcriptions.* All the individual interviews in the main study and 27 of the groups (in whole or part) have been transcribed for detailed analysis. These transcriptions are the primary data-set for our analytic procedures. However, prior to transcription of the interviews with boys, a summary of the main content and process of each interview was undertaken. The summary documented material which was returned to in detail when exploring important themes covered in each interview. It also allowed the interviewer to record impressions of the process of the interview (for example, whether it was 'easy' or 'difficult', whether there were surprising aspects to it, and so on) and has been used to make preliminary connections across different interviews. The summaries are a major source of our knowledge of the impact of each boy on the interviewer, allowing exploration of 'counter transference' aspects of the encounter which might themselves provide clues to boys' emotional concerns. In addition, they allow analysis of the ways in which the boys 'co-constructed' their accounts with the interviewer in the interviews.

2. *Thematic analysis.* The immense amount and complexity of the interview material now at our disposal, representing about 175 hours of individual interview and about 45 hours of group discussion, means that it is impossible to analyse all of it in depth during the life of a project. Instead, we have chosen to take sweeps or 'cuts' through the material guided by theoretical considerations and by key themes that arise from close reading of the interviews. In practice, this means identifying an issue which we wish to explore, extracting all material relevant to this issue from each of our interviewees, categorising this material according to themes to be found within it, and then producing an analytic account of how these themes interweave. There is a quantitative component to this procedure in that it enables us to comment on how frequently boys addressed issues in particular ways. Nevertheless, the main thrust of the analysis here is qualitative, constructing an in-depth account of the way our research participants make sense of the issues we have discussed with them. These thematic analyses are the main source for our presentations in the chapters of this book.

3. *Narrative analysis.* As well as the thematic analyses cutting across our entire sample, we are beginning to explore the accounts of their lives

provided by individual boys. This allows us to examine the contextual biographical factors impacting on their constructions of their masculine identities. We are concerned to identify what Bruner (1990) calls 'canonical narratives' (which are general stories about how lives may be lived in the culture, serving to justify certain behaviours) as well as personal narratives. This work is in its relatively early stages, but some examples of more detailed examinations of individual boys can be found in several places in this book.

Findings

Many of the results of the study are presented in this book, as we address a number of issues which we regard as significant for contemporary debates on masculine identities. Here we want to summarise just a few general 'findings' which we relate to a specific set of research questions around which the study was originally organised. The first of these is simply that 11–14-year-old boys (and the girls we interviewed) have sophisticated understandings of the current contradictions associated with the negotiation of masculine identities. For example, many boys recognised that popular masculinity is pervasively constructed as antithetical to being seen to engage with schoolwork. Yet, some were clear that they wished to attain good qualifications without being labelled by other boys in pejorative terms. Many saw masculinity and toughness as inextricably linked but said that they themselves were not tough, leading them to give self-justificatory accounts of why they might be exceptions to the masculine norm. A common view constructed by the boys related to the racialisation of masculinity, with African Caribbean boys being seen (as in other studies – e.g. Sewell, 1997) as particularly masculine, but nevertheless often being denigrated. These contradictions were related to what we identified as the major canonical narratives about masculinity current in London schools, which can briefly be summarised in three parts:

1. Boys must maintain their difference from girls (and so avoid doing anything that is seen as the kind of thing girls do).
2. Popular masculinity involves 'hardness', sporting prowess, 'coolness', casual treatment of schoolwork and being adept at 'cussing'.
3. Some boys are 'more masculine' than others. This involves both racialised and class consciousness.

Below we briefly report those findings most directly related to our original research questions (given in italics), drawing on all our sources of data as relevant.

1. **Stability and centrality of self-definition.** *What are the positions occupied by the boys in relation to their self-concept as masculine? For example, are they proud of being young men, optimistic about their future masculine roles, or are they better described as 'apologetic' or 'ambivalent'? Do they have developed ideas about what it means to be a young man growing up in contemporary society, and do they regard the issues facing them as different from those facing girls?*

   - *'Hegemonic' masculinity.* Although there is considerable debate in the literature over the existence and significance of an organising mode of 'dominant' or 'hegemonic' masculinity, it is apparent from the interview material provided by these boys that attributes such as 'hardness', antagonism to school-based learning, sporting prowess and fashionable looks remain very influential in determining boys' popularity and also their views of themselves and others as properly 'masculine'. In our work on this issue, we use this material to further illustrate ways in which social class and 'race' impact upon constructions of, and are drawn upon in constructing, modes of hegemonic masculinity. The function of hegemonic masculinity as a method of social regulation amongst young men is also important. It is partly because most of the boys in the study felt that they did not possess the characteristics of 'popular'/hegemonic masculinity that they were at pains to explain how they were nonetheless masculine and gave clear insights into the plurality of ways in which boys negotiate masculinities in London schools.
   - *Differentiating boys and girls.* Talking about girls comprised a substantial part of most interviews. Sometimes the topic of girls was introduced by the interviewer, but often girls were spontaneously discussed by the boys and featured prominently when discussing issues such as popularity, academic work, fighting and sport. For many boys it seemed impossible to talk about themselves without alluding to girls. Boys commonly posed a number of gendered oppositions involving denigration and idealisation of femininity. While boys asserted themselves as tough and active, several of them described girls as more mature, evidenced in their attitudes to

schoolwork and friendships and their ability to be serious and to give emotional confidences. A number of boys seemed to project on to girls a capacity for closeness and sympathy which they denied in boys. We also found that the construction of heterosexual desire seemed to involve a positive affirmation of these gendered oppositions; that is, gender difference was eroticised.

The girls we interviewed constructed similar kinds of gendered dichotomies as the boys, though attaching quite different meanings to these and evaluating the 'feminine' and 'masculine' components differently. Almost all the girls were highly critical of boys for being immature, irresponsible and troublesome, constructing themselves, in opposition, not only as mature, sensible and conscientious, but also more engaging and as having a much wider range of interests than boys. But their negative constructions of boys were usually qualified in ways that undermined simple and straightforward divisions between good girls and bad boys. Often girls attributed boys' 'bad behaviour' to peer pressure with the implication that when they were on their own boys were not bad. Also some boys were constructed as exceptions and seen as 'nice'. As with the boys, however, the girls tended to eroticise gendered difference: they wanted as boyfriends not 'nice' boys, but boys who were funny and sporty.

- *Homophobia.* Our data provides evidence of ways in which boys police their identities by constructing certain boys as transgressing gender boundaries, and rendering them effeminate or gay. Homophobia was extremely pervasive, and we have examined this in relation to fears and anxieties associated with popular ways of being boys.

- *Football.* Football was a key motif in the boys' constructions of masculinities and was raised as a key theme by both boys and girls. Football talk was an important resource drawn upon in the construction of gendered identities, even for those young people who expressed antipathy to football.

2. **Relationships.** *What attitudes are expressed towards men and women, boys and girls? What do these attitudes reveal about the quality of these boys' relationships with others? How much intimacy with other people do they experience in their lives? What, if any, sexual experiences do they have and how do these contribute to their sense of their masculine identities?*

- *Parents.* When boys spoke about their relations with men and women this usually concerned their parents, with most boys constructing their mothers as more sensitive and emotionally closer to them than their fathers who were seen to be more jokey, but also more distant and detached. Twenty-three boys (out of 78) indicated that their fathers were much less available for them than their mothers; only two said that it was the other way round, and many boys wished they could see more of their fathers, with some indicating that fathers did not respond adequately to their needs for help. Nineteen boys specifically mentioned turning to their mothers when things went wrong, for instance over being bullied or getting into trouble at school, compared to four who turned to their fathers. A pervasive finding was that it was culturally accepted within schools that jokes about boys' mothers were unacceptable – to the extent that such jokes were often interpreted as invitations to fight.
- *Girlfriends.* As noted above, supposed feminine attributes were sometimes eroticised. However, even desirable girls were kept at a distance. It was unusual for boys to want girlfriends as 'friends'. Indeed, usually friends were other boys who were positioned (in opposition to girlfriends) as people with whom they could not talk freely about their emotions for fear of ridicule, but also, paradoxically, as people with whom they could 'have a laugh' and feel free. Girlfriends were often seen as constraining boys to act totally 'different'. Potential girlfriends were also imagined as unfamiliar: for instance, very few of the boys we interviewed had or could imagine having a girlfriend in their school.

3. **Security and anxiety.** *What are the areas of security and the areas of confusion and uncertainty in the boys' constructions of themselves as masculine?*

- *Education.* The elements which constitute 'hegemonic masculinity' make those boys who wish to identify with the academic values of a school subject to social disapproval from their male peers. Few managed to be both popular and overtly academically successful. We found that 'having a laugh' was a way of being a boy in relation to adult authority and classroom learning, and was part of an oppositional culture around which high status could be constructed. Conscientiousness and commitment to work were, in contrast, feminised. However, many of the boys also expressed anxieties about impending examinations and whether they would achieve decent grades. In the individual interviews some boys admired girls for working hard, and were critical of boys for their obsessive focus on football and their relative lack of commitment to schoolwork.

- *Style.* Many of the boys we interviewed spoke at some length about their own and other boys' appearances, though they also tended to play down their interest in their looks when comparing themselves with girls. While girls could be constructed as interested in other girls' looks without being labelled homosexual, this was much harder for boys. Many boys spoke about wanting to look good in designer clothes, and took style of dress as a key marker of popularity among boys, and some mentioned working out to get 'six packs' and make their bodies look muscular. However, none said they or other boys found particular boys good looking. Indeed most boys who were asked this found the question strange and seemed uncomfortable. 'Style' is a particularly racialised marker of masculinity, with African Carribean boys being high status in this respect.

- *Pets.* Many boys in the individual interviews spoke with a great deal of affection about their pets. This was a topic which was conspicuous by its absence in the group interviews, and one which several boys mentioned they would not raise with other boys at school because they would be seen as 'wimpish'. In an exercise undertaken by 54 of the boys we interviewed individually, in which boys were presented with 20 photos of men and boys in various contexts, 15 boys selected a photo of a man stroking a cat as being most like them. These boys spoke about the pleasure they derived from caring for pets, being able to stroke them and cuddle up to them and being loved by them. A few boys contrasted the sorts of relations they had with their pets with much less intimate relations they had with people.

- *Parenting.* Many boys imagined being parents in the future. Nineteen boys (out of 54) selected photos of men with children in the photo exercise, explaining that they wanted to be like them, to care for, play with and teach children and show them things and places. Some boys also associated being a father with material success. These idealised constructions of fatherhood were not always matched in the boys' accounts by their own experiences of fathers, which were often permeated by loss and disappointment.

4. **Identifications.** *From where do they draw identificatory models and what use do they make of them? How significant are parents and teachers as influences on their notions of themselves as boys/young men?*

As noted above, almost all the boys constructed oppositions between their relationships with their mothers and their relationships with their fathers, and between mothers in general and fathers in general. It was possible to identify two canonical narratives in relation to parents which were produced in both individual and group interviews:

(1) Emotional closeness (mostly with mothers) as opposed to emotional distance or unavailability (mostly from fathers).
(2) Identification with fathers but not with mothers, particularly through sport (especially football) and having fun. In much of our more detailed analysis, there was evidence of boys wishing for closer contact with fathers than they actually managed to achieve.

Teachers were not considered to provide identificatory models. Many of the boys in the study expressed resentment against what they perceived to be teachers' preference for, and favouritism to, girls. This perceived bias was, in ethnically mixed schools, reported to be racialised. Black boys were seen to be (unfairly) punished more than were white boys.

5. **Influence of social representations.** *How are issues such as education, work, sexuality, violence, 'style' and identification with social values reflected in the interview material? What features of media representation of males contribute to the boys' ideas of their own masculinities?*

Material relating to this question has been covered above. In addition, boys reported themselves only to be interested in media representations which were identifiably masculine. Their accounts indicated that they consumed other media representations only for fun or to laugh at them.

6. **Effects of social class, ethnicity and 'race'.** *What are the contributions of social class, ethnicity and 'race' to the experiences, attitudes and concepts of identity held by the boys? To what extent can they describe these effects directly?*

● *Racialisation.* It seems very apparent that 'race' and ethnicity are very prominent in the thinking of our London boys: their discussions in groups on the topic were animated and rich, and there is ample evidence both of a pool of racialised experiences and of racialised thinking in their individual interviews. In this study, white and black boys particularly attributed the characteristics of popular/hegemonic masculinity to black boys of African Caribbean descent, and racialised Asian boys and black boys of directly African descent as 'not popular'. These racialised constructions were both emotionally marked and interlinked with masculine identities.

• *Social class.* In general, both working-class and middle-class boys expressed caution about, and/or dislike of, boys from other social classes. This was particularly marked among private-school boys for whom social class spontaneously emerged as an important preoccupation. Most of the boys we interviewed in private schools were extremely aware of their identities as private-school boys. A common topic raised by these boys which generated much emotion in the group interviews was the perceived hostility of state-school boys to them. Ten of the 24 private-school boys we interviewed individually complained about this, usually dismissing it as reflecting the unwarranted envy of state-school boys. At the same time, private-school boys positioned themselves as intellectually superior to, and more privileged than, state-school boys, with 14 describing state schools as impoverished, with uncommitted and useless teachers and particularly hard and streetwise boys. While this demonstration of intellectual and moral superiority was common to private-school boys who felt assured of their future economic and career success, some private-school boys also resented being seen as wimpish and snobbish in relation to 'harder' state-school boys. Private schoolboys tended to take it for granted that they had to do academic work, and it was striking how many complained about the lack of free time they had and the pressures they felt under from their parents to work hard. However, as in the state schools, boys who were seen to work too hard were feminised and teased.

The interviewer's experience

Here we want to draw attention to the active presence of the interviewer – a white man responding to the interviewees in particular ways and showing particular emotions. In line with our aspiration to create a collaborative context for the boys to talk about themselves, the interviewer adopted an informal style with an emphasis on trying to understand the boys' lives and generally being sympathetic to them. He saw his task as encouraging the boys to talk about themselves and he worked hard to create a non-judgmental and affirming atmosphere. Rather than treating the interviews as indexing pre-existing masculine identities, we see the challenging conversational/discursive process taking place between the interviewer and the boys he interviewed as itself part of the cultural construction of masculine forms. We are interested, therefore, in the interviewer's response to the boys, and we shall be drawing upon his accounts of interviews for the insights these provide concerning the kinds of masculine identities different boys were producing. For example, using these, we can investigate relations between the same boys and the interviewer in individual and group interviews, and examine what light this throws on gendered performances in these different kinds of interview.

As mentioned above, after each individual interview, the interviewer recorded his impressions of the process of the interview; for example, whether it was 'easy' or 'difficult', whether he liked the boy or not, how engaged the boy was, whether there were surprising aspects to it, as well as summarising important themes covered in the interview. We place some value on using these summaries to track the emotional response of the interviewer to the boys and to the process of each interview. This arises from the idea that this response is a product of the specific combination of boy and interviewer in each case, intersected by the emotional impact of whatever it is that they talked about. More psychoanalytically, it can be seen, at least in part, as a 'countertransference' reaction on the part of the interviewer to the specific unconscious thoughts and feelings projected into him by any particular boy. As the same interviewer was used for every boy and in every group, we have a good opportunity to observe continuities and variations, surprising responses and particularly strong ones, from within a context in which we have a clear idea of our interviewer's characteristic way of reacting.

An example of this process can be seen in the way the interviewer reported developing feelings of attachment to many of the boys he interviewed individually, and especially to those who seemed 'direct', 'open' and were keen to 'confide' in him. Sometimes, the feelings he had for the boys were contradictory, for example when boys were open about their racism, homophobia, bullying and violence. The interviewer also felt contradictory feelings towards the many boys (about a quarter of our sample) who constructed themselves as 'good' (mature, sensible,

autonomous) in comparison to other boys, who they would often charac-
terise as sexist, immature, football-mad, disruptive or easily led. The
interviewer disliked them for being 'elitist' and for reproducing popular
versions of boys as insensitive and thoughtless, and yet most of these
boys were extremely 'open', spoke affectionately about others in ways
which were not possible in group interviews, were positive about girls,
and were critical of bullying and fighting – all things which endeared
them to the interviewer. The following is an example from process summaries on two such boys.

> *I felt a bit annoyed with him for the way he distinguished himself from the
> 'wrong crowd' or the boys who played football and messed around, and I imag-
> ined myself as one of these boys thinking he was a snob. He made me want to
> identify with the boys from whom he was disidentifying himself ... I am not sure
> why I felt so antagonistic to him when he mentioned saying 'Shhh' to those boys
> who spoke while the teacher was talking in class. Surely I should admire him
> for having the self-confidence to be able to do this, and why should some boys
> prevent other boys from listening to the teacher and getting on with their work?*
> (from David summary)

> *He was a boy who was courageously transgressing the normally polarised gen-
> der divisions and I really liked him for that ... I wish it was possible for more
> boys to mix with girls as friends and to be much less invested in positioning
> themselves as different from girls...I also felt slightly annoyed with him for
> being so self-righteous and for constructing an unbridgeable gulf between lik-
> ing football and liking girls as friends.* (from Oliver summary)

Throughout this book, we use the interviewer's subjective responses,
recorded in process descriptions of this kind, as one guide to the emotional underpinnings of many of the boys' narratives.

Structure of the book

In this book, we have sought to describe in an accessible way some of the
main 'findings' of the research, focusing on boys' and girls' accounts of
their experiences of 'young masculinities'. In Chapter 1, we give examples of interviews with boys in groups establishing the 'feel' of talking to
young men. This is explored in relation to the frequent claim about boys'
inarticulacy, and it is argued through the use of the examples that these

notions about inarticulacy arise out of restricted versions of what constitutes 'talk'. The groups waver between crude posturing and deeply thoughtful discussions on the nature of masculine experience in the early teenage years. This material is used to set up an argument that boys' voices, often heard only as threatening, can convey subtle, complex and contradictory narratives of growth. Aggression and the seeds of sexual harassment can be found in them, but so can stories of aspiration, anxiety, loss and hope. The experience of talking to boys is a compelling and rewarding one. The dynamics of the research interview are described – what 'hearing boys' voices' might entail.

Chapter 2, 'Developing "boy-centred" research' is the main place in which we ground our work in the relevant literature, offering a review of recent research on the emergent masculinities of teenage boys. Particular attention is given to the construction of boys as active subjects in the production of their masculine identities. A coming-together of the theoretical positions developed in discursive social psychology, psychoanalysis and ethnography is described, and several major studies drawing on, and contributing to, this theoretical perspective are reviewed. Emphasis is laid on the potential for understanding masculinities as constructed through discursive strategies fuelled in part by psychodynamic as well as social processes.

In Chapter 3, we consider the pervasive notion of 'hardness' in the boys' accounts of themselves, which emerges as a defining characteristic of what has come to be called 'hegemonic masculinity' – the dominant masculine 'ideal'. Our argument is that while boys readily recognise this ideal, they also position themselves in complex ways in relation to it, often resisting it or disparaging it as a way of being for themselves. The contradictory features of their self- and other-description in relation to 'hardness' are documented, as is the powerful cross-cutting of categories of 'race' and 'class' with images of hegemonic masculinity. Football appears here, as in several other chapters, as central to contemporary young masculinities.

Chapter 4 looks at boys' accounts of their relationships with, and perceptions of, girls, in particular how girls are constructed as 'other' to boys and what the content of this otherness entails. Boys demonstrate ambivalent feelings here, sometimes split into idealising girls as people to whom one can talk seriously, while denigrating them for their emotionality, inability to joke, and interest only in 'talk'. We look at ideas the boys have about 'masculine' and 'feminine' talk and about girls' relationships with one another. Boys also differentiate between different 'kinds' of girls (popular, noisy, attractive, etc.) and have much to say about the idea of a gender divide. This is also one of several chapters in which there are revealing differences between accounts derived from boys in individual interviews, single-sex group interviews and mixed-sex group interviews – in this instance particularly revealing how masculine identity construction is premised on the repudiation of liking for girls. In Chapter 5, this analysis is pushed further through a consideration of girls' views, expressed in the mixed-sex group interviews and in the interviews (about boys) with girls on their own. Girls here show especial sensitivity to differences between boys when they are on their own and when they are in groups, and have a lot to say on the vexed topic of boys' 'immaturity'.

Chapter 6 deals with the ways in which notions of ethnicity and 'race' pervade constructions of masculinity in contemporary society. The chapter documents what white, black and Asian boys say about ethnicity and 'race', and how they position themselves in relation to the 'otherness' produced in these accounts. Amongst other aspects of these accounts, we draw out the ambivalence boys express towards the racialised other, the racialisation of 'style', the gendered and sexualised nature of discourses of 'race' and how these are produced differently in group and individual encounters with boys. The function of racism in bolstering white masculinities is a particularly troubling aspect of these discourses.

Chapter 7 describes the way boys monitor their own masculinities and those of their peers through acts of 'policing' centring around the rites and rituals of homophobia, in particular the use of the concept 'gay' in the mutual cussing and teasing of boys. We show that there are many instances where this becomes fraught with anxiety and that there are strong relations between the fear of appearing 'gay' and the parallel avoidance of femininity. Boys' intimate relationships with one another are tightly constrained by this fear, which feeds into wider anxieties about sexuality and gender identity.

In Chapter 8, we pick up on a topic receiving considerable media attention at present, that of boys educational 'underachievement'. There is evidence in our material that resistance to schooling can be a marker of ideal masculinity. On the other hand, many boys show a paradoxical admiration for girls' 'maturity' and their focus on their schoolwork. There is also considerable resentment towards teachers for their perceived discrimination against boys and especially, in ethnically mixed schools, black boys. We suggest that boys' dissatisfaction with hegemonic constructions of masculinity and with the ways in which they felt problematised by teachers and adults presents possibilities for change in boys' educational performance which need not be expressed through opposition to teachers and girls.

Finally in our presentation of our data, Chapter 9 considers relations between boys and their parents. Tales of anger, loss or indifference around 'absent' fathers are documented, as are boys' complex attitudes towards, and expectations of, mothers. Boys clearly struggle to stay in contact with parents who do not necessarily offer them the kind of nurture they wish for, and this affects their own sense of the kind of adults they can become – something we explore in this chapter in the context of an individual boy's very difficult relationship with his father. The Conclusion to our book picks up on the issue of how boys can become different by arguing for the multiplicity of available masculinities, many of which are described with considerable acuity by the boys in our study even when they also distance themselves from them. The prospects for intervention with boys are also outlined in this concluding chapter.

A note on transcription conventions

We have kept the transcripts as simple as possible for the purposes of the illustrative material presented in this book. Throughout, the interviewer (Rob Pattman) is represented as **RP**, with the exception of the individual interviews with girls – which were carried out by Ruksana Patel (**RuP**). Short pauses are shown by spaced hyphens (-), while pauses of more than a second are given numerically (e.g. (2) means a 'two-second pause'). The equals sign (=) is used to indicate two or more people talking over one another. Occasionally there is a notable elongation of a world that seems to have emotional significance; we have recorded this by adding colons into the relevant word, for example s::o and so::rt.

1
Boys talk

Introduction: getting boys to talk

Carrying out in-depth, relatively unstructured interviews with boys might seem in many ways to be an ambitious undertaking. On the whole, boys in the early teenage years do not have the reputation of being good and compliant talkers. As well as boys being commonly seen as control problems, more likely to mess about when free of the disciplinary constraints of strong teachers, the popular view is that boys (and men) are 'emotionally inarticulate', lacking the capacity to 'name' and therefore even to experience feelings and emotions, and particularly to engage in sustained and reflective conversation about their feelings for and relationships with others. Indeed, this might be seen as part of the general 'moral panic' about boys, related to their difficulties of socialisation and educational achievement. It certainly seems, at times at least, to be a view adopted by teachers. For instance, teachers sometimes expressed surprise that we wanted to conduct interviews lasting an hour, implying or explicitly warning us that the boys might not be able to sustain concentration for that long. In one school, the teacher who introduced the interviewer to the prospective interviewees told the boys not to misbehave and to take the interview seriously, as if without that warning they were likely to be difficult to manage. In four other schools, teachers encouraged the boys to 'think carefully' and to try and talk 'fluently', again expressing a worry about their natural inclination to not do so.

This version of young masculinity as characterised by inarticulacy and seditiousness was to some extent shared by the boys themselves. Being interviewed was an unusual experience for the boys in our sample, not just because they had never been interviewed before, but also because talking about themselves and their relationships was not something they usually did. Indeed, as we discuss in Chapter 4, 'talking at length' was frequently seen by boys as characteristic of *girls*, while boys, being more energetic, played football. In these accounts talk was associated with doing nothing and wasting time. The very identities of boys as active and energetic were being forged, in part, by 'feminising' talk and dismissing this as a poor substitute for engaging in activities such as sport. Furthermore, the topics which we wanted to explore in the interviews – self-definitions, friendships, relationships, emotions – were cited by some boys as the sorts of things with which girls and not boys were preoccupied in their conversations. For boys, talk was supposedly merely instrumental:

Scott   *All I need to know is just the basic stuff, you know, like she's well she's fine ... [but] girls want to know all the inside stuff, if girls hear you having a conversation with friends they'll come up to you and if a friend walks off they'll come up to you and say, 'What was that about then?' and if you don't tell them they'll say 'Oh please tell me, tell me, tell me.'*

Despite this stereotype of the grunting adolescent boy (and, it must be said, embarrassingly, against our own expectations), what was striking about almost all the interviews was the engagement and fluency of the boys, not least when providing illustrative accounts of differences between boys' and girls' conversational styles. As will be evidenced throughout this book, while they did not necessarily find it easy to express their emotions clearly, they nevertheless mostly gave it a good try, became very involved in the interviews, and produced accounts of themselves and their experiences which were expressive, convincing and richly nuanced. If they were emotionally inarticulate they were not demonstrating it. In most cases, it felt as if the interviews could have gone on longer; pauses were usually brief and these rarely signalled lack of engagement but usually indicated that boys were struggling to talk about issues which they found difficult. Often when elaborating upon things they normally took for granted, such as gender and ethnic differences or their definitions of boys and girls, boys would pause and think things through anew, producing texts marked by uncertainty but not by confusions born out of laziness or resistance to the interviewer. As Tony said about this:

A couple of questions were a bit hard to answer, like questions about differences between boys and girls. I can't really think of them they just are like that, you know, you - just that's the way you think of them that's the way, it's just the way that the world's like created that way.

Even in the group interviews where there was more opportunity for becoming distracted and for messing around, none of the boys appeared to lose interest, stop participating or become disruptive. In most of the group interviews, the interviewer needed to exercise considerable control, but this was in response to the enthusiasm shown by the interviewees, not the lack of it – for example intervening when too many people were speaking at the same time, or putting questions to boys whose voices were being excluded, or clarifying and picking up on points which were being lost as the conversation changed direction. In some year-7 groups, the interviewer felt like a teacher with a lively and inspired class, the boys constantly raising their hands to signal that they wanted to speak. After the group interviews most of the boys were very keen to participate in the individual interviews, and because of this it was problematic to select only three boys from each age group to be interviewed individually, as originally planned. The interviewer explained that we wanted, if possible, to interview boys from different ethnic backgrounds individually, but in most cases there were boys from the same ethnic background 'competing' to be interviewed, and this often had to be settled on the toss of a coin. A few teachers who had overheard the 'noise' from the group interviews were surprised at how keen and committed the boys were.

We are not claiming that we had some magic approach to the interviews which allowed normally inarticulate boys to find a voice. Rather, it seemed that despite their own views of what might be appropriate to 'masculinity', most boys were eager to accept the offer of a non-judgemental, open interview which gave them a chance to think creatively about their experiences in the presence of a supportive (male) adult. Reasons for participating given by our interviewees were curiosity, a break from lessons, because their mates were doing it, and because they wanted to talk about 'personal things'. On our part, we tried to develop interviewing styles and procedures which would encourage our participants to speak openly about their experiences and concerns. While the interviewer introduced various themes – for example, relations with other boys, girls, adults and people from different ethnic backgrounds – the time spent discussing these and the direction the interviews took was very much determined by the interviewees. Trying to adopt a friendly and relaxed style, the interviewer sat opposite the interviewee with no tables or desks in between; in the case of the group interviews, the interviewer and interviewees sat together in a circle. At the beginning of the interview, the interviewees were thanked for agreeing to participate and the interviewer stressed how we were wanting to learn from *them* what it was like being an 11–14-year-old boy, that there were no right or wrong answers, that everything they said would be kept in confidence, and that they would be given pseudonyms to protect anonymity. After that, and despite some uncertainties, the interviews mainly took off, with boys becoming involved with their own stories and (in the group interviews) those of their peers in animated, often highly entertaining and sometimes deeply moving ways.

Our general stance in all this is to view interviews as 'co-constructions' between interviewer and interviewees, a kind of collaborative quest out of which we hope will emerge narratives of identity which might be quite new and unstable, but are nevertheless part of the complex work of producing masculinities. As will be seen below, there is interesting evidence from the boys themselves concerning how successful this quest was, and – more specifically – how they responded to the interview procedure.

Difficult interviews

A few boys did seem uneasy and unsure how to relate to the interviewer. This was the case particularly with four boys who had been very quiet in the group interviews. Three of these boys were small and slight, and in the individual interviews two of them had complained about being bullied by other boys. While these interviews were experienced by the interviewer as 'difficult', it seems that this in part reflected the shyness and deference of the interviewees. Over time, perhaps as a result of becoming more familiar with the interviewer, even these boys tended to become quite open about topics which they indicated they did not normally talk about with other boys or with adults. The interviewer noted (in his process summaries) feeling frustrated with these more diffident boys for making him feel like an authoritarian figure 'trying to dig stuff out' of them, but also feeling considerable warmth towards them for 'opening up' to him and communicating their anxieties. In each of these cases, the interviewer found the follow-up easier, and thought that the boys became more comfortable and relaxed with him.

Surprisingly, two boys who had been very vociferous during the group interviews – Carl and Jed – were 'difficult' to interview individually. Both of these boys described themselves as hard and sporty, and were witty and obviously popular in the groups. About his relationship with Carl (a black boy) in the individual interview, the interviewer writes:

I felt very different from him, a bit like a prying adult asking slightly stupid questions with obvious answers. I was also quite aware of being white,

wondering if he was reluctant to open out to me because I was white and/or an
adult.

When interviewed in a group, Carl, like the other boys, positioned the interviewer as a fellow male to whom they could express grievances about girls in the neighbouring school, and Carl even teased the interviewer as someone who would be surely laughed at by those girls if he walked past their school at lunchbreak. In Chapter 4, we investigate how different Carl was in the group and individual interviews, especially in relation to the ways he spoke about girls. We suggest that Carl was clinging on to his 'hard' identity which he felt was threatened by the interviewer focusing on him in the individual interview and asking him questions about his feelings and relations. It is likely that this relationship was racialised, with Carl perhaps being particularly suspicious of a white man asking him 'personal' questions.

The interviewer's comments on his experience of Jed include the following:

> *He looked quite uncomfortable, he was fidgeting, his face was red, he seemed*
> *to be struggling and I wasn't sure what to do, whether to draw attention to this*
> *at the risk of reinforcing his anxieties, whether to try to be less like an inter-*
> *rogator at the risk of allowing long embarrassing (for him and for me) silences*
> *to develop ... Quite often I made tentative suggestive responses to my own ques-*
> *tions which he latched on to with relief ...*

As with Carl he found it 'ironic that a popular noisy boy with a "reputation" [my word with which he agreed] should be so quiet with me.' Unlike Carl, who tried not to engage with the interviewer, Jed showed considerable frustration. He was most animated when talking about teachers who saw him as disruptive and were not 'nice' to him, and one key theme which emerged was his sense of annoyance with teachers who expected him to be as good as them at their subject and viewed him as 'stupid' for not being so. It seems likely that he experienced the individual interview as a difficult and frustrating lesson, and imagined the interviewer was like a teacher, trying to show him up. As the interviewer notes:

> *I wondered whether he felt frustrated at not being 'able' to answer the inter-*
> *view questions, if he saw the interview like a lesson in which he was given lit-*
> *tle or no help by expert teachers and expected to do well when he couldn't.*

Maybe I helped to make the interview seem like a hard test by asking more and more questions and I'm sure he picked up on my feelings of exasperation at times.

Carl was interviewed only once; he was absent for the follow-up interview – perhaps deliberately so. In the follow-up with Jed, the interviewer reported being 'amazed' at how different he was – 'open, fluent and relaxed'. Reflecting upon this, Jed explained that he did not know what to expect in the first interview and did not realise that he was free to say what he wanted. He was redefining his relationship with the interviewer in the follow-up, seeing him no longer as a hostile teacher figure.

Some boys were 'difficult' to interview about their attitudes to and relations with girls because they positioned themselves through their *indifference* to girls and girlish things. These boys tended to present social relationships with girls as self-evident and to feminise talk about social relationships – which may be a reason why they were also less fluent in general than most of the other boys. However, it was noticeable that they became more talkative in the follow-up interview, and more inclined to take the interview in unexpected directions. For example, the interviewer reported finding Jim in the first interview 'quite guarded and a bit immature because he said such stereotypically boyish things ... and, looking at the floor as he spoke, he made me feel like a figure of authority which I didn't want to be.' Jim constructed girls as very different from boys to the extent that he seemed uninterested in what they did and what it was like being a girl, as is apparent in the following extract from the first interview:

RP   *Yeah, yeah (2) Do, do you have any friends that are girls?*
Jim *Not really.*
RP   *Why do you think that is? (1)*
Jim *'Cos if I - friends, girl friends, if they weren't interested in football - I won't be able to spend any time with them.*
RP   *Right, yeah - so a girl would have to be interested in football, to be friendly with you?*
Jim *I suppose so.*

The interviewer found the follow-up interview with Jim 'much easier and more enjoyable' and mentioned that 'Jim definitely grew on me and I ended up liking him and feeling for him much more than I had done in the early parts of the first interview.' Jim himself said he found it 'easier' because his relationship with the interviewer had changed – 'the first time you were a stranger and I was a bit shy', and because 'this time, I knew what to say.' Though he still constructed himself and his interests in opposition to girls, he spoke at more length about girls and seemed much less indifferent to them. Unexpectedly, when asked how he got on with girls at his last school he even mentioned joining with them to dance.

Boys' experiences of the interview and the interviewer

We were positioning the boys as 'social actors' in the interviews by encouraging them not only to talk about themselves and others in expansive ways, providing illustrative narrative accounts, but, also, to reflect on how they were identifying and categorising people. When discussing the experience of being interviewed, some boys contrasted the interviews with classes, where, they indicated, they did not have opportunities for expressing themselves, and where the teacher was more authoritarian. Indeed 'talking in class' was often presented as something which usually boys did as relief from the tedium of work but which was proscribed. Presumably, it was because these interviews were being conducted during school hours on school premises that comparisons with classes were so often made:

Paul   *It's like in class there's loads of people and it's like the teacher telling you what to do and you can't really speak like that.*

Maurice   *It was good to talk about, like, I can't really talk to teachers like this..they hardly listen to ya.*

Pete   *Interesting ... it shows ... if you're an adult not a little kid and it's like all these topics that you would react to ... and how you grow up about these topics ... I think it's quite interesting, I prefer to do this rather than lessons.*

Most boys imagined that the interview would be much more formal and often expressed surprise and relief at how 'easy' it had been. Some thought it would be like a school test where they would be subjected to intensive questioning and their 'performance' evaluated:

Matthew   *I thought the quesions were going to be a bit harder, which I wouldn't know the answer to, but it was fine ... I thought if*

> *I answered something wrong then it would just ask me more and more about it and I wouldn't be able to answer them so it would be like getting harder and harder.*

Pete *I thought it was going to be hard. Yeah, but it wasn't that hard it was just personal life. I know a lot about my personal life, haha.*

The fact that they were being asked to talk about themselves and their everyday social relations also surprised a group of boys (age 13–14) from a private school who had seemed quite tense at the beginning, laughing nervously as each boy introduced himself:

Hicham *I thought like, you were gonna ask us, like [**Andy**: Weird] several, yeah, weird questions.*

Matthew *Yeah funny questions.*

RP *Like what kind of questions?*

Hicham *I don't know, I thought you were gonna be really serious an' stuff like that, like schoolteachers. [**Andy**: Yeah] [several giggle]*

RP *Sorry.*

Hicham *I thought you were gonna be like our school teachers, like [**Andy**: Really strict]' 'cos, like, when I read the letter that you was, erm, (1) doctor of something or something like that [giggle], yeah. [laugh]*

Richard *Yeah, in a dark room an' ask all these questions. [loud laughter] [twenty questions]*

Hicham *Like my cousin did psychology for A level an', like, she said all her, erm (1) professors like were really weird an' stuff like that.*

Richard *She was just trying to scare you.*

RP *So you don't think I'm weird then?*

Andy *No. [loud laughter]*

RP *That's really nice of you. [several laughing]*

Richard *That's alright.*

RP *So, I mean, what kind of questions did you expect that I'd ask?*

Richard *I don't know. [several giggle]*

Andy *Really, really terrible. [**Colin**: do you know girls?] [laughing]*

RP *Sorry?*

Several *Do you actually know girls, yeah. [**Matthew** giggles]*

Hicham *In the letter you said like you would report some stuff to the authorities, school authorities.*

Matthew	*Yeah, so [giggle] do you smoke, do you drink? Something like that.*
Richard	*I thought it would be, you know, do you take drugs ?*
RP	*Oh right, yeah.*
Matthew	*Yes - no answers.*
Richard	*I do. [loud laughter]*
RP	*You said, yeah, you said that you thought I'd also ask about girls a bit, and I did ask about girls.*
Colin	*Well, no not, you really didn't ask that much about them.*
Richard	*Not what you do with them kind of thing.*
RP	*Oh, you expected it to be like that, yeah?*
Matthew	*Yeah.*
RP	*So is it, was it better than you thought it'd be then?*
Several	*Yeah, yeah.*
Matthew	*Yeah, far better.*

In this extract, Hicham is referring to the letter we sent to the boys about the research, which set out points about the interview being non-judgemental, non-evaluative and confidential. Part of it ran as follows:

> We shall be asking questions about the kinds of things you like doing in and out of school, your relationships with other boys, girls, and adults such as teachers, parents/guardians, what you hope for your future as well as any worries you might have. There are no right or wrong answers to these questions and we hope you will be able to answer these as freely as possible. We want to make it clear that your answers will be held in strict confidence. If, however, cases of abuse or extreme bullying are reported to us we shall have to refer these to the school authorities.

These boys commented on how different the interviewer was from their (strict) teachers, and, also, from an image of the psychologist as a detached expert making them and their behaviour the objects of a 'scientific' discourse. By distancing the interviewer from this image they were implying how *surprisingly* 'normal' he was. This was partly because he was not problematising them by asking them questions about 'knowing girls' (which they appeared to use euphemistically for sex), and about drugs – questions characteristic of a view of adolescence as a period of hedonistic self-indulgence and lack of control propelled by an 'inevitable biologically-driven conflict' (see Griffin, 1997). When drugs and sex were discussed in the interviews, it was when they were introduced by the boys, often when they were talking critically about *other* boys (or girls) who took illegal drugs and smoked tobacco, or who were 'obsessed' with sex. However, the boys themselves had clearly expected our interview to go down the more traditional lines; Hicham's recollection of the passage in our covering letter raising the possibility of reporting instances of 'abuse or extreme bullying' to the school authorities is more evidence of this.

All the boys (14) who expressed a preference for one interview over the other, said that they liked the follow-up interview better, because of their familiarity with the interviewer and the sorts of questions, and also because they felt more the subjects of the study:

Jerry   *I liked this one better than I did the other one, 'cos I knew what it was going to be like. I wasn't as nervous and things … now I know what it's like and it's quite fun.*

Jack   *There were more things to say than the last interview because that's the first time really you asked me, and I wasn't quite sure but this time I'm sure.*

Pete   *I know what's going to happen now … it's just like me opening my big mouth for ages speaking about my life stories.*

It appeared that the experience of being positioned as social actors in the interviews actually helped to make some of the boys more willing and able to reflect on social identities and relationships that they tended to take for granted. Matthew said he preferred the second interview because the experience of the first interview had changed him and he was more observant and reflective:

Matthew   *This interview was easier because I've had time to think about what I said last time …*

RP   *What have you thought about?*

Matthew   *Oh, the people I hang around with, who I talk to sort of, I've sort of noticed a bit more. [RP: Have you?] Yeah, sort of I, I instead of just talking to someone I sort of realise what I'm doing now. [RP: Oh right?] So sort of … also a bit more sort of self-confident and things.*

RP   *Why's that?*

Matthew   *I don't know really, I'm sort of - I talk to people - and I see what they're like, and I know exactly what they're like … 'cos I sort of* notice *more … I now find it easier to talk to people because I notice what they're like more.*

Performing in interviews

One issue which was raised many times by teachers and which is very characteristic of our data, is that there were differences between what boys said (and how they behaved) in individual interviews as compared to group interviews. In part this relates to Matthew's point above, that the very fact of being interviewed often produced changes in boys' thinking. It also linked with a more general observation that boys often spoke about 'acting' differently in different situations and with different people. For us, this is an important reminder that the interviews themselves were sites for 'acting' or 'performing' and that the boys' behaviour in different kinds of interview or at different times might reveal different facets of their masculinities. In other words, we do not see their performances in individual interviews as somehow having been more 'authentic' than those in groups (or vice versa), but rather see each setting as drawing out different manifestations of masculine identity construction – different ways of 'doing boy'. In holding to this view, we are following the work of recent identity theorists such as Judith Butler (1993), who stress the complex and active ways in which gender is produced and performed through repetitive acts, giving it the appearance of something solid which individuals possess. In our research, this means examining the boys 'performances' in the different interview contexts, and in relation to the specific demands made on them by their conversations with our white, male interviewer, as modes of gendered work, rather than as expressions of some underlying, true 'gender identity'. So, when a boy says different things in a group compared to an individual interview, and behaves in distinctly different ways, this is not because he is being truthful in one situation and false in the other, but rather because he is taking up different (sometimes contradictory) discursive positions in different contexts, and modifying and also resisting these.

Being serious and 'softer' in the individual interviews

The view that boys were better able to express their 'real' identities in the individual interview was expressed by some teachers who warned the interviewer that boys would be easily influenced by other boys in group interviews. The 25 boys who expressed a preference for the individual over the single-sex group interviews claimed, however, that this was not because they were impressionable, but because they had more opportunity to talk, and also because they could talk about 'personal' things in a 'serious' way and were not constrained by fear of other boys 'laughing' at them:

Michael *This [individual] one was more personal, and the one in the group was joking around having a laugh.*

RP *More personal?*

Michael *Like you telling about your family and everything and your views on issues.*

RP *That would have been difficult in a group?*

Michael *Yeah ... I dunno it's like, um, if you said something, like, people might start laughing.*

　　　...

Ibrahim *When we're in a group it was sort of, like, if I said, like, about girls or anything they would start laughing or, and then go to class and say like, um, 'Ibrahim said that about girls in front of the man.'*

These boys were producing 'softer' versions of masculinity, in the sense of being less loud and funny and speaking about emotions and relations in ways which would be derided, as some boys specified, as 'soft' and wimpish with a group of boys or even usually with adult males. In the individual but rarely the group interviews, boys spoke not only positively about girls, but about girls who were friends, their relations with their girlfriends, their grandparents, anxieties about bullying, anxieties about home and pets. In addition, it was mainly in individual interviews that boys derided other boys for being uncommunicative, thick-skinned, aggressive and uncaring.

It seems clear that at least some boys were enabled to be 'softer' in the individual interviews because the interviewer himself was informal and boy-centred, asking questions about feelings and relationships. Some of the boys who expressed a strong preference for the individual interview and enjoyed being able to talk more 'seriously' about themselves, seemed to like the interviewer for being serious, caring and interested in them, and liked being able to 'confide' in him. Alan, for instance, had spoken with much anger about his father, and at the end of the interview revealed that these were feelings he normally kept to himself:

Alan *I trust you a great deal ... I haven't told my mum hardly any of what I think of my dad so you're kind of special really.*

RP *Why do you think you've been able to tell me?*

Alan *'Cos you seem so nice and you're kind of what I would like to be, you're a nice man.*

From the general context of Alan's story, described more in Chapter 8, it seems likely that he was projecting 'softness' on to the interviewer, who was constructed as 'special' because he was able to talk to him about being 'soft' without being derided. What appears to be particularly significant for Alan, in his construction of the interviewer as 'special', is the intersection of the interviewer's gender and characteristics he likes or values: here was a *man* who was being 'nice' and with whom he wanted to identify.

Given the ubiquity of constructions of girls and women as 'better listeners' than boys and men (see Chapter 4), the positioning of the interviewer as a sympathetic listener and confidant was sometimes ironic. The interviewer drew attention to this with John who mentioned how he could only talk to girls and women about the anxieties he experienced about not seeing his separated father:

John   *I much prefer speaking to girls about my problems than I do boys, especially to older women ... like my mum, my mum's friends, even my nan.*

RP   *I was wondering how you saw your relationship with me 'cos you're telling me things which are quite, um, quite intimate things about yourself?*

John   *Yes, I don't mind speaking here to you because hopefully you don't start, like, if you replay this tape you won't start laughing about ... as you said at the first interview this will be in strict confidence and anything you want to say, so, like I take your word for it ... I trust you just to show students and stuff. So I'm not fussed. So yeah, it's a good relationship between me and you because we can just talk, so it's good.*

John did not allude to the interviewer's gender and, like a number of other boys, focused on the interviewer as someone whose *role* it was to take boys seriously and not to laugh, as presumably he imagined boys (and men) might otherwise do. Though he spoke about the interviewer as an *interviewer* and not a particular man, John attached considerable importance to the relationship he established with him. As the interviewer records:

> *After the interview it seemed he did not want the relationship to finish and said twice that he would be available at any time should I wish to do more interviews with him.*

Other tendencies related to expressing 'softer' versions of masculinity in the individual as opposed to the group interviews could be observed quite strongly in the boys' behaviour. In the individual interviews, but rarely the groups, boys:

(1) seemed cagey and uneasy (six boys were described as particularly difficult to interview and other boys, at times, seemed unsure or unwilling to elaborate and open out);
(2) constructed themselves as 'good' in the sense of being more mature, responsible, harder working and more pleasant to girls than many other boys (17 boys);
(3) expressed dissatisfaction with popular ways of being boys (16 boys);
(4) idealised girls (11 boys);
(5) spoke about close relationships with parents, grandparents, pets, children and girls (more than half our sample).

Some of these differences were overlapping. For example, boys who idealised girls tended also to be critical of popular ways of being boys, and some of these boys constructed themselves as 'good' compared with other boys.

Being 'free' and 'funny' in group interviews

In contrast to the comments above, 29 boys said they liked the group interview better, mainly because they felt 'freer'. It was after being interviewed in groups that the boys expressed most surprise at enjoying the interview, finding it 'fun' and being 'free' with their mates, having expected it to be serious. This was no doubt partly because it was the first interview – they knew what to expect for the individual interviews which followed – but also because the boys tended to be much louder, livelier and funnier in the group interviews. Many boys enthused about the 'fun' they had 'having a laugh' with the other boys in the group. Laughter was not, here, presented as constraining, but as facilitating talk. The boys who preferred the group interviews also said they liked being able to engage in and be part of a conversation, rather than being singled out to answer questions:

Dean *When you're with your friends you have a laugh as well make stuff funny, and you have more to talk about, you just start chatting and get to know them a bit more and find out what their opinions are.*

Norman   *[In the group interview] you weren't just relying on your own ideas, you could sort of use your ideas with other people's.*
Julius   *In the individual interview it was more personal but in the group interview everybody was laughing about just talking ...*

These comments demonstrate the importance of boys sparking off each other. In contrast to the teachers who indicated that boys in groups were dominated by 'peer pressure', these boys tended to speak about their relations with other boys in the group as interactive, 'using your ideas with other people's', with other boys being seen as catalysts 'triggering off something that you might want to say'. In the group interviews the boys were collectively producing and enacting 'cultural stories', with different individuals contributing to common and clearly familiar stories about identities, relations and experiences. All the boys we quoted from, above, were confident contributors in their groups, and the discussion in all the groups in which these boys participated was lively, loud and funny, with the interviewer often doing little more than seeking clarification, as the boys built on each other's contributions.

Talking man to man in the group

In the group interviews it was possible to observe what boys were like with other boys, which boys were funny and how they were funny, how certain boys tended to dominate the conversation and others became quiet, and also how boys supported each other, offering mutual recognition of experiences as well as indicating how varied their experiences were, drawing upon and collectively constructing common cultural stories as well as managing differences. In these the interviewer intervened much less, with the conversation between the boys often developing a momentum of its own. The interviewer, however, regulated the conversation by introducing topics, picking up on points, asking for clarification, challenging, pointing out differences between what different boys were saying, putting questions to particular boys and trying to draw in the quieter boys. The interviewer's identity as an interested adult male outsider was, as in the individual interviews, highly significant. Like the boys, the interviewer found the group interviews often very funny, especially when they were telling 'well worn' stories about familiar themes which 'sent up' their teachers and parents. Telling these stories to him, an interested and informal adult, perhaps made them seem more funny and subversive.

In the group interviews, the boys were much more invested in asserting themselves against girls, something which they themselves attributed
to the fact of the interviewer being a man. Indeed it was this which the
members of the following group of 13–14-year-old state-school boys said
was most significant about the interview:

RP   *How did you find it?*
Joey   *Just found it easy.*
Marvin   *Good.*
James   *Good.*
Benny   *It was very good.*
James   *It's not like talking to a teacher [**Maurice**: it's not like talking
            to a woman, if you was like a woman we couldn't talk about
            the things we've talked about], we couldn't talk to a teacher
            about porn mags and things like that. [laugh]*
Benny   *Yeah, we couldn't say things about the girls 'cos she might
            disagree.*

They proceeded to try and place the interviewer as a familiar male figure:

Joey   *We ain't ever talked to someone like that.*
James   *No.*
Maurice *My dad. [laugh]*
Marvin   *It's like talking to a brother or uncle.*

In the individual interview, Maurice spoke about his father, like many
boys (see Chapter 8), as a jokey figure and identified with him as someone with whom he could share 'rude' jokes, in contrast to his more serious mother. The laughter which followed his contribution indicated that
the boys could not consider speaking to their fathers about the sorts of
issues they had been discussing, perhaps because their fathers were seen
as more authoritarian than the interviewer, or because jokey fathers were
regarded as people with whom they could not have reflective conversations about their concerns and relations. Saying it was like 'talking to a
brother or an uncle', Marvin was perhaps reflecting upon his relationships with men with whom he could more easily confide.

The construction of the interview as an all-male affair became even
more apparent when the interviewer asked them if the presence of girls
would have 'made a difference'. There was a resounding 'yes'.

James   *They'd be hogging the tape not giving us a chance to speak.*
Benny   *They'd be saying, 'Oh that's not true you lot do this, you lot do that.'*
RP   *I'm going to be interviewing a mixed group of 3 girls and 3 boys. I was wondering =*
Joey   *= They'll be a big argument in that.*
Benny   *Oh my God.*
Marvin   *Ohh.*

In this, as in many other single-sex group interviews, girls were constructed as opponents who blamed boys for being immature, perverted and sexist, and were supported by teachers. This was part of the collective gender performance in which boys engaged, constructing themselves with much humour in opposition to easily offended, serious, obsessively talkative and bossy girls. Their horror at the prospect of girls and boys being interviewed together derives from and reflects the particular gender-polarised positions and identities they were establishing in the single-sex group interviews.

Mixed-gender interviews

Despite these dire predictions, seven of the nine mixed-gender interviews we conducted were engaging and not particularly hostile, and most boys were surprised at enjoying the mixed-gender interviews and how 'open' they had been. For example, Andy, reflecting in the individual interview on being interviewed in a mixed-gender group, said:

Andy   *I thought no-one would say nothing ... someone might have said something and then that've been a shock to everyone and they would've gone out and told someone else ... then everyone'd know.*
RP   *Why wasn't it like that?*
Andy   *Didn't know why no-one was scared to speak, but then as soon as people started saying some stuff what I didn't think they would've said, then I just started saying whatever.*

We further examine the ways boys and girls positioned themselves in relation to each other in mixed gendered interviews in Chapter 5.

Talking about bullying in individual rather than group interviews

The contrast between what boys were like in the individual and single-sex group interviews was especially apparent with the 12 boys who spoke, in the individual interviews, about being bullied. Only one of these boys elaborated on this in the group interview, in response to the other boys who were criticising him for 'grassing' on their friends. Recording how different one such boy, Chris, was in the two types of interview, the interviewer writes:

> *In the group interview he seemed very different, bright, cheery integrated with the group ... he said in a loud, jokey way that he was the 'hardest'. In the individual interview he was sad and serious and spoke about being bullied ... for being small, weak and having a gap in his tooth. I wouldn't have imagined that a boy who was picked on for being 'weak' could have been so noisy and cheerful when claiming, with tongue in cheek, to be the 'hardest'.*

When asked if he could have spoken in the group interview about being bullied, Chris looked shocked as if this was completely out of the question, and when asked why not, said, 'Cause like they might laugh when they get out and tell people that were picking on you that I had told you.' In contrast to the group interview, in which he had joked with the other boys, in the individual interview he indicated he was afraid of other boys laughing at him.

Oliver, who spoke in the individual interview about being bullied for mixing with girls instead of playing football (see Chapter 7), enthused with the others in the group interview about gory films, blood and guts. Whereas in the individual interview he emphasised how much in common he had with girls and how different he was from boys in general, in the group interview he constructed himself, like the other boys, as different from girls who were described as easily scared. In the individual interview he praised girls and criticised boys for being 'idle', 'rowdy' and obsessed with football. When he was asked in the individual interview if he thought he was different in the group interview, he said that in the group interview he could not speak 'freely', whereas in the individual interview 'no-one knows except me, you and the tape':

> *Like when I said that I hate boys, about playing football and that, all the people who play football would gang up on me and beat me up. When I said that I act like a girl, that I like girls better than boys, they'll gang up on me and beat me up for that.*

Oliver's contention that he could speak 'freely' in the individual interview, assumes that he is basically the same in both contexts, only more
able to express himself in one than the other. Yet, whereas when interviewed individually he provided rich narrative accounts of befriending,
mixing and identifying with girls, in the group interview he was deeply
engaged in stereotypically boyish discussions. Indeed, one of the boys
who had participated in the same group interview, complained (when
interviewed individually) about Oliver and another boy 'talking about
bazoukas and machine guns and that' when 'you wanted to find out how
a boy's life was.' Ironically, while this boy contrasted Oliver's 'silly' talk
about guns with talking 'seriously' and 'personally', Oliver, when interviewed individually, derided boys for being silly and obsessive, particularly in relation to football (see Chapter 7), and expressed a strong
preference for the individual interview because it was 'more personal'.

It was inconceivable for Chris, Oliver and other boys to talk about being
bullied in the single-sex group interviews, we want to suggest, not just
because of their fear of reprisals, but because they were constructing different versions of themselves in different interviews. Some boys mentioned
being able to talk about bullying and other anxieties to girls
and women who were often idealised as sympathetic and caring. We examine later how different boys were with girls than when they were
just with boys, by investigating boys' accounts of this (in Chapter 4) and by
addressing the gender dynamics in mixed-gender interviews (in Chapter 5).

Resisting 'softer' relations with the interviewer

It may be that some boys felt 'freer' in the group interview precisely
because of being drawn into 'softer' relations with the interviewer. In one
all-boys' state school, boys passing by knocked on the window, laughed
and banged on the door when the individual interviews were being conducted. One of the boys being interviewed, Bob, said that they were just
joking: 'they'd know nothing's going on ... ' The interviewer's request, at
the end of the group interview, for volunteers to be interviewed individually had been met with some surprise and laughter and he had been
warned that other boys might think 'something's going on' in the individual interviews. When the interviewer probed what this might be, Bob
seemed embarrassed, reassuring him they were not being serious:

Bob   *They know it's not going on, but they just like say, just like, um (1)
just cuss you (1) something like.*

RP *Just cuss you, yeah?*

Bob *Yeah.*

RP *Why would they do that?*

Bob *Don't know, people just like cussing each other.*

RP *Yeah, 'cause if they think that =*

Bob *= 'Cause they think if they cuss them then they feel more like, um, powerful than the other person.*

RP *Right (1) so, so they think that, that I am trying to seduce you or something, is that what they think?*

Bob *Yeah, something like that.*

RP *Yeah (1) what, what why do you think they think that?*

Bob *(1) They just, (2) feel powerful [**RP**: Yeah] since, um, if, if they cuss me and I answer back then they have that power over me to say what they want about me.*

RP *Right (1) but why do you think boys are concerned about (1) calling people gay, and also thinking that, imagining that I =*

Bob *= It's being powerful ain't it? (1) like.*

RP *Why, why particularly gay?*

Bob *Um, 'cause (1) it's just (1) they don't like (1) it's easy cuss calling someone gay.*

In the above individual interview, the interviewer reflecting upon himself being positioned as gay was particularly discomforting for Bob. Talking about 'gay' as 'just a cuss', Bob was playing it down and making less threatening his relationship with the interviewer who was making him uncomfortable by asking him about the reactions of the other boys. (Talking about 'gay' as 'just a cuss' was extremely common. In this particular school some of the boys likened it to swearing, but unlike swearing it did not incur detentions.) When the boys were opening the door and banging on the window, Bob fluctuated between smiling as he caught their eyes and looking straight-faced as he turned to the interviewer, identifying with the boys outside, while also positioning himself as serious and reflective in relation to the interview. If we allow, as Bob suggests, that the boys are 'just cussing' or joking and know nothing is 'going on', this begs the question of why they act in a jokey way *as if* 'something is going on'. Even if they were 'just joking', they were drawing attention to and trying to disrupt the relationship between the adult male interviewer and the boy. These performances were no doubt about boys asserting themselves as heterosexual, something we examine in Chapter 6 where we describe the prevalence of homophobia among the boys we interviewed and its significance in policing masculinities. But the disruptive and jokey behaviour of the boys 'outside' may also have been fuelled by a sense of exclusion, of missing out on the close attention the interviewee was receiving. A few boys in other schools mentioned their classmates who had not been interviewed being envious and eager to know what questions were asked.

Finding it difficult to speak about topics in the multiethnic group interview

It was often in the individual interviews, as opposed to the multiethnic group ones, that boys spoke about their experiences of racism. For instance Han, a Chinese boy, talked at some length in the individual interview about being teased at school for his accent. This included being hit by some boys. He was small, wore glasses and was softly spoken. His parents lived in Hong Kong and he had come to England two years previously to attend school and live with his aunt and uncle. He did not play football and said he only had one friend at school with whom he played table tennis. In contrast, he said he had many friends at the Chinese school he attended on Saturdays, and played football with them. He preferred being with Chinese boys, he said, because he could communicate with them in his mother tongue. He had been extremely quiet in the group interview, where the topic of racism had hardly been discussed. When it had been introduced by the interviewer, the boys asserted that racism did not exist in their school because it was private. The interviewer asked Han if he could have spoken about 'being bullied' in the group interview, and he replied 'Yeah I could ... so the group can hear and, er, sometimes hurt me ... stop it, stop it.' This seemed like a wishful fantasy.

It was not just small and quiet boys who were unable to talk about experiences of racism in the multiethnic group. In one interview, comprising four white and two black boys aged 13–14, the interviewees introduced themselves as friends who could joke with each other and went on, amidst much laughter, to give their nicknames and the reasons for these. Don, one of the black boys, who was later described as the best footballer and one of the hardest boys in the year, was called 'monkey', but no reason was given for this. The interviewer asked why he was called that and records feeling uncomfortable:

> *I felt a little uncomfortable doing so as if I would undermine the camaraderie.*
> *Clearly this was a racist name and it seemed inappropriate to be getting the*

white boys to admit they were being racist to Don and maybe also embarrassing Don.

One of the boys responded 'Cause he looks like one', and more quietly, with a slight laugh, 'nothing racist'. Don smiled. In the individual interview, Don was asked how he felt about being called monkey, and he said he did not like it and neither did the girls. Lance, a popular and sporty black boy who carried much authority in the multiethnic group interview, talking at length and rarely being interrupted, said in the individual interview that he could not have talked about racism in the group interview:

Lance   *...A lot of them are white and a lot of them don't know.*
RP   *Is it not possible to talk about racism with white people?*
Lance   *It's something that's tried to be ignored ... It's such a sensitive issue ... because it's like you are trying to say I am racist ... and like you are not calling them people racist, you are just saying, like, you're just saying that pointing out racism where it is.*

Lance was the only black boy in the group, and there were relatively few black boys in his school.

Monoethnic interviews with black and Asian boys and the significance of 'racial' identities and racism

'Race' was more likely to be introduced by the interviewees and featured more prominently in the individual interviews with black and Asians than white boys. It was also given a particularly high profile in most of the monoethnic group interviews. Three schools would not give us permission to conduct monoethnic group interviews on the grounds that they were 'racially' divisive, but it was in these interviews that many of the boys provided particularly rich and emotionally engaged accounts of 'racial' identifications and racism. In the three group interviews we conducted with black boys only, racism was introduced by the boys early on when talking about the school and, in particular, teachers. This also happened in a group interview where, unusually, there were more black than white boys – six black, two white and one Asian boy. In the two interviews we conducted with Asian boys only, racism was also a significant topic, but mainly spoken about as something they experienced outside school.

In the monoethnic interviews with black boys only and Asian boys only, it was noticeable how friendly and supportive the boys were towards each other. In one of these, the Asian boys introduced themselves as friends and commented on how each contributed to the dynamics of the group. In these interviews, the stories they told about themselves in and outside school frequently featured other members of the group. Often they spoke specifically about their experiences as black or Asian boys, and these seemed to reinforce feelings of commonality and friendship. The Asian boys in one group became particularly engaged and animated when talking about their common experiences of visiting relatives in India and Sri Lanka. In this they confirmed and validated each other's identifications as 'outsiders and English', and the effect was to generate strong feelings of mutual interest and support. Talking about racism also had this effect. In the monoethnic interviews, forms of racism articulated by one boy were immediately recognised by the other boys, as illustrated in the following extract from an interview with some 13–14-year-old black boys:

Jonathan	*Like, er, when, em, the boy hasn't done anything, he's sitting down, and say like a white boy an he, and he threw something, and the black boy gets the blame for it and he's doing his work.*
RP	*Right.*
Jonathan	*And the teacher starts having a go at him and sends him out of the room.*
RP	*How do black boys respond to that?*
Anthony	*Get angry.*
Nigel	*And sometimes you wish you was a girl so you can just punch her in her jaw.*

Talking to a white interviewer

One perhaps surprising feature of these supposedly monoethnic interviews with black and Asian boys was how keen these boys were to talk about 'race' and racism with a white interviewer. In one interview with black boys, the interviewees were quite reticent at first and said they had little time as they would have to leave for assembly. But as the interviewer picked up on their grievances about school and racist teachers, they became extremely engaged and elaborated on a range of issues related to 'race' and racism. When the interviewer offered to stop early, they asked if they could continue. The feedback was very positive at the end of all the monoethnic group interviews. For example the following black boys said:

Stewart   *It was good 'cause you could speak your mind.*
Kevin   *That was the first time I could speak my mind.*
Nathan   *We all shared the same views.*
Kevin   *If anybody is racist to us we've got the right to beat them up.*

Despite their fluency with our white interviewer, in some of the interviews with black boys, white people were seen as untrustworthy and difficult to talk to:

Marcus   *When you're talking to white people now, you can't talk to them at all ... if you're talking to them and you say something about someone else, they'll run, go and tell them.*
Michael   *You say something, about someone what's the same colour, they'll [white boys] go to them and tell them...and then there's all problems and growing up.*
RP   *Like what?*
Michael   *You want to fight or something, like, they'll get NF down the school.*

The boys were talking about white boys, with the interviewer as a white man apparently exempted. But whites in general were also criticised for their privilege and complacency. One black boy said 'white people have got it easy and they don't realise how easy they have got it', and when asked to elaborate, said:

> They might, if they live in a black area, they might get racism but it ain't going to stop them from getting jobs ... if you've got a white boss, yeah, that person might like black people but he might give it to a white person out of obligation, but that's how easy they have it. Or they're in school they don't really, if they've got a white teacher they aren't going to get racism are they ... ?

When asked at the end if they could have 'said more things' to a black or Asian interviewer, the boys in the monoethnic interviews said no. This may have been because they did not want to seem 'offensive', but speaking to an interested white adult about 'race' and racism, as well as being inter- viewed about themselves, was perhaps a new experience for these boys, and this may have made them even more keen to talk about this and to elaborate points they might assume a black person would take for granted. Mac an Ghaill (1988), a white man studying black students, also points to the significance of being seen to be concerned about racism: he was told by the black women students he was interviewing at the college where he was teaching that his 'anti-racist stance within the college was of primary significance in their deciding to participate in the study' (p. 181).

Monoethnic interviews with white boys

One of the interviews with white boys was 'accidentally' monoethnic because at the private school where it was being conducted there were hardly any black or Asian boys, and none had been recruited for the inter- views. In this interview 'race' was not a high-profile issue, and when it was introduced by the interviewer, the interviewees (aged 11–12) focused upon being English and not being white, thus reflecting the taken-for- grantedness of whiteness. In the other two interviews with white boys only, 'race' and racism were more to the fore, with the boys criticising black boys for developing exclusionary cultural styles, for being racist and aggressive to whites and for drawing on slave discourses to justify this as 'pay back'. They also complained about authority figures like teachers and the police being more lenient with blacks than whites for fear of being seen as racist. Both these interviews were in schools where less than half the pupil population was white, and one of these schools was in an area where there was strong support for the National Front. It was in this school that 'race' and racism dominated the discussion, no doubt encouraged by the fact that the teachers had not given the boys our letters explaining the focus of the research, and had told them they were going to be interviewed about 'race'. During the interview, the boys (aged 13–14) were very excited and spent much time and energy denying they were racists in ways which seemed to parody antiracist discourses:

Gerry   *[gets close to the microphone] Give racism the boot.*
Martin   *[also gets close to the microphone] No-one's a colour, they're just a person. [starts mimicking a soul singer]*

These boys were particularly aware of 'performing' to the tape, speaking closely to the microphone and wanting to listen to themselves afterwards.

They enjoyed being 'outrageous' in the interview (as one of them indicated at the end) and at the same time tried to present themselves as not really racist, leaving it unclear as to whether they were in fact parodying antiracist discourses. There was much laughter when one boy, Derek, said '60% of black men have sausage lips', but, at the same time, recognition that this was 'out of order' when the interviewer began to pursue this:

RP   *What - what do you - what's sausage lips?*
Tony   *No, it's out of order - they're out of order.*
Derek *Not me.*
Jimmy *Don't print that shit man.*
Derek *No, I was joking, 60% of black men get along with the white men - a lot.*

Presumably Derek felt able to mention 'sausage lips' because the interviewer was white. Also he was saying something risky, as evidenced by the laughter as well as the distancing of the other boys from him, and his retraction of his comment. At the end of the interview, some of the boys who had been most critical of black boys remained behind when Derek had left, and proceeded to distance themselves further from him by saying he was in the NF. It is likely the boys perceived the interviewer (who described this as 'one of the most anarchic interviews I've done') as a figure of authority with liberal ideas about 'race', and perhaps because he was not 'outraged' by their racism but pursued it in a non-judgmental way, liked him and wanted to present themselves as not really racist. Hence the contradictions between their (outrageously) racist posturing and their (ambiguous) denials.

Conclusion

The rich, fluent and emotionally engaged accounts provided by the boys we interviewed refute popular notions of boys as being emotionally illiterate. Boys themselves 'feminised' talk, in particular talk about relations and feelings, and were often surprised at how articulate they were and how much they had to say in the interviews. This, in our view, demonstrates how dependent talk is upon context. Being interviewed about themselves usually three times – once in a group and twice individually – for a total of three hours or so, was experienced by most boys as different and enjoyable, and also as creative. They were surprised to have an adult centring on them as social actors, rather than testing them, problematising them, firing questions at them and putting them on the spot. The boys changed during the course of being interviewed as they became familiar with the interviewer and his questioning, and as the interviewer got to know them and became able to identify and discuss issues which were key for them. This was apparent in the preference expressed by a number of boys for the follow-up interview, compared with the first individual one.

We have addressed the interviews themselves as specific contexts which encouraged certain kinds of talk and ways of constructing and performing identities. We argued against seeing the interviews simply as opportunities for boys to put into words thoughts and feelings they already had and perhaps did not normally express. The boys were *working,* producing versions of themselves as they talked. The interviewer was not just a facilitator but a *co-constructor*, for example pursuing certain topics the boys raised in certain ways, challenging them on specific issues, avoiding being judgmental, being informal, and communicating emotions. As we have described, the boys' behaviour and disposition, and what they said, varied considerably between different kinds of interview – individual, single-sex and mixed-gender group, monoethnic and multiethnic group. In these different contexts they were establishing particular relationships with the interviewer as well as, in the group interviews, with the other interviewees, and enacting various versions of masculinity. The different kinds of interview thus provided opportunities for us to see various types of gendered performance. For example, in the individual interviews we found boys were more serious, more critical of boys in general and more willing to talk about things which might be derided as wimpish or soft with other boys present. In the boys-only groups, on the other hand, we identified the following types of gendered performances. These were not mutually exclusive, and usually the interviews were characterised by a combination of these performances:

1. Constructing hierarchies between themselves. Sometimes this was explicit when, for example, the boys introduced themselves and each other in terms of 'hardness' or footballing ability.
2. Joking. The single-sex group interviews were characterised by the boys themselves as jokey, and there was often a great deal of laughter in these, with boys 'cussing' each other and teachers, and telling stories – often clearly 'well-worn' stories about familiar themes – which 'sent up' their teachers and parents. Telling these stories to an interested adult perhaps made them seem more funny and subversive.

3. Collectively asserting themselves in relation to girls. We have mentioned how girls were often constructed as opponents in group interviews with boys, and this is a topic we explore in Chapter 4.
4. Friendliness. Many boys enjoyed the single-sex group interviews because of the camaraderie they experienced, and, as we noted, this was particularly noticeable in the monoethnic group interviews with black boys and Asian boys.

As well as demonstrating that boys are not – despite the popular stereotype – poor talkers and emotionally illiterate, we also want to argue against the construction of boys as problematic and insensitive in groups of boys and as more authentic on their own. This was a view not only held by teachers, but by girls and boys themselves (see Chapters 4 and 5). In our study, boys were often friendly and supportive of each other in groups, and this did not necessarily depend on them being antisocial towards others, for example constructing girls or teachers as common opponents. However, the process of problematising boys in groups may become a self-fulfilling prophecy with boys in groups becoming increasingly alienated from figures of authority as well as girls. The question we want to raise is not how do we stop boys mixing with each other and being disruptive, but what makes boys so different on their own with an adult or a girl than in groups of boys, and what can be done to make them less so? While those we interviewed commonly defined boys as loud, sporty, aggressive, funny, strong and anti-work, these were not fixed and essential masculine characteristics, but narrow though extremely influential discursive constructions. It became apparent that simply talking about experiences helped many boys to consider what alternative ways of 'doing boy' could be available to them.

2

Lads, machos and others: developing 'boy-centred' research

Introduction

This chapter provides some background to our project by investigating recent research which has explored the construction of masculine 'identities' through ethnographic, observational and interview methods. We are particularly interested in research that addresses the topic of boys' experiences by allowing them to speak about it openly and in detail, rather than research which, for example, measures achievements, attitudes or behaviours. We are also concerned to maintain a view of masculinity in its relational aspects – that is, to understand how it comes to be constructed in relation to femininity- and how, in the context of 'masculinity' itself, there might be many varied 'masculinities', alternative ways of 'doing boy'. Other key topics explored in research on masculinities and gendered identities include the ways in which what counts as being female or male is contested and resisted and how gendered identities are differentiated by, for example, social class and 'race'.

This work addresses boys and young men not as detached subjects whose language describes a reality 'out there', but as people whose identities are continually reinvented in the language they use as they construct and re-construct gender and sexuality. The accounts boys give of their experiences are placed in the foreground in this research, which as will be seen has largely taken an ethnographic form. However, the theoretical frame in which much of this work is cast is one in which 'experience' itself is made problematic; that is, it is assumed that all descriptions of experience are themselves 'discursive constructions', ways of making sense of things, of articulating specific versions of self, identity and the world (see Scott, 1992). This is the sense in which recent ethnographic and qualitative research on boys has attempted to 'de-centre' the masculine subject, focusing on what boys' accounts of their perceptions and experiences reveal of the social construction of masculinities. Carrying

50

out 'boy-centred' research, therefore, does not imply uncritical acceptance of boys' versions of themselves; rather, it builds on the idea of masculinities as something achieved -a practice or practices (Wetherell and
Edley, 1998), a set of 'performative acts' (Butler, 1990; Nayak and
Kehily, 1996) or an activity of 'doing' gender (Bohan, 1997).
Masculinities have become contextualised as specific plural identities
which intersect with class, ethnicity and sexuality and which are taken up
and performed in particular ways in locations such as the school or the
streets. Boys' accounts and ethnographic descriptions of their activities
give access to this performance, but still require interpretation. Thus,
while this research addresses masculinities as everyday practices in
which boys are engaged, emphasising agency and the meanings boys
attach to their actions, it recognises also that their actions are constrained
by the discursive positions available to them, and further that boys'
investments in these positions are perhaps only partially conscious.

One implication of this is that it is important for politics and for
research to hold onto the notion of men as 'victims' as well as 'oppres-
sors' in a patriarchal culture. Polarising gender into 'rational male sub-
ject/contentless female other', as has been the tendency in some
otherwise critical work, obscures the multifariousness of masculinities
and also the way in which their organisation is premised to some degree
at least on the preservation of selfhood in the face of the fragmenting
forces of contemporary 'postmodern' culture. Rattansi and Phoenix
(1997), for example, point out that late modernity is characterised in
sociological literature by complexity and flux to a much greater degree
than that prevalent in the capitalist modernity of the immediately preced-
ing era. This is linked in part to the erosion of traditional class-based
identities and to increasing male unemployment as a result of the decline
of heavy manufacturing industry, and to the transformation of gender
identities with the increasing participation of women in work outside
the home. Since, according to Seidler (1994) and others, being a man
has meant identifying with what 'we do', these trends are likely to be
experienced as particularly threatening – as a form of psychic death and
also as a constant reminder of how empty masculinity is. Late modernity
has also been characterised by an explosion of identity politics centred
particularly on the assertion of feminist, gay and lesbian and black
identities all of which have an impact on the sustainability of more traditional notions of masculinity. It is in this confusing and challenging
context, with its potential for enabling boys to take up less constrained
gender positions but also with its threat to the taken-for-granted privileges

of power, that the need to prove or assert masculinities becomes more pressing.

Boys as active subjects

The best research on boys as active subjects is interpretive and critical, prioritising the meanings boys attach to their actions and locating these in relation to structures or institutionalised practices embodying power relations. Where such research has been carried out it has addressed masculinities as identities which intersect with ethnicity, class and sexuality, and which can function as collective responses in particular cultural environments, notably schools, with their rhetorics of meritocracy in work and sport. The semblance of self-contained, self-confident masculinities is deconstructed by showing how they are created relationally and how they are policed, and by revealing the anxieties and vulnerabilities of boys which cause them to police themselves. Masculinities are consequently presented as powerful but fragile, asserted and constituted in opposition to each other and to versions of femininity.

Paul Willis' *Learning to Labour* (1977), was one of the earliest and most influential texts presenting boys as active and de-centred subjects. His aim in this was to develop an explanation of the reproduction of class relations in school through a detailed ethnographic account of the lives of a group of white working-class boys (the 'lads') who were 'destined' for generalised labour. The 'lads' inverted their school's middle-class standards, mocking the ways in which teachers treated pupils as children and in so doing asserting their more 'adult' identities. One of the defining characteristics of being 'one of the lads' was the ability to 'produce a laff', often at the expense of the 'ear'oles', the school conformists. The 'lads' were contemptuous of the 'ear'oles' because of their presumed inexperience of adult pleasures (drinking, [heterosexual] sex) which were counterposed to a commitment to schoolwork and an acceptance of the authority of the teacher. This opposition was gendered, the lads associating manual labour with 'masculinity and toughness', and the 'ear'oles' engagement in school as 'cissy'. Willis argued that the lads were drawing upon cultural constructions of masculinity which idealised manual workers' 'sacrifice and strength', so becoming a source of heightened self-esteem. The lads asserted their masculinity in the stories they told not only about resisting mental work but also about their relationships with women. 'Lascivious tales of conquest or jokes turning on the passivity of women or the particular sexual nature of men are regular topics of conversation' (p. 43).

Willis argued that the lads were realistic in their rejection of the school's investment in the discourse of meritocracy, seeing through to how it operates as a means of social control. It has been suggested, however, that in his emphasis upon the lads' resistance, Willis was romanticising them and not giving sufficient priority to the sexism and racism through which their masculinities were constituted. Willis explained the lads' culture in terms of class based resistance and not, as Skeggs (1992: 191) puts it, as 'legitimation and articulation of power and domination' – a notion drawing on the more fluid, Foucauldian conceptualisation of power which has become influential in the past two decades. Skeggs also argues that Willis failed to address the importance of sexuality in the formation of gendered identities in schools, for example colluding with the lads by not addressing how young women as active subjects resist and negotiate school (see Griffin, 1985). He implicitly confirms young women's marginality by prioritising class over gender as a dimension of power and an aspect of identity. Thus, the 'othering' of femininity by the lads is represented in Willis' account as part of the process through which class relations are produced – through which certain young men draw upon and create a working-class identity – rather than as a particular mode of masculinity.

The intersection of gender, class, 'race' and sexuality

More recent school-based ethnographies on boys, for example Mac an Ghaill (1994) and Sewell (1997), have examined how gender intersects with class, 'race' and sexuality in the formation of masculinities. Following Willis, this research has explored how the identities of particular boys have been produced collectively as ways of dealing with and negotiating their particular environment. But whereas Willis focused on the 'lads' and not those from whom they differentiated themselves, this research has distinguished more clearly between different masculinities. Both Mac an Ghaill and Sewell illustrate how these masculinities are structured as relations of power and how they are mediated by sexualised constructions of femininity.

In Mac an Ghaill's study, the 'Macho Lads' (from working-class backgrounds) regarded schoolwork as not 'real work', but as 'girls' work' and were contemptuous of school conformists. The 'Real Englishmen' (from middle-class backgrounds) differentiated themselves from the Macho Lads in terms of their attitudes to and relationships with women, with comments such as, 'they're really crude bastards with the girls ... they all go round thinking that they're real men, getting women and all that. It's all talk ... we're the real men' (p. 79). Somewhat ironically, they asserted their masculinity and a sense of cultural superiority by distancing themselves from boys who were regarded either as 'crude with girls' or as posing as real men. The 'Real Englishmen' also resisted their 'feminist' parents, who they claimed were 'emasculating' them by encouraging them to repress their 'real' sexual feelings. A third group, the 'Academic Achievers', who were from a skilled working-class background, were ridiculed and bullied for their participation in conventionally 'feminine' subjects. They learned to resist the ways both students and teachers positioned them as effeminate by parodying this identity. At the same time, however, they asserted their masculinity in more conventional ways, for instance by distinguishing male and female interests, which they associated respectively with the intellect and emotion, in subjects like English and drama. They disparaged the Macho Lads, 'the embodiment of manual labour and low life futures', calling them 'dickheads'. Finally, a fourth group, the 'New Enterprisers' were 'most active in the gender appropriation of recent curriculum reforms', for example colonising the computer club. They also constructed their identities in opposition to the Macho Lads who, they protested, gave the school a 'bad name' (p. 64).

In an ethnographic study which focused on the culture of a group of young men doing modern apprenticeships, Haywood and Mac an Ghaill (1997) found that constructions of heterosexuality were particularly significant in delineating the group identities of the young men. As with the various groups Mac an Ghaill identified in his school-based study, these were constructed in relation to each other. Haywood and Mac an Ghaill view the modern apprenticeship as a 'sexual apprenticeship', and argue that 'this was made visible in the way "Fashionable Heterosexuals" and "Explicit Heterosexuals" positioned a group of apprentices as "Sexual Outsiders"' (p. 583). Whereas the 'Fashionable Heterosexuals' displayed their heterosexual desirability through consumption of popular styles of dress, going to nightclubs, pubs and driving cars, the 'Explicit Heterosexuals' 'tended to base their heterosexuality on a demonstration of extreme perversity, violent misogyny and a racialised sexuality.' Rather like 'the lads' in Willis' study, they challenged authority by making explicit sexual references such as drawing penises on the board and 'searching for sexual double entendres in comments made by trainees and apprentices' (p. 582). Heterosexual performances such as these have been found to be significant in the construction of the identities of much younger and sexually inexperienced boys. For example, Emma Renold (2000) found that 9–10-year-old English primary-school boys 'formed their heterosexual identities' through 'symbolic sexual performances', 'public sexual innuendoes,' 'sexual storytelling' and 'sexual objectification of girls and women' (p. 321). In her observational study of pre-primary children, Valerie Walkerdine (1981) found boys subverting the woman teacher's authority by objectifying and sexualising her. Hayward and Mac an Ghaill examine how the boys identified themselves as heterosexually competent through sexually harassing other boy apprentices – the 'Sexual Outsiders' – whose 'presentation of themselves was not dependent on visible assertions of heterosexuality' (p. 583). These boys were ridiculed by the 'Fashionable Heterosexuals' for their presumed feminised or heterosexually unfashionable and unattractive looks, and by the 'Explicit Heterosexuals' in 'more explicitly sexualised ways' as gay.

Addressing black masculinities as collective responses in a racist culture, Tony Sewell (1997) explores how black boys (aged 15 years) 'survive modern schooling'. He found that many of these boys located themselves in 'a phallocentric framework', positioning themselves as superior to white and Asian students in terms of their sexual attractiveness, style, creativity and hardness. (In Mac an Ghaill's study, those Macho Lads who were African Caribbean expressed similar sentiments.) They referred to white boys as 'pussies' (female) and 'batty men' (homosexuals) and, in illustrating this, spoke of white boys' fears about 'doing daring' or up-front scams (pp. 11–12). This kind of masculinity was most clearly exemplified by the 'rebels', who cultivated and played with machismo styles (e.g. listening to 'hard ' rap with misogynistic lyrics, boasting about their heterosexual prowess, developing particular styles of walking). Sewell claims they were resisting racism, but, at the same time, playing to and reinforcing white racist stereotypes of black men. They resented being 'othered' by teachers, being perceived as threatening and being picked upon because they were black, but for some of them the knowledge that teachers were afraid of their appearance, style and 'gesture' was a source of power and an incentive to perform in threatening ways. The 'hyper-masculinity' of the 'rebels' was rejected in school by the 'conformists', the majority of African Caribbean boys, who spoke of the importance of investing in schooling in order to better themselves in a racist society, and also partly by the 'innovators' who desired academic success but were attracted by the rebels. Like Willis' 'lads' and Mac an Ghaill's 'macho lads', the rebels deployed the rhetoric of experience to assert themselves in relation to other African Caribbean boys, while the 'conformists', like Mac an Ghaill's 'academic achievers', drew on the rhetoric of reason in positioning themselves in relations of power with respect to the rebels.

The hegemony of whiteness, as of masculinity, has previously been exemplified in its taken-for-granted, unmarked character. Recent research has focused on how white boys construct their racialised identities. This has again highlighted the way identities are unconsciously constructed in relation to the other. In interviews with white skinhead 14–25-year-old young men in Birmingham, Anoop Nayak (1999) found that while these boys disparaged black boys for acting or performing, for example 'swinging their arms like ... apes', they did not see themselves as enacting whiteness. 'White identities are naturalised in the phrase "We act like we act", which disguises the regulatory styling required to sustain these identities and allows whiteness to be presented as the "norm" ' (pp. 88–9). Whiteness was reified and taken for granted. Les Back (1994) found that for white, working-class young men living in south London, African Caribbean men were 'constructed in the terms of the fear and desire couplet', in contrast to Vietnamese young men who were 'typically vilified as feeble, soft and effeminate' (p. 181). Being an African Caribbean male was associated by these white men with hardness, assertiveness and sexual attractiveness – characteristics which they valued highly. Back suggests that this was why many young white men were attracted to black style.

In a paper examining the identities and emotions of the five 'prime suspects' in the Stephen Lawrence murder, David Jackson (2000) explores the kind of white masculinities these young men inhabit and how they were constructed in relation to versions of the black masculine 'other'. Rather than addressing these young men simply as racist monsters and emphasizing their arrogance, as the popular media tended to do, Jackson contrasts 'their outward bravado' and 'inner anxieties'. Analyzing their racist language and posturing, as caught by secret police videos, he argues that the intensity of their racism towards black people was fuelled by their own insecurities as white, working-class young men, desperate to be seen as 'confident', 'flash' and 'making it'. Jackson argues that the 'prime suspects' were engaged in a 'white warrior discourse' as they sought to 're-constitute themselves as vigorous, manly and powerfully dominant, especially in their gendered selves and white English identities' (p. 21). This involved 'projecting their ambivalence and self-doubts onto ... fantasized black men'. Jackson situates their racism arising from a sense of loss in the context of the decline of English imperial power, and the contemporary proliferation of multicultural discourses. Their sense of loss is reinforced by their perception that 'other' cultures are being celebrated in the name of multiculturalism at the expense of their 'own' (see Hewitt, 1996). Their anxieties about 'loss' and their desire to assert themselves in relation to black men, were no doubt reinforced by popular associations of toughness and smartness with black boys. As Jackson writes, 'some black men were seen to have more street credibility than the suspects who are more concerned with giving an appearance that they've made it' (p. 17). In developing anti-racist approaches for working with young white racist men, research such as Jackson's and Hewitt's suggests that these must not be 'overly rational' and dismissive of their racist beliefs, but must 'work with the underlying fears and anxieties about being seen as humiliated that motivates many white, working-class men today.'

The construction of Asians as weak and effeminate and African Caribbeans, in contrast, as macho, has also been observed by Mac an Ghaill (1994), Paul Connolly (1994) in an ethnographic study in a primary school and Phil Cohen (1997) in a study of white working-class adolescent boys in London. Like Back, Cohen found that a number of the white boys he worked with were attracted to African Caribbean styles because of macho associations, while despising and rejecting Asians as 'wimps'. The white boys told stories about street fights with black African Caribbean boys in which they both admired and despised them. They were seen by the white boys 'in terms of an aggressive street presence, whilst Asians, in contrast, were portrayed as performing bizarre rituals behind closed doors...' (p. 159). Connolly (1998) found that whereas white and black boys fought and had cussing matches in public places, they would 'swoop' on Asian boys, hitting them and calling them racist names. As Connolly notes, the 'style of such confrontations prevented South Asian boys from effectively defending themselves and therefore "proving" themselves as competent fighters' (p. 126). Asian boys, he argues, had become partially 'the focus through which other boys were able to develop and reassert their own masculine status. Arguably, being masculine could be reinforced by some boys through distancing themselves from South Asian boys just as much as it could from girls more generally' (p. 125). Teachers also contributed to the feminising of Asian boys by praising them for their hard work, constructing them as quiet and little and needing to be befriended, and disciplining them usually in private not public. They tended to attribute Asian boys' bad behaviour to peer pressure and played down its significance, using words like 'silly' and 'immature', thus maintaining perceptions of them as essentially 'hardworking and helpful' (p. 119). They were most likely to single out black boys to be publicly chastised who, in turn, resisted this, confirming teachers' expectations of them as unruly.

The vulnerability of masculine identities and emotional expression

Research such as that of Mac an Ghaill and Sewell has indicated the vulnerability of masculine identities, which always need to be proved or asserted and so reinforce and obscure the anxieties and tensions which underlie them. There is evidence in these studies that masculinities may become shored up and exemplified in the most polarised and misogynistic ways by boys who collectively feel undermined in and out of school. Mac an Ghaill argues that despite the apparent camaraderie which male peer groups offer, they are actually experienced by many boys as unsupportive; in his study, several boys expressed feeling 'lonely' with their 'mates'. This was because of the pressure which they felt in these groups to assert masculinities by avoiding all talk about feelings. Angela Phillips (1998) points to a dichotomy between boys' constructions of themselves as 'loyal' and the male peer group culture which tends to militate against displays of intimacy or concern for others. In interviews with 13–14-year-old boys about their working practices at school, the boys reported that they 'don't help each other and laugh at people who need help'. The boys were 'aware that girls have more intimate relationships which they tend to describe disparagingly'. For example they were preoccupied with girls 'whispering,' implying they were 'underhand and sneaky.' Such constructions of girls, Phillips suggests, 'betray their feelings of exclusion'.

The peer group, as Holland *et al.* (1993) found, enabled young men to talk about heterosexual desires, but such talk was structured by the need to affirm manhood. Like Mac an Ghaill and Phillips, they found that young men experienced the single-sex peer group as a competitive space in which they were expected to prove themselves. This was reflected in their stories of first sex which were about proving their masculinity: 'perhaps the most significant difference between the stories of first sex told by young men and young women was that the former spoke of masculinity and the latter of the self' (Thomson, 1996, p. 6). Julian Wood (1984) in his study of boys' sexual cultures in a London sin bin (a school for 'disruptive' children) found that when boys spoke about girls in single-sex group interviews, they were sexualized by objectifying and fragmenting them, and 'the reproductive and excremental aspects of the female body were constantly referred to by the boys in a fixated-disgusted tone edged with nervousness and surrounded by giggling' (p. 65). This kind of sex talk was contrasted by Wood with an occasion when one boy spoke alone into a tape recorder about the type of women he fancied. This boy spoke much more affectionately about girls, and distanced himself 'from the most one-dimensional view of women that he perhaps feels is de rigueur in the company of his mates: that is, a view that *completely* reduces women to their bodies' (p. 80). Peer-group talk about girls was titillating and was a way in which boys constructed themselves as powerful in relation to the girls they dissected, but this seemed to be at the expense of being able to express feelings of affection.

The notion that boys are vulnerable and weak precisely because they cannot express their emotions and anxieties among their peers, is, as Thomson *et al.* (1998) found, a popular one among girls. Interviewing young teenage boys and girls in England and Northern Ireland about their moral values and identities, they found that girls saw women as strong as well as mature because of being able to 'express "feelings" and to construct and negotiate "problems" ' with their peers. 'The contrary demands of masculinity to hold feelings was understood to stunt emotional development' (p. 8). Boys were seen by the girls as immature because of being preoccupied with their 'public image', with the implication that girls could be much truer to their 'private selves'. Yet, paradoxically, 'emotionally leaky' boys were despised by the girls as 'wimps'.

In an interview-based study involving 14–16-year-olds in London schools, Becky Francis (1999) also found that boys were constructed – by both boys and girls – as immature and inauthentic in groups, and as developing a culture of 'laddishness' which militated against intellectual achievement. 'Laddishness', Francis writes, 'evokes a young exclusively male group and the hedonistic practices popularly associated with such groups, for example "having a laugh", alcohol consumption, disruptive behaviour, objectifying women ...' (p. 359). She notes that 'laddish' values have had a high media profile, popularised in various sitcoms as well as being condemned as part of the contemporary moral panic about boys 'underachieving'. Francis asked her subjects whether they agreed with the view expressed by a British education minister that 'laddish values' were impeding boys' learning. Two-thirds of the pupils, including about two-thirds of the boys agreed. Though laddish boys were criticised, especially by girls, for being immature, 'acting hard' and 'showing off' to impress other boys and girls, the students also implied that laddish behaviour was 'important and desirable in male friendship groups and for attracting girls' (p. 370). It seems they positioned themselves in complex and multiple ways in relation to notions of 'laddishness'. Francis herself reflects on how she and the teachers 'often found the laddish boys particularly appealing and amusing' (p. 371).

While 'laddish' boys may be seen as heterosexually attractive, some researchers have found that many boys construct 'falling in love' as making them less 'laddish', more mature and autonomous. Interviewing college boys about their experiences of 'falling in love', Redman (1998) found that the ways they spoke about this 'seemed to involve the boys in asserting a form of masculinity that was in competition with other more laddish forms' which these boys disparaged as immature (p. 11). Redman suggests that the appropriation of 'romantic masculinities' and the consequent rejection of 'laddishness' 'allowed the boys to reinvent themselves' in a way which was consonant with the academic demands of college. Interviewing young men and women in their late teens and early twenties about sexual relationships, Holland *et al.* (1998) found that 'the development of an intimate relationship with a woman is a means by which many of them [young men] are able to distance themselves from the values of their male peers' (p. 90). Love relations and relations with peers appeared to be expressed in opposition to each other. With their male peers, they could not even communicate feelings of love and respect for girlfriends for fear of ridicule (see also Wight, 1994). Wood (1984) suggests that the desire for heterosexual relationships among boys may be reinforced by dissatisfaction with relations in the all-male peer group:

> The fact of not being able to show 'softer' aspects of self to one's mates may push the boys towards a heterosexual relationship with an 'ordinary girl' who can listen to them and allow them to relax certain constraints of macho. (p. 79).

Walker and Kushner (1999) argue that having a girlfriend enabled a boy to 'escape the ritualised banter of his mates and indulge in extended conversation'. This they see as being significant in enabling boys to be more 'self confident' and 'individualistic' (p. 53): 'armed with her acceptance of his private self, he can venture back into the group' (p. 54).

Walker and Kushner (1997, 1999) found the dichotomy between asserting or proving masculinities and expressing feelings, especially in male groups, tends to be experienced by boys themselves as an acute disjunction between a 'public' and a 'private', 'authentic' self. For example, they found that many 12–15-year-old boys whose 'public' identities were openly displayed and asserted as confident and optimistic, heterosexual, macho and sociable, nevertheless 'privately' expressed anxieties stemming from their 'public identities'. Among these anxieties were concerns about their academic progress and their future employment prospects, in opposition to which they asserted their confident and hedonistic 'public' identities. However, while it is important to recognise the significance of the public/private dichotomy in the ways boys construct and experience their identities, it is equally important not to reify the public and private by associating the private self with authenticity and stability and the public self, in contrast, with artificiality, peer pressure and external manipulation. When Walker and Kushner write about boys' 'construction of a private self', they risk decontextualising it, identifying it with 'what you think and who you are' in opposition to what 'you say and what you do' with your peers. Not only is it theoretically important to give weight to the construction of selfhood in different contexts, it is also empirically the case that boys may experience being able to be 'who they are' in the context of the peer group (see Chapter 1). For example, Pattman (1991) found that boys reported being able to communicate 'the one thing you think about most' and 'the first thing that comes into your head' when talking about sex in the peer group. Even though boys' peer-group talk about sexuality may be jokey, misogynistic and often involve shared insults (see Holland *et al.*, 1998), it tends to be constructed as private and about 'real feelings' precisely because talk about sexuality is circumscribed in other contexts and with other people.

Recent literature indicates that the 'authentic' individual is itself an attractive masculine identity (one which the 'Real Englishmen' in Mac an Ghaill's study appeared to adopt). It is often taken up in quite élitist ways by boys who fail in terms of hegemonic versions of masculinity. Other boys are re-constructed as weak, manipulated by the crowd, obsessed with image and inauthentic. For example, Edley and Wetherell (1997) reported how some sixth-form non-rugby-playing boys challenged the domination of rugby players at a private single-sex school by portraying them as 'unthinking conformists, incapable, or even scared perhaps of doing their own thing' (p. 211). The implication was that they (the non-rugby players) were, in contrast, 'mentally strong' and individualistic. Interviewing men, Wetherell and Edley (1999) found that 'demonstrating one's distance from macho stereotypes' was a common discursive strategy, and argue that this may be 'one of the most effective ways … of being a "man" ' (p. 351). Rather than seeing these men as 'beyond gender power', they focus on how they were asserting their superiority, demonstrating individuality and autonomy' as well as maturity, by constructing themselves as different from these stereotypes. Referring to Seidler (1989, 1994), they note the celebration of individuality and autonomy is 'not just a legacy of liberal Enlightenment discourse,' but 'a mode of representation long colonised by men' (p. 350). They question Connell's assumption that the sorts of macho stereotypes from which many men and boys distance themselves represents hegemonic masculinity. 'Perhaps what is most hegemonic is to be non hegemonic! – an independent man who knows his own mind and who can "see through" social expectations' (p. 351).

Femininity and homosexuality

Several studies (e.g. Willis, 1977; Mac an Ghaill, 1994; Sewell, 1997; Redman and Mac an Ghaill, 1997) have focused on how masculinities are constructed as relations of power around opposing discourses which deploy the rhetorics of experience and reason in various ways, and also on how femininity is constructed as other, even by those adopting apparently 'subordinate' masculinities. Femininity comes to be associated with particular boys in opposition to whom 'real' masculinities are asserted. These boys are seen as 'gays and cissys', terms which Epstein (1997) shows are often interchangeable. The fragility of masculinities in this sense has been highlighted by research which has pointed to the homophobic concerns of boys. In interviews with gay men about their experiences as boys at school, Epstein found that homophobia was expressed 'towards non-macho boys and was in terms of their similarity to girls' (p. 109). She indicates that it is by foregrounding and examining misogyny and homophobia and how they are interlinked that we can begin to address and deconstruct taken-for-granted heterosexual masculinities. The dual others to normative heterosexual masculinities in schools are girls/women and non-macho boys/men. It is against these that many boys seek to define their identities.

The importance boys attach to homosexuality has become apparent through the ways they position men researching gender and sexuality (or acting as facilitators in 'boys' work'). Mac an Ghaill (1994) found that he was constructed as 'soft' by a number of the male students with whom he interacted, and claimed that this 'seemed to operate as a code that legitimated his personal engagement with the boys in a "non-masculine" mode of talk' (p. 95). It seems that in this context 'soft' had quite positive connotations – there was no indication that the young men Mac an Ghaill spoke to (even the Macho Lads) sexualized this identity and felt threatened by, or were hostile to, him. But in an ethnographic study 'probing ... norms of masculinity' of boys aged 14–16 in two schools in Glasgow, Daniel Wight (1994) was questioned about his marital status in order, as he perceived it, to ascertain his sexuality. He responded by saying he was married with two children 'which led them to conclude (correctly) that I am heterosexual' (p. 707). The effect of this statement on Wight's relationships with the young men in his study is open to debate.

Male facilitators of young men's groups, whose aim has been to encourage self-reflection and talk about feelings and relationships, have also been viewed suspiciously as gay. Epstein (1997) refers to a workshop she attended on anti-sexist work with boys in which the facilitator claimed that in order to retain any kind of credibility with the boys with whom he worked he had to 'drop remarks about having a girlfriend' and even to state that 'we know that none of us here are gay' – an ethically dubious approach. Wight (1994) points out that explicit references to homosexuality by the young men in his study were rare, but this, he suggests, did not indicate their lack of concern with sexual orientation in establishing their identities, but rather how compulsory heterosexuality is taken for granted as the cultural norm. In contrast, Nayak and Kehily (1996) in a study on the ways homophobia was expressed in a secondary school, found that homophobia had a high profile in heterosexual male student cultures: 'we were struck by the everydayness of homophobia and wondered why it was so prevalent' (p. 211). In a conversation with girl students (aged 15) about boys' homophobia, the girls indicated in a way which mocked boys how tied up their construction of themselves was with showing themselves not to be gay. Boys, they pointed out, invented certain boys as gay and proceeded to relate to them as if they were 'contagious': 'they go "STAY AWAY" (demonstrates crucifix sign with fingers) or something like that' (p. 216). They were derisive of the ways boys lumped together boys with 'squeaky voices' or who were not 'very well built' or quiet in class, and of the very explicit ways they distanced themselves from them. Nayak and Kehily concluded that homophobia was a kind of performance in which many young men were constantly engaged which 'gave masculinity the appearance of substance' (p. 225). The fact that the young men felt compelled continually to perform, and the fusion of these performances with ('unmasculine') anxieties and contradictions – for example making the sign of the crucifix, being anxious about having to watch an HIV video, running into the girls' toilet to avoid a 'homosexual encounter' – suggested how problematic the achievement of a masculine identity was. Playing upon and drawing attention to the anxieties which underlie these homophobic performances is a way in which girls resist boys' misogyny, although girls themselves often seek to avoid being labelled as 'lesbian' (Lees, 1986).

In an ethnographic study of sexual bullying in secondary schools in central England, Duncan (1999) found that while the 'most prevalent and hurtful accusation levelled at boys by both sexes was to be called gay' (p. 106), the idea that some boys might actually *be* gay 'was inconceivable'. When Duncan mentioned to the boys he interviewed that it was claimed that 10 per cent of the population was gay and that this might be reflected in the school, the boys 'responded with frightening alacrity that they would attack them, even if they had been close friends up to that point' (p. 108). Mary Kehily (1999) also found that the teenage boys she interviewed, in her school-based ethnography, were 'anxious to place homosexuality beyond the bounds of their immediate environment'. When she asked, 'what if one of your mates told you that he was gay?' the boys expressed 'shock' – 'having a gay friend was unimaginable' (p. 14). The shock was defused through humour as the boys sought to redefine relationships they took for granted. Drawing on 'stereotypes of gay men as contagious and sexually voracious', they joked about not wanting to be 'left alone' with their mates, 'especially if you're sleeping around at your mates'. It is hardly surprising, given the 'presumption of heterosexuality' and the disgust and abhorrence which boys expressed when this was challenged, that no boys in these studies identified as gay. Indeed, reflecting this, gay boys are conspicuous by their absence in school-based ethnographies, Mac an Ghaill's (1994) research with 16–18-year-old young men being an exception. Duncan indicates that boys' homophobia in schools also operates to 'shut down' 'signs of incipient emotional sharing between boys', confining boys to a thin and impoverished range of expression for their feelings' (p. 124).

A further example of the enactment of masculinity in relation to particular fears and anxieties associated with femininity can be found in the 'cooties' rituals which Barrie Thorne (1993) observed in an ethnographic study of an elementary school in the United States. In 'cooties', 'specific individuals or groups are treated as contaminating or carrying germs' (p. 73). While girls and boys may give cooties to one another, girls are treated as 'the ultimate source of contamination' (p. 74) – they are the ones who infect boys. Cooties are spread usually when someone has been touched after being chased in the playground, though cooties can be warded off by shaping one's fingers to eject a 'cootie spray' or using 'cootie catchers' made of folded paper. The parallels between these rituals and those that Nayak and Kehily observed to ward off homosexuality are striking. In this case, girls in general, and in particular overweight or impoverished girls who became labelled 'cootie queens' or 'cootie girls' (there were no equivalent 'cootie kings' or 'cootie boys'), were the pollutants from which boys physically protected themselves and, in so doing, displayed their masculinity. Not only did they differentiate themselves from girls in this way, but they constructed certain boys (from whom they distanced themselves) as girl-like by pushing them next to the contaminating space of girls, making them sit next to them. These subordinated boys included recent immigrants from Mexico and a boy 'who was overweight and afraid of sports' (pp. 74–5).

Nayak and Kehily draw upon the work of Judith Butler (1990) to suggest that it is precisely through repetitive performances of this kind that gender is produced and enacted; that is, gender is a performative act. Homophobic and misogynistic repetition of the kind observed by Nayak and Kehily, may be understood as a continual attempt to construct an ever elusive masculine ideal. As Nayak and Kehily (1996: 227) write, 'the performance provides a fantasy of masculinity which can only be sustained through repetition, yet always resonates the echo of uncertainty'. Similarly, Donna Eder *et al.* (1995) in a study of gender relations among adolescents in a school in the United States, suggest that boys' homophobic practices demonstrate that there is no essential masculinity and, hence, that boys have actively to attempt to shore up their masculine identities: 'since these labels are viewed so negatively by adolescent boys, their extensive use suggests that strong pressure is needed to reinforce traditional masculine behaviour' (p. 64).

Recent research in Britain and Australia has noted a tendency for boys to construct themselves as victims of sexism, and in response to this, assert themselves in macho ways. In a questionnaire-based study in Britain, involving 1400 boys, aged 13–19, Buchanan and McCoy (1998) found that boys with low 'self-esteem' are most likely to 'comfort themselves with the knowledge that they are indeed true mega macho males' (p. 34) and to 'feel most threatened by women's struggle for equality' (p. 39). In an ethnographic study which focused on 12–15-year-olds in four secondary schools in working-class catchment areas in Britain, Shirley Prendergast and Simon Forrest (1997) found 'a growing sense of bitter injustice among boys' which 'could be heard in the ways in which boys described what they saw as teachers' differential behaviour to girls and boys' (p. 185). The boys reported teachers favouring girls and being nice to them, talking and listening to them more, giving them higher marks and being less likely to punish them than boys. The girls they interviewed corroborated this, but explained that boys were treated less favourably not because of teachers' prejudices but because the boys were more disruptive and troublesome. In her interview and questionnaire-based study of 13–14-year-olds in a mixed school, Angela Phillips (1998) found marked differences between boys and girls on the question of whether teachers favoured girls, with 69 percent of boys and only 21 percent of girls agreeing with the suggestion that teachers paid 'more attention to girls'. While the boys, in their questionnaire responses were more critical of women than men teachers for favouring girls, in the single-sex group interviews which Phillips conducted with them, they blamed men teachers more for preferring girls and in particular for flirting with them. Phillips suggests that 'accusations of men teachers flirting with girls from boys' may be 'tied up with a sense of disappointment felt by boys' who 'want to be treated like men but find themselves reduced to the status of child in relation to teachers and often their female peers' who see themselves as 'more mature than the boys' and able to 'establish more equal relations' with teachers (p. 12). As we discuss in Chapter 5, the construction of girls as mature in relation to boys, and their identification with teachers, has been noted by a number of researchers doing ethnographic work in schools.

The mixed group discussions which Prendergast and Forrest held on the topic of gender relations, were highly charged and gender polarised, with girls criticising boys for, among other things, 'behaving badly in class', 'showing off', 'fighting', 'being sexist', 'not listening' and 'taking the mickey', and boys blaming girls for 'leading boys on', 'winding boys up', 'talking all the time' and 'being disloyal'. Prendergast and Forrest suggest that these sorts of gender polarised engagements may have become more 'conflictual' over the past decade, because boys (and especially working-class boys) have, with the restructuring of the economy, 'lost ground compared to girls', and also because girls 'no longer have quite the same romantic desires and investments in the boys that they know, and have come to articulate more about their own needs and interests' (p. 192). They found the frustration of the boys was also apparent in the 'fatalistic ways they spoke about their future lives', and the 'meaninglessness of school when they saw boredom, unemployment and poverty ahead of them'. All the girls, 'in contrast when asked about their future ... had plans'.

Evidence that the sort of anger and bitterness Prendergast and Forrest observed in the boys they studied may be, in part, a response to the increasing confidence and independence of girls, comes from an Australian school-based study. This was conducted by Kenway *et al.* (1998), and focused on the impact of feminist reforms in schools – the introduction, for example, of single-sex group work and events and the promotion of subjects and activities constructed as traditionally masculine for girls. Such reforms were found to make many boys 'cynical, resentful and alienated, hostile and punitive' (p. 152). Mobilising a 'discourse of victimhood', many boys sought to 'rebuild male solidarity' (p. 154), blaming teachers and girls for the perceived injustices being perpetrated against them and reasserting 'traditional masculinity' and being more demanding in class. While the boys blamed girls for excluding them from single-sex activities and lessons, they also 'fiercely and often brutally protect their boys-only places and pleasures' (p. 149), notably the playground and sport. They also interpreted single-sex events and classes in terms of a 'deficit view of girls' – girls were seen as , 'too shy, too weak and too worried to make it with them in the main game of schooling' (p. 149). Kenway *et al.* are critical of gender reform programmes, as practised in schools, for tending only to problematise boys in relation to girls and therefore fueling boys' resentment of girls and influencing them to become more macho. Such programmes need to encourage boys to reflect on their masculine identities and their pleasures and fears.

Constructing the fiction of an essential masculinity from multiple positions

How young men construct the fiction of an essential, unified masculine self on the basis of an absorption with control of the body is a major theme in this research field. Connell (1995) writes about how particular hegemonic masculinities focus around a muscular male body essentialised and reinforced in opposition to an 'emphasized femininity'. 'What it means to be masculine', he suggests elsewhere (Connell, 1987: 27), is, quite literally, to embody force, to embody competence'. Being physically big, as Nayak and Kehily observe, can take on a symbolic character, for example acting or performing in ways such as shouting or laughing loudly, which make one look big and draw attention to oneself.

A number of other researchers have noted the significance attached by boys to body shape and, in relation to this, ability at sport as indicators of masculinity (e.g. Thorne, 1993; Canaan, 1991; Eder, 1995; Kessler *et al.*, 1985; Messner *et al.*, 1990). Whitson (1990) claims that for boys and young men:

> for whom other sources of recognised masculine authority (based on earning power, adult sexual relations or fatherhood) are some ways off, the development of body appearance and body language that are suggestive of force and skill is experienced as an urgent task. (p. 23)

Canaan (1991) suggests that for the working-class young men in her study, their bodies were 'the main source of their power and esteem', since their male identities were partly affirmed through manual labour (p. 122). These young men, aged 16–21, identified themselves and other young men in terms of their relations to 'hardness'. Hardness or lack of hardness was associated with fighting ability and was sexualized, with the hardest boys being constructed as the most heterosexually attractive. A distinction was commonly drawn between those boys who were admired for 'being hard' and those who were despised for 'acting hard', between those who are able to demonstrate their hardness in fighting and those who were not. Of course in critiquing certain boys for 'acting hard', we might suggest, following Wetherell and Edley (1999), that they were asserting themselves as 'individuals' and 'their own men' in relation to them. Frosh (1997) interprets the concern of boys and men with body size and muscularity as representing a kind of estrangement from their bodies. They are striving to make their body 'the instrument of the will, to be honed and worked upon so that it will be able to achieve what is expected of it', repressing and opposing 'its illnesses and its emotions, its uncontrollable aspects' (p. 72). This is supported by Jackson (1990) who, in an autobiographical piece, reflects on how, as a boy, he 'hardened' his body through 'everyday sporting practice' (p. 207) and became habituated to imposing 'my will on my body and other people rather than listening to it and learning to acknowledge its needs' (p. 220). Paradoxically, however, as Mary Kehily (1999) found in interviews with teenage boys about sexual encounters with girls, female bodies were 'idealized' and male bodies 'denigrated'. While women were constructed as 'smooth', 'rounded' and 'nice', men become 'hairy', 'smelly' and 'nasty'. It would appear the idealization and eroticisation of bodily difference was closely linked to the extreme disgust which Kehily found boys expressed about same-sex sexual attraction among men. Though male bodies were denigrated, they were also, as the research we have cited suggests, objects of desire for boys. This research indicates that physical toughness and self-confidence are linked and counterposed to intellectual or academic commitment, which comes to signify weakness and effeminacy.

As Sewell (1997) and Connolly (1998) found, these oppositions are racialised. The African Caribbean boys in Sewell's study, as we have seen, were aware of being perceived as threatening by teachers. Sewell observed that teachers' anxieties towards black boys often 'focused on their bodies', viewing them as big and seeing their size as threatening. It seems that the performances of the African Caribbean boys, and especially the 'rebels', became reified and associated with 'race' grounded in body type. These boys also constructed themselves as bigger and stronger than white boys, and took pride in this. Focusing on the performances of black boys and men in the USA, Richard Majors (1990), like Sewell, elaborates on these as compensatory responses to racism through which they assert themselves in 'expressive and conspicuous' ways as black males. These centre around physical appearance and disposition and have been described by Majors (1990) as 'cool pose':

> Black men often cope with their frustration, embitterment and alienation and social impotence by channelling their creative energies into the construction of unique, expressive and conspicuous styles of demeanor, speech, gesture, clothing, hairstyle, walk, stance and handshake. (p. 111)

He argues that sport is particularly important for black males for demonstrating 'cool pose', citing the expressive styles of black basketball players. But Majors also notes that the emphasis on sport and cool pose among black males is often self-defeating because it comes at the expense of educational advancement. Furthermore, the construction of oneself as an 'expressive' male takes place in opposition to versions of effeminacy and, as Majors shows, reproduces inequalities between males and females as well as male hierarchies.

Connolly (1998) found that football, which was dominated by African Caribbean boys and was 'highly valued among the boys' as it provided 'one of the central aspects of their identities', was understood by teachers as helping to integrate 'problematic' black boys (p. 134). Not only did black boys' participation in football help to produce them as sporty, tough and active in opposition to being academic, but also in opposition to 'weak' Asian boys. Asian boys were 'almost systematically excluded from playing football', and when asked to explain this, African Caribbean and white boys denigrated them as weak, like girls: 'they can't run fast' or 'they're small' (p. 129).

In an interview-based study with boys in primary and secondary schools in Australia, Gilbert and Gilbert (1998) found that 'while the experiences of gender of particular boys is complex, and changes with context, the performance of masculinity is always constructed in relation to a dominant image of gender difference' (p. 143). In particular, boys constructed girls as bookish and clever, and themselves, in contrast, as active and sporty. Girls' cleverness was not admired, but attributed to their inactivity – 'they have nothing else to do' but work. Gilbert and Gilbert examine how this construction of girls makes boys anti-academic: 'the more able boys engaged in disruptive behaviour to show they were like the others and the collective lack of effort tended to disguise the shortcomings of, and save face for, the low achievers' (p. 140). Boys also asserted themselves by denigrating and ostracising those boys who were constructed as academic. They were seen as inactive, like girls, and antisocial, doing schoolwork rather than participating with other boys in sport. In some of the individual, though not the group, interviews boys revealed costs incurred by positioning themselves as 'active' boys, for example, not being able to say they liked aspects of school, such as reading, to other boys. One boy 'identified as a worker' tried to 'evade any stigma' by claiming he worked 'to get it done' in order to do 'other things', the implication being that he did not work because he derived pleasure from it. 'Ultimately he was saved', Gilbert and Gilbert note, 'by being acknowledged as a sportsman' (p. 134).

Researching the significance of football in the lives of 10-year-old primary boys, Jon Swain (2000) found that 'girls were actively excluded from football' (p. 104) and also that certain boys who were 'barely granted a look in during the games' (p. 105) were 'frequently publicly derided and ridiculed for their lack of skill and prowess'. They became 'feminised' and subject to homophobic abuse. These boys spoke about the good footballers, the popular boys, as ' "flash", "showoffs", "bullies", "acting hard" and as "not letting us play football" ' (p. 107). It would seem that much like the non rugby playing boys in Edley's and Wetherell's study (1997), they were resisting the popular boys and relieving their own anxieties by constructing them as not genuine. Significantly, Swain found that academic ability and commitment were not feminised by these 10-year-old boys, nor were they constructed in opposition to being sporty. Indeed, the committed footballers were 'also high academic achievers, they enjoyed school and school work, and for the most part worked hard in the classroom, even if they affected an air of insouciance' (p. 106). In contrast, the unpopular boys were not only 'not very good at football or games', but 'were not such high academic achievers, did not do so well in class, were lacking in confidence and generally seemed more imma-ture' (p. 107). It may be that masculinity and femininity become increas-ingly polarised around sport and work in secondary school and are more fluid constructs earlier on.

In the above studies, boys' engagement in sport is not taken for granted, as if simply reflecting a male propensity for physical activity. Rather particular sports are conceptualised as key sites for the construc-tion of masculinities. In a paper on the significance of football among 9–10-year-old boys in London primary schools, Epstein *et al.* (forthcom-ing) found that in one primary school 'doing boy acceptably (to other boys and to many girls too) involved playing football as well as knowing how to talk about the professional game knowledgeably.' 'Establishing oneself as a good footballer ... established one as a real boy' and as het-erosexually desirable. Epstein *et al.* suggest that the exclusion of girls from football did not lead to girls being uninterested in it, for, while the boys played football, 'much of their talk was about the boys, their prowess as footballers and their general attractiveness'. But in another primary school they studied, football appeared to be much less significant in reproducing gender polarized identities. This was partly because girls-only football sessions were organised by a popular woman teacher; not only did this challenge the view that football could only be played by (active) boys, but it meant boys were 'compelled to find other activities,' some of which involved playing with girls.

It may be, as some researchers have argued, that in middle-class schools, because of their academic orientation, opportunities for 'doing boy' in popular ways are circumscribed. Here the boys are encouraged to take a 'calculative attitude' and 'rationality and responsibility rather than pride and aggressiveness' are encouraged (Connell, 1989: 296–7). At the same time, though, sport in these schools creates, as James Messerschmidt (1994) explains, 'an environment for the construction of masculinity that celebrates toughness and endurance' (p. 87). But as if to compensate for the relative failure to 'do boy' in popular ways at school, and to 'validate a boy's "essential nature" ' (in Messerschmidt's words) , middle-class white boys often engage in successful pranks, mischief, van-dalism, minor thefts and drinking outside school (p. 89).

It is not, however, always the case, as Peter Redman shows, that academic commitment is seen to signify weakness and femininity in

opposition to being sporty, disruptive and funny. As Redman's autobiographical account of his appropriation, in an all-boys grammar school, of
'muscular intellectualness' implies, being intellectual may be a way of
proving oneself and asserting a masculine identity which has much in
common with competitive sport (Redman and Mac an Ghaill, 1997).
Redman writes about how he admired and identified with a history
teacher because of his intellectual self-confidence and his ability to 'push
people around intellectually' (p. 163). For Redman, who was bad at
games and uninterested in hard sciences, this teacher made accessible an
'alternative yet "proper" form of masculinity' in a school with a public
school ethos of competitive sports – a particularly rich example of the
deployment of the 'rhetoric of reason' in constructing a powerful masculine identity. However, it is worth noting that in this autobiographical
piece, Redman's interest in and engagement with the humanities, as a
sixth-form student, is read only in terms of this becoming a source of
'real' masculinity and of 'muscular intellectualness' and not (or not also)
in terms of possibilities for reflecting upon and discussing (in however
sublimated ways) social relations, feelings and emotions. According to
this account, Redman was attracted to his history teacher because he
' "de-feminised" academic work in the humanities and refuted the label,
"a bit of a poof" ' (p. 171), not because he exemplified a different version
of masculinity, was more liberal than other teachers, was more self-
reflexive and treated students more democratically. Attraction for this
latter set of reasons seems like a plausible reading which is denied by
exclusively focusing on masculinities as identities forged only in opposition to a femininity constructed as unitary and essentialist.

Conclusion

Research on boys as active subjects involves making masculinities plural
and understanding and addressing them as relational identities which
boys construct and inhabit. While such research aims to be interpretive
and empathic in order to understand what it is like to be a young man
from the point of view of boys themselves, it is critical of the ways particular masculinities come to be constructed as if they were pre-given
identities with essential attributes inhering in them, necessarily different
from the femininities of girls and women. By addressing how and why
these gender-polarised identities are asserted, performed and consoli-
dated in relation to girls and other boys, research which treats boys as

active subjects constructs masculinities as produced out of specific discursive strategies. Essentialist versions of 'masculinity' are, however, not dismissed as intellectual aberrations, but re-conceptualised as specific and pervasive ways of 'doing' gender. In particular, research on young men as actors has pointed to the tensions and costs involved in taking up polarised gender positions, including the costs to others – girls and 'subordinate' boys. Young men have been seen in these research accounts as both powerful and vulnerable, oppressing others and, at the same time, clinging desperately onto their masculinities by repudiating 'non-hegemonic' aspects of themselves and projecting these onto others.

The research reviewed in this chapter has critically deconstructed the ways masculinities are made into, and lived as, natural or essential identities. However, it sometimes makes depressing reading, partly because it appears to perpetuate the practices it critiques as features of masculinity. The danger is that research becomes so preoccupied with the ways boys aggressively and competitively assert themselves that it fails to acknowledge the possibilities of 'softer', less polarised and more 'transgressive' masculine identities, except as subordinate masculinities in opposition to which hegemonic masculinities are always enacted. Even Redman's and Mac an Ghaill's account of finding and inhabiting an alternative masculinity in a culture dominated by a competitive ethos in sports and 'hard' sciences, emphasises how this reproduces rather than subverts preoccupations with competition and potency. While it is important that research draws attention to the oppressive ways masculinities are constructed, it also needs to be attentive to the ways, contexts and times in which boys inhabit alternative (not necessarily subordinate) masculinities and the attractions of these to them. For example, research such as that by Walker and Kushner (1997), Wight (1994) and Pattman (1991) suggests that boys inhabit 'softer' masculinities, are less misogynistic and more likely to express anxieties connected with health, work and relationships when talking to an adult interviewer than in the peer group. Walker and Kushner (1997), Wood (1984), Redman (1998) and Thomson *et al.* (1998) found boys are also able to be 'softer' and less competitive with girlfriends. Walker and Kushner argue that the effect of having a girlfriend was to undermine boys' investments in competitive masculinities and reduce the disjunction they experienced between their practices in different settings. Thus, by emphasising the multiplicity and fluidity of identities of specific boys, being aggressive and competitive may be understood not only as contradictory and anxiety provoking, but also as (an unstable) part of a boy's repertoire of masculinities.

Our focus in this chapter has been on the research carried out by others on the construction of masculine identities. In the remainder of this book, we present an account of our own research, striving to make heard the voices of the young people we have interviewed as they reflect upon many of the issues which we have discussed in 'academic' terms so far.

3

'Hegemonic' masculinities

As we have already noted, it is now commonplace in many countries for media, governments and educationalists to make pronouncements that take it for granted that there are major problems with boys. Indeed, it often seems that there is a 'crisis' of masculinity that centres on education, but also relates to issues of violence, criminality, uncertainties over relationships and identity, sexuality, employment and increasing levels of suicide. Regardless of what individual boys are like or how they live their lives, they can hardly fail to be aware that they are commonly constructed as problematic and that this is attributed to certain deficiencies of 'masculinity' itself. But is there any evidence that there is such a cultural construct of 'masculinity' on which boys draw, and if so how do boys – who as we have seen in Chapter 1 can be active and reflexive in thinking about themselves as masculine – talk about how they deal with the resulting constraints and choices? This chapter draws on the accounts of the 11–14 year old boys in our study to address these questions.

How can we understand masculinities?

The research and theoretical ideas described in Chapter 2 suggest masculinities are not simply naturally occurring. Instead, they are constructed in social interactions and achieved through the use of the cultural resources available to particular boys and men. For the boys in our study, these included the ideologies of masculinity prevalent in their schools and classrooms, the social structures in which they lived and their own social positions. Furthermore, there are different kinds of masculinities available to boys and men. Literature on masculinity generally finds that there is a 'dominant' form of masculinity that influences boys' and men's understanding of how they have to act in order to be 'acceptably' male, and that this dominant mode is associated with heterosexuality, toughness, power and authority, competitiveness and the subordination of gay men. This is often referred to as 'hegemonic' masculinity (Connell, 1995). Yet, most boys and men cannot hope to fit into the masculine 'ideal' and many men who are powerful within society do not have the characteristics of toughness and physical dominance associated with it (Cornwall and Lindisfarne, 1995). Despite this, many researchers continue to draw on the concept of hegemonic masculinity because it captures the power of this masculine ideal for many boys and men (Gilbert and Gilbert, 1998; Wetherell and Edley, 1998). Connell (1995) argues that hegemonic masculinity is important to the fantasy lives of many men and that men often position themselves in relation to it, even if they critique or subvert it (see, for example, Wetherell and Edley, 1999). Since boys and men are positioned differently in relation to hegemonic masculinity, it is not surprising that there are different kinds of masculinities (Connell, 1995; Mac an Ghaill, 1994).

We found that the boys we interviewed provided support for the existence of 'hegemonic' masculinity as a powerful idea that regulates boys' behaviour and for the notion that different masculinities are produced through performances that draw on the cultural resources available. The rest of this chapter takes this up by examining boys' accounts of the impact of hegemonic masculinity and how they dealt with it.

Constructing narratives of popularity

Bruner (1990) suggested that any society produces stories of how lives should be lived within the culture. According to this view, these 'canonical narratives' can be identified in individual accounts alongside more 'personal narratives' arising out of speakers' own biographies. This distinction can helpfully be applied to the narratives produced by the boys in our study in that they are personal and nuanced, yet illuminate the canonical narratives of masculinities common in London schools. Most striking in this respect is the way in which 'hegemonic masculinity' of the kind described by Connell (1995) is recognisable – often when describing what it means to be a 'popular' boy. Since 'hegemonic masculinity' is not an everyday term, we did not ask the boys in our study to define it. Instead, we asked them about masculinities in both general and specific terms. Examples of relevant questions here are, 'I wonder if you could tell me how you get on with other boys, for instance at school or with friends you see outside?' or 'Are some boys popular? How do they get to

be popular?'. There was strong agreement among the boys we interviewed that 'popular masculinity' requires attributes such as 'hardness',
antagonism to school-based learning, sporting prowess and fashionable
style. Being bigger than other boys could also be helpful. More broadly,
as mentioned in the Introduction, the following canonical narratives
about masculinity could be identified from our interviewees as current in
London schools:

1. Boys must maintain their difference from girls (and so avoid doing
   anything that is seen as what girls do).
2. Popular masculinity involves 'hardness', sporting prowess, 'coolness',
   casual treatment of schoolwork and being adept at 'cussing', dominance and control.
3. Some boys are more masculine than others. This involves both
   racialised and class consciousness.

The features boys identified as making for popularity were thus strikingly
similar to those identified by Connell and many other masculinity
researchers as features of hegemonic masculinity. Perhaps because of
this, they were used by boys not only to explain popularity, but also as a
measure of whether they themselves and other boys at school were 'properly' masculine. This was a racialised construction in that boys of African
Caribbean descent were presented as the group most likely to embody the
characteristics of popular masculinity.

The issue of boys' educational performance will be dealt with in
Chapter 8, while their relationships with girls is dealt with in Chapters 4
and 5. This chapter concentrates on how boys construct narratives of
hegemonic masculinity and how they deal with their own and other boys'
positioning within these narratives. As will be seen, having hegemonic
attributes is produced as an explanation of what makes certain boys popular, but the two concepts are not quite the same. At various points, hegemonic masculinity as defined earlier ('associated with heterosexuality,
toughness, power and authority, competitiveness and the subordination of
gay men') is seen as problematic for popularity – for example, when it is
embodied by a particular boy in too extreme a way, or when it precludes
other desirable attributes such as being 'easy to get on with', or when
white boys express resentment of black boys for their 'cool' style and
supposed toughness. The two examples below, both from 14-year-old
white middle-class boys, show how boys draw easily on an image of
hegemonic masculinity when describing 'popular' masculinity ('hardness', attractiveness, sporting prowess and being 'the best'), yet also fill

out the detail with personal narratives in which other attributes are seen as important. They thus demonstrate how some boys could nuance their accounts so that the canonical narrative was sufficiently broadened to include their everyday cultural practices:

RP   *What kind of things make boys popular in your school?*

Luke   *Um (2), amongst boys or amongst girls or in general? [RP: Both really.] Um (25) amongst the people who are like (3) hardest, or (4) who girls think or boys think are, like, attractive and things, like, that um (2) like if someone's really good at football, then people will think you're a really good <u>football</u>er and they probably, um (2) yeah, that kind of thing people, like (1) being the best person, the <u>best fighter</u> or <u>best runner</u>, things like that.*

RP   *So it's all tied up with sport then? Sporting ability and also hardness as well?*

Luke   *Yeah, that kind of thing.*

RP   *And those are precisely the kind of things that you distance yourself from. You don't see yourself as being like that at all. [Luke: Yeh] So how would you describe yourself in school?*

Luke   *Amongst my friends I would say I'm quite, like, popular but amongst the general school, I wouldn't say I am.*

         …

RP   *What boys are popular in your school, in your class and how did they become popular?*

Maurice *I dunno. David's quite popular 'cos he's (1) like pretty hard, but he's quite good at sports as well. He's best in our year [RP: Is he?] at football.*

RP   *Ah, is he, yeah?*

Maurice *And he's fast an' that.*

RP   *Yeah. (1) And that's how he's popular, because he's good at sports and he's quite hard?*

Maurice *Mmm*

RP   *Right. (1) How's he hard?*

Maurice *Fighting an' that. [RP: Yeah] I wouldn't wanna have a fight with him 'cos (1) [RP: Yeah] ya know (unclear) but…*

RP   *Why, why are hard boys popular?*

Maurice *Dunno, just, dunno, just are. It's not most time how hard they are 'cos (2) well my mate, my mate Jimmy he's in the other class, I'm probably harder than him but, he's, he's just as*

> *popular, 'cos, dunno 'cos easy to get on with an' that. All the*
> *girls, like if say I'm talking to the girls an' that, they can talk,*
> *I can listen to 'em an' all that. Easy to get on with, an' that.*

RP   *Easy to get on with girls.*

Maurice   *Say like you got a good personality, then makes you quite pop-*
          ular, say like you're funny or something [RP: Right] as well.

Maurice's account agrees with Luke's notion that popular masculinity at
each of their schools is related to sporting prowess and 'hardness'.
However, he adds that it is also helpful to be able to talk to girls and to
have a 'good personality', suggesting that hegemonic attributes are not
necessarily the only ones promoting popularity. They are nevertheless
very powerful, coming to mind first whilst the non-hegemonic attributes
are produced as elaborations or even exceptions.

Further characteristics associated with popular masculinity were 'coolness' and style of clothing, with a few boys also mentioning appearance,
particularly related to height, strength and weight:

RP   *Can you tell me what makes boys popular?*

Joey   *(2) Clothes.*

RP   *Clothes? What sort of clothes then?*

Joey   *Designer clothes.*

          ...

RP   *Okay. So, some people are cool are they?*

Calvin   *Yeah, some people think they are cool.*

RP   *Right. Do they think you are cool?*

Calvin   *No. Some people do. Some people don't. I just think I am*
          ordinary.

RP   *Right. How do people become cool? What do they do to become*
          cool?

Calvin   *They like, get Adidas designer clothes and show-off...*

Recent research (e.g. Miles, 1998) indicates how important is youth
style to the construction of young people's identities. Storm-Mathisen
(1998), for example, in a Norwegian study, found that buying pressure for
clothes was symbolic as well as practical, and clothes helped to differentiate young people into 'cool', 'normal', 'wanna-be' or 'nerd' groups –
although those deemed attractive by their peers could get away with
wearing anything. It is, therefore, not surprising that 22 of the 78 boys we
interviewed said they formed opinions about people according to the

brand names they wore and focused a lot of attention and energy on this. Attractiveness and size were also reported to be important to popular masculinity and to maintaining hegemonic authority:

RP   *How do you think that is? Why do you think the bullies are the good looking ones?*

Alan   *I don't know. I think it's the same as the girls. They know they are and they wanna make theirselves appeal to the good looking who are usually bullies.*

RP   *Does that make them popular with boys - the fact they're good looking?*

Alan   *Yeah, most of the time it does.*

RP   *Yeah, yeah.*

Alan   *Even my friends, they'd rather be speaking to someone who's good looking who you hate, than to be with someone you like who's not so good looking. There's a couple of us who'd rather have a conversation with someone who's got spots than someone who hasn't*
          …

RP   *This physical side, is it important to boys do you think. Are boys concerned about size? It's something that came up quite a lot in the last interview.*

Leroy *Yeah, I think so, I think the bigger you are, you command more respect kind of thing. I think boys tend to look up to someone who is a bit bigger, a bit more conspicuous, that everyone can see. Look up to you kind of thing. I mean if you're small you go pretty much unnoticed, or people just tread on you and think you're not worth anything.. It happens to boys all the time you know like 'Shut up Johnny you're really short.' Whereas the same thing never happens to you, unless of course you are disliked by some- one else. But usually that kind of thing never happens when you're big, it means something. Really, I'm not saying you're more intelligent, but the fact that you are there boys tend to look up to you and think 'Oh My God' kind of thing.*

RP   *That's one of the reasons why people look up to you, because of your size?*

Leroy *I think size is something to do with it, not quite so more, because I'm not the tallest in the year anymore. I was for three years, well I guess you know that kind of thing happened.*

Boys who demonstrably had some of the characteristics identified in the quotes above were likely to report that they were popular:

RP   *Right. Does, um, because you're good at football does that make you quite popular at school?*

Benny *Yeah it does 'cos everyone's like 'Oh I want him in my team otherwise we're not gonna get nowhere really.' Like 'cos in PE, um, nine times out of ten my team will come higher that'll be good.*

Since so many features of popular masculinity were identified by the boys, it may seem that 'popularity' is not an exclusive category and that almost all boys have the opportunity to be popular on the basis of characteristics or dress. However, to be really hegemonic required that boys have several hegemonic characteristics. To be powerful in some ways but not others could place boys in contradictory positions. This is demonstrated in the following quotation where the boy concerned (James) has previously claimed to be 'looked up to' by others on account of being 'hard', but then reveals that he gets called names ('stupid' and 'thick') by both boys and girls. As will become clear particularly in Chapter 8, academic work was generally not considered to be part of hegemonic masculinity, something noted by Willis (1977) in his ground-breaking research. Nonetheless, popular masculinity does require an insouciant sharp-wittedness that runs counter to 'stupidity', and this seems to be drawn out of the image of the hegemonic ideal as fast and cool, never to be a dupe. James, who is not a subtle boy, is therefore contradictorily positioned in relation to hegemonic masculinity and, as a result, helps to illuminate its plurality:

RP   *What sort of things might people say to you that might get you angry?*

James *I suppose if people say stuff to you, it gets you angry.*

RP   *What sort of stuff would people say to get you angry?*

James *I dunno, anything, horrible things ... There's a boy he might say 'you're thick' or 'stupid' or things like that.*

RP   *That happens sometimes?*

James *Yeah.*

James, then, demonstrates the point made by Wetherell and Edley (1999) that hegemonic masculinities are contradictory and nuanced. His account furthermore illustrates the importance of contextualising hegemonic masculinities. Schools are institutions where young people

have little choice but to spend several hours per week together and
are dependent on managing their social relations as painlessly as possible. Not surprisingly, they produce contradictions and constraints in
the possibilities open to young people, as well as vigilance and policing
of each other. James' account demonstrates how, despite his influence
over some of his peers, he is vulnerable to the power of others to call
him names.

It definitely was the case that boys reported that to be good at football,
'hard' and confidently cheeky to teachers frequently won boys' admiration, even if this was grudging. However, there were characteristics generally associated with hegemonic masculinity which did not necessarily
make boys popular. Many boys gave accounts of boys who were 'too
tough' and who maintained a place high in the masculine hierarchy by
being too physically threatening. Such boys were frequently reported to
be resented and disliked by the boys giving these accounts. In the quote
below, Norman is analytically insightful as he makes this distinction
clear. In doing so, he introduces the notion of 'hard' masculinity as 'an
image that people choose', indicating that he views it as actively performative and optional:

RP   *Right. (3) What, what makes boys popular at school?*

Norman   *Well there's, there's sort of two different types. There's people*
             who, um are (1) popular through their image. So say if they're
             really hard, everyone'll be friends with them. Because it's the
             *best side of someone to be on. [**RP**: Right, yeah] But um …*

RP   *Because - is that because they're afraid of them?*

Norman   *In a way. I mean. There are some quite nice people, that are*
             hard in the year. But, um, there are some people that people
             *feel really obliged to be, to be nice to. [**RP**: Right. Why?] Just*
             for that reason. And then there's also, um (3) other people
             who, who are just nice to people. And you can't help being
             friends with them.

RP   *OK, yeah. OK, I'd like to ask you about both kinds of boys.*
             Firstly the boys who, who have a hard image. How do they
             kind of cultivate that image. What is it to be hard?

Norman   *I dunno. It's, it's just your, general manner. Really. I mean you*
             don't necessarily have to be in lots of fights. Although you say
             *you are. [**RP**: Yeah] It's just your general image that comes*
             across to other people.

RP   *How, how does it come across? What, what, what do they do?*

Norman *Just the way they walk, talk, act, everything. [**RP**: Yeah, yeah] I mean it's just pe - people choose an image an' then work on that image. Everyone does.*

RP *Do they tend to be quite big, these boys then? Or…*

Norman *Not necessarily. It's just an, an image that people choose. 'Cos, 'cos everyone's chosen an image an' worked on it.*

RP *Every, everyone. Every boy, yeah?*

Norman *Yeah.*

RP *So what kind of image have you chosen?*

Norman *I don't really know. I've just sort of, adapted to how, how people act towards me.*

Negotiating the limitations of hegemonic masculinity

While some boys succeed in being popular and/or making other boys fearful of their 'hardness', it seemed to be difficult to be accepted (or to accept others) as really possessing ideal masculinity. Indeed, boys did not necessarily claim to aspire to hegemonic masculinity, even though they tended to take it as the standard against which to evaluate themselves and other boys. They therefore positioned themselves in relation to 'popular' and 'hard' masculinities in various ways, showing considerable evidence of what Wetherell (1998) terms 'troubled' subject positions – points in conversations when subject positions become difficult and have to be repaired. In our interviews, this was often manifest in the ways boys strove to explain that although they did not fit the bill for a hegemonically 'ideal' male, they were nevertheless acceptably masculine. For example, the complex relationship between managing to be popular and successfully performing hegemonic masculinity is demonstrated by the fact that many boys wanted other boys to consider that they were really tough, but not senselessly violent. Their accounts tended to indicate that they had, at some point, 'proved' their toughness and no longer needed to do so. Some of those disliked for being too tough were claimed by other boys to be inauthentic – pretending to be tough but really not being so (which is why they had to keep on proving their toughness). A few boys also provided insights into boys' attempts to be authoritative with each other and other boys' resistance to this:

RP *Define boys*

James *Um, (4) um, (1) most boys are bossy so, watch out for the bossy boys*

RP	*Most boys are bossy?*
James	*Yeah, most of them*
RP	*Right. So, so you don't like most boys?*
James	*Um, I get on with some - bossy boys 'cos they're not really bossy towards me.*
RP	*Oh really, yeah. Why do you think that is?*
James	*Um. I don't know (1) it's like, um, (3) I don't know//*
RP	*Yeah. Are you bossy?*
James	*I can be sometimes when I'm annoyed.*
RP	*When you're annoyed, yeah? Who, who're you an-, who are you bossy to?*
James	*Mm. The people that are bossy to me.*
RP	*Right. What do you do when you're bossy?*
James	*Um, like if they tell me to shut up I tell them to shut up.*

More generally, the four most common ways in which boys established their authenticity as masculine whilst diverging from the masculine ideal (in Edley and Wetherell's (1997) terms, 'jockeying for position') were as follows:

1. Some disparaged those who they said were 'just pretending' to be hard and argued that, while they themselves were not 'the most popular', they were at least authentic.
2. Many were acutely sensitive to how 'hard' they were in relation to other boys. Some boys managed to deal with not having the characteristics associated with popular masculinity by locating themselves high up the hierarchy of 'hardness'.
3. A minority attempted to subvert hegemonic masculinity by considering themselves above it.
4. A few boys managed both to be seen as 'popular' and to attain well at school. These boys were usually reported by others to be 'nice' as well as being exceptionally good at football. They tended not to let other boys see that they enjoyed doing well at school.

These strategies are discussed immediately below.

Disparaging those who are 'just pretending' to be hard

Although most of the boys we studied did not consider that they were hegemonic and could see that some other boys were 'acting hard', they did not reject the notion of hegemonic masculinity as unrealistic and unattainable. Instead, the idea that there is a genuinely 'hegemonic masculinity' furnished them with a reason to put down other boys as 'not really hard'. This also allowed boys who felt that they were themselves not 'hard' to consider themselves 'genuine'. In the next example, the 14-year-old white boy who is speaking makes an accusation that some white boys 'act' hard by imitating boys who are perceived as 'genuinely hard' – in this case, black boys of African Caribbean descent. This imitation, attempting to cross racialised categories as it does, makes it even clearer that hardness is not a 'genuine' feature of these boys, but an act:

RP   *Right. Do you think some boys do they [want to] be something else?*

Bob   *Yeah. Yeah, try and act hard or try and talk in a, like some people like try talkin' like a Jamaican accent or=*

RP   *Do they?*

Bob   *Yeah and like kiss their teeth like Africans, like Afro-Caribbean do, try and copy them.*

RP   *This is English boys tryin' to be like that. White English boys?*

Bob   *Yeah. Some do. Yeah.*

RP   *So why is that then? Why do they try and be like that?*

Bob   *Dunno because they look as... quite hard people and if they try and, if they act like that then they're gonna, people are gonna think, 'Oh look they look hard. Don't look at them else they're gonna start trouble.' So that's probably why.*

Although the boys who produced such accounts thought that 'acting' demonstrated *in*authenticity, they nevertheless were able to see hegemonic masculinities as a performance, rather than as 'real'. This allowed some who did not regard themselves as 'hegemonic' to maintain untroubled subject positions as authentically masculine. However, this did not mean that they recognised that hegemonic masculinity is itself illusory. Instead, they continued to assume that it is 'real', but simply out of reach for most boys. Looking down on boys they saw as pretending allowed them to continue 'jockeying for position' in relation to hegemonic masculinities, while denying other boys' claims to hegemony. This notion of striving for self-coherence and authenticity was particularly used by private-school boys who were attempting to assert hegemony through educational attainment and condescension towards state-school boys.

Positioning themselves as high up the hierarchy of 'hardness'

While they did not claim hegemonic masculinities, 11 boys clearly set up hierarchies of 'hardness'. This particularly suited boys who were attractive, big and good at sport and those from disadvantaged backgrounds. For some, it was arguably the only way in which they could assert any hegemony in their lives (cf. Gilbert and Gilbert, 1998; Katz and Buchanan, 1999):

RP   *People don't like you if you're not hard?*

Ferai   *Yeah. But I'm like - in that group interview I was about the third hardest there and (1) it was Tony and John, they're strong and I'm like quite strong but I don't beat people up. Like only playin' around stuff.*

RP   *So how do people become hard? Is it because they're strong then or...?*

Ferai   *Yeah and they're popular and - yeah 'cos they're, 'cos they're strong. They're strong and they're good at football.*

RP   *Okay. But you said you don't go around beating up people so how do people know that you're strong?*

Ferai   *Because when I'm, when I'm muckin' around I like, I'll put them in head locks and stuff and they can't get out.*

Subverting hegemonic masculinity by being above it

One strategy used by some boys (12) to resist the notion of hegemonic masculinities was to claim to be above it. Boys did this in a number of ways: they asserted their authenticity (in contradistinction from acting), claimed a particular skill, made claims to maturity or to being egalitarian or enforcing justice. The boy quoted below (discussed in detail in Chapter 7) refused to assert a masculine identity and aligned himself with the girls in his school. He dismisses other boys as so obsessed with football that they cannot get on with anything, whereas he at least knows how to get on with his academic work (and values working):

Oliver *Yeah. Like, as I said in the group, I don't play football... I hate football. What's the point - of eleven men running up and down a bit a gre-, a bit a grass, kickin' a ball? There's no point a that. A::n', everyone teases, everyone goes 'Oh, you can't play* *football' an' that, when I'm talkin' about interesting stuff with the girls. An' goin' I.T. Club wiv my friends, an' that. (1) And, (5) boys just, (1) ah, what can I say? (2) Boys (2) are just, ah, what is it? (2) Idle. Boys are just too idle.*

RP   *Right. What d'you mean by that?*

Oliver *Idle. They go out, they play football an' that. After that, they come back in the lesson, don't do no work. If the cup-, if the cupboard's open, I could go and pull out one boy's book who plays football for my class [**RP**.: Mm] and you'll see about that much work done from 'im, about that much.*

RP   *Right.*

Oliver *I'll pull out anovver book, who don't play football and you'll see like pages of it done.*

RP   *Yeah. Yeah. So, how is it that, that, um, football - boys who like football don't work? I mean, wh, why is it? =*

Oliver *= They talk about football in the class.*

RP   *Yeah.*

Oliver *'Cos I sit next to a boy who plays football but, an' 'e don't, and 'e gets, 'e gets all the work done, but after 'e's finished the questions on the board, 'e don't go to the book and look up questions what 'e could do. 'E just sits there, leans back on 'is chair and talks about football.*

RP   *Is it not possible to, to like football and also to like work?*

Oliver *No, 'cos , it could be, but, the boys, when the boys come into the class, they don't, as soon as they sit down, football. Football. But when I come and sit down, 'Alright, Miss, what we doing today, Miss?' 'Er, doing this, Oliver'. 'Okay, then'. Do it all. At the end of the day, I've worked hard, when the boys are stayin' be'ind, doin' their work, havin' detentions an' that. [**RP**.: Mm] An' I don't think that you could like football and still get on with your work.*

This is rather similar to the use of the 'rhetoric of reason' identified in Sewell's (1997) study to refer to strategies used by boys who disparage others' obsessive interest in sport and similar signifiers of hegemonic masculinity because it is a fool's option, leading nowhere. The position of the boy quoted above – as intermediate between the boys and girls in his class – served to protect him from competition with other boys, to whom he claimed to be superior rather than subordinate. However, he did not appear to be entirely comfortable or happy with his positioning – perhaps not surprisingly since he did not really fit in with any group.

Versions of 'having it all': hegemony and academic achievement

Despite the difficulty of maintaining non-hegemonic positions but still managing to retain a sense of personal value, some boys (10) gave accounts of themselves which indicated that they were generally considered, and considered themselves, hegemonic and popular and yet also achieved well at school. Any differences they identified from the hegemonic standard were ones that allowed them confidence in their own superiority. This was a position most easily sustained by boys who attended private schools, although it was also managed by some boys in state schools. They made claims to 'having it all' in very different ways. One black 14-year-old, for example, said that he was popular because he was good at sports and indeed he was mentioned in other boys' interviews as being popular, good at sport and very strong. He was, however, meta-analytic and self-deprecating about his sporting performance, explaining that it was because he was shy that he tried to 'show off' in sport and demonstrating an awareness of how one can be different in different contexts. He also said that he was seen as sensitive and sympathetic by other boys:

RP   *Yeah, yeah. And you said that, that, that people can - if they've got problems, if they've got problems, they've got worries, that they can, they can express them to you, can they? What sort of problems do the people take to you then?*

George   *Er, usually when like, someone's bullying 'em an' stuff like that. An' they come to me, explain what happened an' ask me to help them, or say, go and talk to the person that's - bullying them or something.*

George also said that he was happy when he came top in something in class, but did not talk about this at school. Another boy identified him as popular because he was so 'nice', as opposed to 'hard' boys who you feel 'obliged' to like and who sustain their popularity by cultivating their hard image. In addition, he was funny because he seemed to mock himself for 'acting mature' and was not trying to 'boost his image', laughing at himself when he used 'long words' in science lessons. In this case, it seemed that George was allowed by other boys to be a good all-rounder because he appeared not to take himself too seriously. His open sensitivity and sympathy were accepted by other boys because of his popularity, which it also reinforced.

In another instance, a white 14-year-old boy who had come to Britain from Eastern Europe explained how he had asserted his 'hardness' when other boys thought that he was weak. As a result, he was now able to get on with his work and to be polite to teachers (which was what he wanted to do) while remaining popular. It is noteworthy that his narrative establishes his 'hardness' in much the same way as those who jockey for position by positioning themselves as high up the 'hardness' hierarchy:

RP   *Right, right. How, how do you think, um, other boys see you then?*

Mo   *They, they, because, um - first when I came here they thought that I was like, one of them - what they call as stiffs.*

RP   *Stiffs? What's that?*

Mo   *They call the boys stiffs who are like, (1) always sucking to teach-ers. [RP: OK, yeah] Always being always polite an' everything. But I say, that's how I am, that's my personality. If you don't wanna be my friend, then that's up to you. And then, now, they thought I was kind of weak, so they didn't hang around with me an' everything. So I just - I proved that I'm not none of them things. But I still respect my teachers. I still am the same person. So now they hang round with me.*

RP   *OK. How did you prove that you weren't weak? ...*

Mo   *Um, I didn't show I was scared of anyone. I, I let them know that, er - I'm harder than them an' everything but I didn't=*

RP   *=Oh did you, really?=*

Mo   *=But I didn't, didn't, I didn't do it in a physical way.*

RP   *Yeah. How, how did you do it?*

Mo   *I just told 'em. I just told them. So, like, I mean people, like some people go around beating up people, bullying them. They just do it to impress their friends and say that they're hard. [RP: Mmm] But I don't do that. I just - I just tell 'em.*

RP   *You tell 'em what?*

Mo   *I just tell 'em that um, the thing that um don't mess with me an' everything. [RP: Right] And they, they're my friends now. I've got like, no boys that are against me. [RP: Mmm, mmm] They like me. They know, they know, they know that I'm harder than them an' everything. And they, they still respect me. I still respect them. [RP: Right] We're all friends. [RP: Yeah] I mean some bully goes around beating up one boy. But no one else likes him. They're all scared of him. No one talks to them. And that's how they lose all their friends.*

RP   *The bully loses friends, yeah?*

Mo   *Yeah. It doesn't have to be that way. You can still be hard, but you can still have friends. But don't do it in a physical way.*
RP   *So, so do you think you're quite hard then?*
Mo   *I'm quite, yeah. I'm like, one of the hardest in the year.*

This group of boys thus demonstrate that those constructed as fitting within the category of hegemonic masculinity are not only differentiated by racialisation, but by the strategies they use and the ways in which they are positioned. The next section turns to a consideration of how social class relates to hegemonic masculinities.

Hegemonic masculinities and social class

In their study of 174 Quebec boys, Laberge and Albert (1999) found 'that the boys' understandings of hegemonic masculinity differed according to their class milieux' (p. 248). Middle-class boys (and those they refer to as upper-class) were more likely to value leadership, sociability and intelligence as characteristics that defined masculinity and virility. Working-class boys, on the other hand, were more likely to suggest that masculinity was about being able to demonstrate strength, attract girls and look 'cool'. Laberge and Albert explain this in terms of the differentiated possibilities, interests and experiences of boys from different classes. Middle-class boys aspired to upward mobility through qualifications, while the working-class young men often lived in neighbourhoods characterised by violence and had subordinated positions. According to Laberge and Albert, presenting themselves as physically and verbally tough can be read as a desire to express power over others within a context of relative powerlessness. This interpretation is supported by the findings of Katz and Buchanan (1999) who, in a questionnaire study of 1344 British boys, found that the boys they labelled 'Low Can-do' (who were predominantly working-class) were more likely to feel marginalised and envisage a bleak future for themselves. They were also more likely than 'Can-do boys' (who came from all social class groups) to believe that boys and men are expected to match up to one idea of maleness. It was also the 'Low Can-do' boys who were most likely to try to prevent their girlfriends from continuing to study. In a complementary argument, a Danish researcher, Nils Kryger (1998) argues that working class boys' commitment to demonstrating physical prowess has to be seen in the context of the manual labour that, in previous generations, they would have been expected to do.

The findings from the studies by Laberge and Albert (1999) and Katz and Buchanan (1999) alert us to how social class intersects with different conceptions of hegemonic masculinities. Numerous studies have identified working-class masculinities typified by the toughness and violence identified by Laberge and Albert (e.g. Willis, 1977, Cohen, 1997). However, Mac an Ghaill (1994) demonstrates that the intersection of social class and masculinities is rather more complex (at least in the British context) than it appears in Laberge and Albert's study. For while the group heuristically typified by Mac an Ghaill as 'the Macho Lads' fit with the working-class masculinity they identify, working-class boys were also represented amongst his 'Academic Achievers' and 'New Enterprisers'. This finding is a reminder that boys are agents in their own lives, rather than being passively and helplessly inscribed within pre-written gendered, social class or racialised scripts which are the inevitable result of their histories. It also illuminates Stuart Hall's (1992) claim that the question of identity is not simply about who someone is or has been, but is centrally about the future in terms of the self-production of new identities. It is, however, clear that some boys and men use masculinity symbolically to subvert and resist their subordinated positions as, for example, did the 'offenders' studied by Collison (1996).

In our study, we interviewed boys from the working classes and the middle classes, who attended both state and private schools. An important difference between young people in state and private schools related to their future aspirations. State-school boys, particularly those from the working classes, tended to have aspirations related to future relationships (such as getting a girlfriend) rather than employment. Nine of the 54-state school boys wanted to be professional footballers and one a professional rugby player. Only one private schoolboy mentioned football as a possible career option, and he indicated that he might go into coaching. Boys from the private schools (and middle-class boys from state schools) were more likely to take future relationships for granted and to aspire to professional careers. Perhaps because they attended schools known to have high educational standards, the boys in our study from private schools expressed more concern about their schoolwork load. They tended to stereotype state-schools and particularly boys who attended them as rough, violent and tough. This did not mean that they saw themselves as soft and not properly 'masculine', but they considered themselves to be less violent and more intelligent. They also recognised a need to work harder academically than their state school equivalents, as if the set of expectations into which they were immersed was one of career success, with pressure coming from peers as well as from parents. The following boy (Albert) from a single-sex private school demonstrates a contradiction much more frequently voiced by boys who attended private schools than those who attended state schools, between the necessity of attaining good qualifications (particularly since their parents were paying to ensure this) while adhering to a definition of (popular) boys as non-academic. In the course of this, he states that his school is a 'weak' one, rather than a 'hard' one, and that he does not like being positioned as weak:

Albert *We have like a weak school and not a hard school.*
RP *Meaning?*
Albert *Um, well we got a reputation of being a very good academic school and not having any good, good hard people so, um, it's quite annoying 'cos it's quite rough actually, we do rough sports and we're quite hard.*
RP *Why do you think you got that reputation?*
Albert *'Cos loads of our pupils are really weak, like really academicos, this counts as a really academic school.*
RP *Why are there so many pupils in this school like that?*
Albert *Don't know.*
RP *You feel quite annoyed about that, do you?*
Albert *Yeah 'cos loads of us, like we don't deserve this reputation.*
RP *How do you respond?*
Albert *Well you don't really do anything 'cos these kids most of them are from the estate and they've loads of mates and stuff... you'd probably get beaten up.*

For boys from state as well as private schools, from the middle classes and the working classes, the importance of maintaining youth styles that required wearing expensive brand names made poverty and affluence relevant to the construction of masculinities, regardless of whether or not the boy providing the account wanted to think in terms of social class. Fashion has long been viewed in the context of power relations: it can serve as a resource by which social groups can maintain or challenge dominant or subservient positioning (Miles, 1998). In that context, the postwar rise in living standards allowed people from the working classes to use fashion as a means to engage in identity construction and resistance to social norms (Hall and Jefferson, 1976; Hebdige, 1979). While, more recently, it has been argued that 'youth subcultures' are more fluid and spontaneous than had previously been thought (Willis, 1990; Widdicombe and Wooffitt, 1995), it is clear that 'youth style' is differentiated in shifting ways by gender and social class and that it is racialised.

This differentiation constitutes one of the ways in which 'hegemonic masculinity' varied in our study. For there was a consistently held idea amongst boys that there were particular brands that were acceptable markers of style, even though what these were varied slightly from school to school. Despite what many boys said, there seemed to be a strong link between access to fashionable brands and social class. For example, the following 13-year-old, white working-class boy from a state school constructs for himself a position which disavows thinking in terms of 'rich and poor' in favour of an individualistic approach. However, he differentiates between the clothes labels that 'you would think' rich and 'spoiled' and those which are poor – which would be 'cussed' in a way which undermines his own insistence that these things have nothing to do with economic resources:

RP   *Okay. (1) D'you, d'you think that, there's certain boys in this school come from, richer and - some boys from poorer backgrounds?*

Dean   *Erm, (1) I mean, (2) in my, in my way, there's no poor and there's, no rich.*

RP   *Mm.*

Dean   *Everyone's on the middle, everyone's just the same. Doesn't matter 'cos they got more money, or 'cos - and, their parents have lots of money, it matters about you. And what you gonna do for your job, and then, then you'll find out if you're richer. And stuff. I mean, people who have, all the - Ralph Lauren T-shirts, Pod shoes and stuff like that, - you would think, 'oh, they're rich, 'cos they always get this and they always get that and they're always spoiled' [RP: Mm]. And, the people with all - the, erm, the Adidas and, not so well (1) fashionable clothes - with, not with the right name, (1) [RP: Mm] erm, (2) they would be - counted as poor. (2) Or cussed.*

The next boy (12-year-old, white working-class) has to deal with being excluded from wearing the designer clothes he would like through lack of money. His account indicates that other boys attempt to disparage him because he does not wear the most expensive labels. It is probably because he is unable to afford them that he knows precisely how much these branded clothes cost, and that, despite claiming that he is not bothered about them, he ends the extract with a list of the Calvin Klein clothes he will soon be getting.

RP   *Do you think there are people at school who come from different backgrounds to you. Some that are richer some poorer?*

Don   *Yeah, There are some people richer than me. Because they like, in the school party, people come in with Chino on. Where my mum orders from the catalogue, she can't really like, buy Chino, the Jeans are, £60 a time, the tops are about, £50. So that's £110 for the top and jeans.*

RP   *Do people come in wearing that stuff do they?*

Don   *Yeah, the school disco. I like the clothes I have. Girls wear - they like the clothes that I wear because I've got - jeans and an orange stripe top.*

RP   *The boys that come in the Chino gear how do they make you feel then, how do you feel about that?*

Don   *I don't feel any different. And they go, 'Oh what's that name brand you're wearing? I've got Calvin Klein on.'*

RP   *That's what they say to you?*

Don   *I say, 'Oh no', they go 'Western Trading what's that?'*

RP   *Do you think they feel superior to you then?*

Don   *Yeah, I just say to them look as long as I wear good clothes, as long as I've got a decent pair of clothes and trainers it really don't matter what name brand it is. I think I wear brand things. I wear Reebok trainers I've got a pair of Kickers. They were £85. I've got a nice uniform and for my next birthday I'm going to get, like, a Calvin Klein jumper, T-shirt and pair of socks and Calvin Klein jeans.*

However, some middle-class boys from affluent backgrounds – particularly from private schools – looked down on working-class boys for buying designer clothes. In the quote below, Matthew, suggests that he does not need 'to prove a point' by conspicuous consumption of designer clothes. The fact that he is able to be meta-analytical about the boy with an assisted place gives him the power to confirm his sense of economic and moral superiority (based on house size and school and not wasting money, respectively). His demonstration of hegemony is common to private-school boys who feel assured of their future economic and career success; it also confirms again how boys could assert different kinds of hegemonic masculinities, often in contradictory ways:

RP   *I wonder - if you - see yourself as belonging to a particular, social class at all?*

Matthew *E:rm, sort of - middle class, really.*

RP   *Right. Why's that?*

Matthew   *Well, we're not - I'm not sort of rich, and, then again I'm not sort of poor, so, sort of in the middle.*

RP   *Right. So how do you - kind of recognise, someone who's middle-class, then?*

Matthew   *E:r sort live in the sort of - er, a normal - normal sized house which is enough to sort of - you know one bedroom each, say that's sort of normal; and (2) er, they go to, this school, which, because, it's like, you know it's quite expensive so - so there's no - not many lower-class people, there.*

RP   *Right. So, so what are lower-class people - like how would you?*

Matthew   *They live in smaller houses and things [**RP**: Yeah] and, are, go to different schools [**RP**: Yeah] and (2), um (1) things like that, and they try - most of the time - you notice that lower-class people* wear *designer clothes - they sort of waste their money on designer clothes.*

RP   *Oh right.*

Matthew   *Because they think, 'Oh if I wear designer clothes then I'll - hang out with more people' [**RP**: Mm] different, but, most of the time they just hang around with their groups - of lower.*

RP   *So do you think they, they waste their money?*

Matthew   *Yeah.*

RP   *Lower-class people yeah?*

Matthew   *On sort of, er, stupid colours and things [**RP**: Yeah] and, on, designer clothes.*

RP   *Is it boys, lower-class boys who waste their money?*

Matthew   *Yeah. On sort of expensive shoes, expensive T-shirts - you know silly things which cost a lot.*

RP   *Yeah.*

Matthew   *'Cos they want - they want to look, as if they're not, lower class, and sort of,* upper *- so it's lo - so people look at them and say, 'Oh wow they must be really rich because they have all these really expensive clothes', but most of the time they've just wasted all their money - on buying this one set of clothes - and they sort of - wear them all the time.*

RP   *What about middle-class boys, do they - not wear designer clothes?*

Matthew   *Well you don't - I, I sort of don't really need to, 'cos, I don't need to prove a point (2) and I could if I wanted to but I don't*

want to because I - 'cos if you - if you wear designer clothes
then you're constantly cautious - not to go and play football or
not to do this or not to do that - 'cos you don't want to get them
*dirty or anything. [**RP**: Mm] So I just sort of, not wear just*
normal clothes.

RP   *What do you mean by proving a point?*

Matthew *E:rm, well you prove a point because if you're, if you're wear-*
ing all this designer clothes it sort of proves, to other people
that you're cool but, you, I don't really need to because I - I
don't really care, what other people think - 'cos I - I just sort
of, I talk to my friends, I'm with sort of my friends, and I don't
care what other groups of people - you know that - if they, they
can carry on wearing their designer clothes 'cos I don't - I
personally don't think it's cool to wear - a lot of designer
clothes because - most of the time you - like on uni-, non-
uniform day - you notice all the people with designer clothes
just don't *do anything 'cos they* don't *want to get their*
*designer clothes dirty [**RP**: Mm] which is just stupid, 'cos*
there's no point in wasting all your money on clothes and you
don't sort of, wear *them properly - you just - walk around with*
them and, never step in a puddle or something.

Some middle-class boys from affluent backgrounds expressed a casual
and confident sense of superiority over boys who do not attend private
schools, as in the following (racialised) example; Crispin is a 13-year-old
white middle-class boy:

Crispin *White people here are different than a lower down less-*
educated school that would be the same as the black race
as well as with the white race. Except in the lower schools
education sort of thing there are more Chinese, Asian sort
of thing.

RP   *How are white people different here from people in the lower*
schools?

Crispin *Um, well, my sister works on supply she teaches French, they*
give her crap, they do their work on a piece of paper, they don't
have exercise books, they just screw it up and put it in their
pockets. They don't do that here. Shout back at the teachers,
swear at the teachers. Leave the classroom, don't go to school.
They don't care. As I say that's with both races.

At state schools, some working-class boys reported experiences of class differences as power relations, recognising how middle-class boys might feel superior. Paul's account, below, is characteristic here in ambivalently presenting himself both as excluded by the speech of the 'posh kids', and also feeling 'pity' for them because they think that being posh is all that matters. This discursive strategy seems to allow Paul, an 11-year-old white working-class boy, to feel more powerful, because he can see through the posh kids' charade:

Paul   = *Like middle class. I don't like, in the morning like, all the posh kids on the bus like speakin' all like, posh like. They always talk about funny stuff and me and my mates don't get it, like, we just walk out, like, it makes us laugh and we don't wanna make them feel bad so we just go outside ... Feel pity for them 'cos they're all boastin' about their computers and feel like they can boss you around 'cos they're more classier than you.*

It is striking that, in an era when many politicians are claiming that class differences have been eradicated, boys from state and private schools were mostly unfamiliar with each other and positioned each other mainly through stereotypes. This social class/private–public-school distinction indicates a plurality of hegemonic forms of masculinity. These were linked to style and, hence, required some money. However, some were also linked to a tough/weak distinction (in favour of state-school boys), while others entailed the construction of cultural capital (in favour of public-school boys – cf. Mac an Ghaill's (1994) 'Real Englishmen'). At state schools, some working-class boys reported experiences of class differences as power relations where they appeared to dislike middle-class boys, but recognised that they could sometimes exercise power in useful ways.

Conclusion

This chapter is concerned with the ways in which the 11–14-year-old boys in our study positioned themselves and were positioned in relation to 'hegemonic' masculinities. We have been arguing, through the presentation of some of our interview material, that the construction of hegemonic masculinity is a complex and active process, most frequently discussed by boys as the elements of 'popular masculinity'. These processes are cross-cut by 'race' (in ways discussed in Chapter 6) and social class as well as deeply embedded as a mode of regulation of boys' identities and relationships. Hegemony is clearly a socially produced set of practices and boys are to a considerable degree aware of this. They were able to articulate how 'popular masculinity' comes about, and also resist some of its modes of expression. Strikingly, most boys discussed hegemonic masculinity as if it was a possession that few boys could hope to obtain: it was rare for boys to consider that they possessed the attributes associated with it. However, the power and pervasiveness of this notion made it difficult for boys to escape without having their gendered repertoires limited by it. Many boys who did not see themselves as possessing the attributes associated with the hegemonic ideal nevertheless negotiated places for themselves as non-hegemonic, yet clearly 'masculine'. For example, some suggested that 'hard' boys were often inauthentic, or ridiculed the 'ideal' in the name of more successful developmental strategies such as doing well at schoolwork. It was undoubtedly the case that most of these boys claimed some components of hegemony, for instance that they were actually 'hard', but did not need to show their hardness, or that they could be dominant through academic work.

The ways in which boys warranted their positions in relation to hegemonic masculinities demonstrate how accounting for themselves frequently produced troubled subject positions which had to be repaired for boys to maintain a sense of their identities as valuable (Wetherell, 1998). The versatility of boys' strategies for constructing alternative masculine identities in the face of the power of hegemonic masculinity was quite impressive, albeit that these strategies were largely dependent on being able to recast apparently 'non-hegemonic' attributes as in some way 'genuinely' masculine. This suggests both that there are a variety of ways in which the characteristics of hegemonic masculinity can be expressed, and also that the power of the hegemonic ideal dwarfs that of truly alternative ways of 'doing boy'.

4

Boys talking about girls

Introduction

Taking identities as 'relational' and as 'marked by difference' (Woodward, 1997), research on the identities of boys has focused on how these are produced in relation to particular versions of the feminine 'other'. In this research, as described in Chapter 2, boys' accounts of girls and women are treated as integral to the process through which boys construct their masculine identities. Such research has challenged common-sense assumptions that gender identities are relatively fixed, self-contained traits which individuals possess and which cause them to behave in similar and pre-ordained ways.

In this chapter, we examine how the boys we interviewed spoke about girls – which they did a great deal, both in answer to our questions and spontaneously (especially in single-sex group interviews). We are particularly interested in how the boys differentiated themselves from girls, for example which 'differences are manifested and represented' and 'which sorts of differences count' (Woodward, 1997). As we investigate boys' accounts of girls and their gendered identifications and disidentifications, we shall be examining the kinds of gender-power relations being produced. We are interested in the recurring gendered oppositions which appear in the boys' accounts, but shall also address the different ways in which boys position themselves in relation to these oppositions. Also, taking the interviews as particular contexts in which gender is performed (Butler, 1990), we shall examine how boys speak about girls in different interviews – group and individual – and how this reflects on the different kind of masculine identities they produce.

Sporty boys and unsporty girls

When comparing themselves with girls, boys frequently (33 of the 78 interviewed) claimed that an important difference was that they were interested in sport whereas girls were not. This comparison usually arose in the context of a discussion about what boys and girls *do*, and quite often led to boys presenting girls as if they were of a different, and rather mysterious, species. Harry, for example, said they 'talk about things' and they 'don't like sport things', and when asked what they talked about, said he had not 'spied on them' – he had no idea. Joey said he did not know what girls did at lunchtime: 'We see them all there in a crowd talking and we look at them and they're gone.' What the boys did seem to agree upon was that girls were not really up to much: nine boys, for example, prefaced their account of girls' activities with the word 'just', contrasting it with their own active and purposive pursuit of sport (especially football):

Craig   *They [girls] like going out with their friends and just walk around the streets, but I like playing football, going to a film or something and they just walk around doing nothing.*

Dean   *Boys like sports ... if you're a girl you stay in one place and just talk.*

This opposition between the active and productive use of time in playing football, characteristic of boys, and girls' aimless sitting, walking and talking, is familiar from the general social discourses on masculine agency and feminine passivity, and in men's failure to recognise women's talk as interpersonal *work*. 'Just' talking was understood as talk for its own sake, as having no other purpose and therefore as pointless and obsessive. When boys talked, it was for a reason: 'Boys talk ... if there's something really to talk about', said Dean.

As part of the process of dismissing girls' activity as meaningless and second-rate, the explanation for why girls 'just' talk instead of playing football was generally given as to do with essential sex differences. They were simply not up to it, being physiologically and temperamentally unsuited for football. When boys spoke about this it sometimes seemed as if they were speaking of girls as if they were little children. For example, in a single-sex group interview with boys aged 11 and 12 at a mixed state school, the boys told the interviewer, in tones of outrage, how teachers supported girls who wanted to play football with the boys. They then went on to elaborate on girls' ineptitude.

Dave   *It's funny watching them.*

Craig *Like the ball's in the centre spot and they all, and they all think the ball's up there so - they all run up there and the ball's still in the centre.*

Dave   *Yeah they don't, they don't =*

Rob   *=And when they go a tackle, it's not like two people tackling, they all go into a bundle.*

Craig *Or if if, um, a boy taps it to them, they* scream. *(1) [screaming sounds]*

Rob   *They panic.*

Dave   *They panic every time they get the ball.*

The boys took up very traditional positions in this conversation, forging versions of themselves as knowing and mature in relation to physically uncoordinated, hysterical and childish girls who could not grasp and abide by the basic rules of football. Their air of authority contrasted with the mock screaming as they mimicked girls getting hurt or receiving the ball and not knowing what to do. This was quite different from boys' serious commitment to football which was associated, in contrast, with playing it hard, competitively and expertly. They went on to construct girls as being obsessed with their looks in a way which made them fragile and pathetic:

Jim   *Yeah, and another thing with the girls, when they play football they get scared to get muddy, some of them, and when they get muddy they =*

Dave   *= When they fall over they get dirty and then, 'Oh I've got to go home and wash my nails', and end up going half-way through a match 'cause they gotta go home and wash their nails.*

Craig *Some girl was playing basketball with us and she went to catch the ball and she hurt her nail and she goes, 'Oh I'm not playing any more'.*

Dave   *And usually when they break their nails they like, 'Oh no, I broke my nail. Gotta start all over again'. Big deal!*

Craig *They've always got nail varnish on.*

Girls' obsession with their looks

The view that girls were obsessed with their looks was frequently expressed. Ten boys interviewed individually spoke of how much time girls wasted on their looks, as if this was as unproductive as 'just talking'. Stressing how little time they spent on their appearance compared with girls, some boys again began with the word 'just'; here, however, 'just' had positive connotations: 'Girls take ages to get ready, boys just are ready' (Derek). 'Girls put on tons of make up, boys just like to be neat and clean' (Mustafa). 'Girls want to make themselves look big by spending so much money on clothes, we just wear designer labels and jeans' (Praful). 'Women wear lipstick and make up and all that … I just put some clothes on and go out' (Olu).

Though these same boys also spoke, with much enthusiasm and knowledge, about various designer labels they wore, they positioned themselves as not obsessed by their looks, redefining their interest in clothes almost as functional. They thus constructed themselves as more active than girls in the sense of not being tied down by their looks. But also, expressing too much concern about one's looks might indicate sensitivity to the physical attractiveness of boys, an impression which, as we see in Chapter 7, boys were keen to avoid. While girls could be construed as interested in other girls' looks without being labelled homosexual, this did not apply to boys. Only one boy, Daniel, mentioned spending much time on his appearance, explaining that his friends 'cussed' him for taking so long to get ready to go out to raves. But this boy was popular for being funny and good at sport, and perhaps for being good looking; under these circumstances, it seemed, he could get away with the 'eccentricity' of keeping his friends waiting while he concentrated on his appearance, having it defined positively as 'individualism' – itself an important goal for boys.

Humourless and mature girls

Recent ethnographic research has pointed to the centrality of humour in the lives of boys, and has examined how boys perform gender by being funny. Back (1994) found that young men engaged in a great deal of 'duelling play', in which they could safely say things that would otherwise have generated conflict. These joking exchanges could also be used to defuse tension if boys provoked confrontation in that they could disclaim malice by insisting that they had been 'just joking'. This also had the effect of silencing objections to the content of malicious jokes and duelling play since to react powerfully and negatively against what is 'just joking' is to show oneself to be humourless. In a study of 15 and 16-year-old school students, Kehily and Nayak (1997) found that young men used elaborate forms of game-play which incorporated ritualised verbal and physical assaults. Aggressive or combative humour was thus central to the construction of masculine identities and hierarchies.

As with football, many of the boys we interviewed constructed humour as exclusively masculine, and implied girls were not sufficiently robust to engage in jokey banter. When boys spoke about their experiences talking with girls, usually they reported feeling less free than they were with other boys. This was partly because of interests they had in common with boys and not girls (sport, gory films and computer games), but also because they had to be careful what to say to girls. Sixteen boys explicitly problematised girls for lacking a sense of humour, which made them (the boys) feel uncomfortable. Dean contrasted boys being funny with girls '*just*' talking, and reported feeling 'easier' with boys:

Dean   *Girls aren't funny ... they're really into, um, just talking to you ... they just really wanna get to know you, they're not really jokeative. They wanna get right to the point.*

RP   *Do you think that's a good thing or?*

Dean   *I mean it's good yeah, but I wouldn't mind if girls were funny, 'cause then - you could act the same as you would with boys ... they wouldn't mind if you told jokes about them.*

Girls were constructed as lacking a sense of humour in a way which made them weak and easily buffeted by boys' humour. As one boy, Pervaiz, asserted, 'you've got to say the right things to girls so as not to get them upset', and illustrating this, he recalled:

We were making fun of the Backstreet Boys [a popular boy band] the other day on our table and she was quiet after that so we knew she was sad, and I said 'OK you like your kind of music and I like mine', so you've got to be careful but boys will just go 'Oh no your music's rubbish'.

In this story, Pervaiz positions himself like the other boys, jokey and tough in relation to the easily upset, emotionally buffeted girl, but also as different from them, more direct and robust. Claiming that some girls' interests in music and film focused on the male stars, he also represented boys as more discerning and, in this respect, more mature:

Some girls just go to see a movie 'cause of a boy like Leonardo de Caprio. I asked them if they've read the reviews and they haven't, they just want to see it ... No boy goes 'I like Arnold Schwarzenneger', they just want to see the film.

Ten boys interviewed individually made similar kinds of comparisons between boys and girls in relation to tastes in music and film. The ridiculing of girls for their assumed obsession with pop and film stars was particularly marked in the single-sex group interviews and the force of this appears to be rooted in jealousy and a desire to put girls 'in their place'. The soap and pop star Peter André was most commonly mentioned, with several boys questioning the authenticity of his mythic 'six pack', and reinterpreting his muscular appearance as a pose, rather than as signifying tough masculinity. The irony here was that it was precisely because he was so popular with girls and came to symbolise male heterosexual attractiveness, that they were so invested in undermining his masculinity. The boys were, in a way, 'jockeying for position' with Peter André.

Girls were seen by many boys as more 'mature' and adult-like than them – more serious, more committed to schoolwork and less interested in having fun and joking – although sometimes this was also seen as a ruse to court popularity with teachers and parents. Almost a third of our sample of 78 described boys as being less serious than girls, and of these nine referred to boys as 'immature'. This was associated with risk-taking, not thinking about the consequences of their actions, not thinking seriously about the future and misbehaving at home and school. Using the term 'immature' made some of these boys critical of boys' silliness, and sometimes the same boys who had complained about girls' lack of humour praised them for being mature. A few boys, however, revelled in being 'immature'. For instance, Norman said he was 'not in a hurry to grow up' which he associated with 'sitting around and discussing things'. Being immature was something he could only experience with other boys, but not girls: 'you can't go into central London with them throwing jelly beans at people in suits'. This seemed like a metaphor for fun and immaturity counterposed to smartness and authority. Messing around and having a laugh were frequently mentioned when boys were asked to say what they or boys in general liked doing, and was often presented as a capacity lacking in others, notably adults, girls and 'stiffs' or 'boffs' (conscientious boys).

The denigration of those committed to the school's work ethic as being unable 'to have a laugh', was vividly illustrated in Paul Willis' classic study of the anti-academic culture of a group of working-class 16-year-old boys. These boys, the 'lads', juxtaposed themselves to the school conformists, whom they characterised as incapable of 'having a laff' (Willis, 1977). In our study, too, 'having a laugh' was a way of being a boy in relation to adult authority and classroom learning, and was part of an oppositional culture around which high status could be constructed. Conscientiousness and commitment to work were, in contrast, feminised. Twelve boys described girls as more conscientious at schoolwork than boys, with boys being seen as having a lower boredom threshold than girls and as being preoccupied with other things. Five of these said that boys needed to talk and have a laugh while they were working and another five mentioned that it took boys longer to settle into work after playing football. The gendered oppositions these boys constructed were between commitments to work and play, with sport, like laughter and talking in class, being seen as breaking the monotony of work.

While the capacity not to take things seriously was usually presented as characterising *boys*, some boys complained about girls 'having a laugh' at their expense. Examples they gave were girls laughing at boys as they walked past, throwing conkers at boys, kicking the ball away when the boys were playing football, calling boys ugly or gay and saying they had small penises. A few boys seemed to enjoy being teased by girls, imagining they were flirting with them, but most were angry with them, and constructed them not as funny, like boys, but as pathetic and childish, and as quiet and shy when they were on their own. One girl was criticised by a group of 11–12-year-old boys for being too much like a boy for playing football, wearing trousers and boys' aftershave, and because she messed around and cussed them. 'She hangs around with boys... and let's say you're walking past her, you know she might say something rude to you for nothing.' This girl was being constructed as 'rude' rather than jokey, it would seem, precisely because of her gender.

Antagonism was also expressed towards girls because they supposedly could get away with being noisy in class. Perhaps the force of this derived from feelings of being discriminated against and unfairly stereotyped by teachers as immature, as in the following exchange from a group interview with 11–12-year-old boys:

Greg   *They [teachers] don't see when they hit us [**Vandad**: They don't expect girls =] but when we try to hit them they see it.*

Vandad   *They don't expect girls to be bad, so.*

Greg   *'Cos they're always like shouting out and mouthing but boys always get caught for some reason...'cos boys' got deeper voices than girls so teachers can hear them easily.*

James   *Think girls are just more crafty aren't they [**Vandad**: Yeah] to get away with things and boys just can't.*

Vandad   *They all suck up to the teachers and then they - you know - hide
behind their backs.*

Four boys countered the view that girls were better pupils by constructing
boys as more 'active' than girls and taking this not as meaning they were
committed to sport rather than work, but that they were more confident
and willing to answer teachers' questions and to improvise in drama. In
Chapter 5 we refer to a mixed-gender interview in which the girls accuse
the boys of being immature, and the boys retaliate by presenting themselves as more 'alive' in class.

Praising girls

Though girls were characterised as easily buffeted by negative emotional
reactions, lacking a sense of humour, obsessed with their appearance,
useless at football and more inclined to 'just talk' with one another, it was
not the case that boys necessarily considered girls to be subordinate or
inferior to themselves. We want now to examine the characteristics of
girls which some boys admired, and how these boys constructed their
own identities in relation to idealised versions of femininity.

In the accounts of these boys, girls were viewed as sensitive and caring, willing to talk and listen, as well as more responsible and committed
to academic work. The popular discourse which positioned boys as
active, tough and funny and girls as passive, boring and fragile was
reformulated so that being active came to be redefined as 'hyperactive'
and being tough and funny was associated with teasing, thoughtlessness,
insensitivity and lack of concentration. Twenty-one boys in our sample of
78 spoke highly of girls, most comparing them favourably to boys. Just
over half of these boys were from all-boys schools, yet these boys comprised only about one-third of the total sample. It can be seen that when
boys were praising girls they were also expressing dissatisfaction with
popular ways of being boys, whether this was made explicit or not.

Lamenting being at an all boys' school, Sadam said, 'You can't talk to
them [boys] really 'cause whatever you says to them ... they are not interested, like, they are only interested in football ... but with a girl you can
still, you can talk to her about anything really.' Sadam did not play football because of his supposed lack of ability, and had been teased by other
boys for this. He mentioned liking girls partly because they did not tease
him for being bad at football, and also because 'I can talk to girls about

stuff like bullying or taking drugs, smoking. If you go up to a boy and go "someone asked me to take a drug", they'd just go, "take it or leave it" '. Girls were also sometimes idealised as the missing 'other', offering something boys could not. For example, reflecting upon being at a boys' school, John, who saw himself as hard and popular with boys, said:

> *I mean you hardly hear - you always hear deep voices in a boys' school. [RP: Mm] And to suddenly hear a different voice (1) like a girl's voice, that could be fair. But most boys' voices are just deep and (1) ugly.*

Constructing themselves very much in opposition to girls, a number of 'hard' boys, seemed to project onto girls a capacity for closeness and sympathy which they denied in boys. John was critical of boys for being jokey and insensitive, as we elaborate later in this chapter, yet also expected and wanted them to be like that.

Being different from other boys in relation to girls

In some of these accounts, boys positioned themselves as different from other boys in relation to girls. This largely meant claiming to be more mature than other boys, knowledgeable about how to talk with girls in sensitive ways, having time for girls and not acting stupid with them. Leroy, a relaxed and sophisticated boy who seemed much older than his 14 years, said he felt more mature than other boys, focusing on the '*stupid*' ways other boys were with girls:

Leroy   *I just kind of feel more mature than they [other boys] do. Some of the things they do, the way they act around girls, going really stupid in the park ... they go absolutely bonkers around them. I'm just not like that ... Wolf whistling, yelling names, blowing kisses and when they don't reply they start insulting them ... it just seems really stupid to me.*

Though he constructed himself as more serious and mature than other boys in relation to girls, he still identified as a boy who did '*silly*' things. The examples he gave of being mature with girls were of him engaging in 'serious' conversation with girls on the school bus, talking about sex with a focus on the 'personal' and not 'just', as with other boys, 'the physical' and about 'A' levels. But he also mentioned feeling 'awkward' about the probing and personal way these girls spoke about sexual relations. He was, like many of the boys in our study, seeing 'talking with girls' as difficult and serious and 'engaging with boys' as easy and funny. The example he gave of being silly was with a group of boys, and it was this, he stressed, which enabled him to be silly: '... if one of your friends jumped into a pond, there's a good chance you might jump into the pond too because everyone's doing it'.

Like Leroy, Zac negotiated between being more mature than other boys (in relation to girls) and being like other boys (when he was with them), but for Zac the focus was on being 'dirty' with boys and not girls:

> *Obviously girls like nice boys you know. And I try to act really mature around girls. I try to - you know be nice to them and not say that I like this and that really dirty stuff because they don't like that and that's the way you've gotta work with girls really.*

Zac said he had to persuade girls that he was not like other boys who were perverts and immature. He still identified as a boy who was 'really open about sex' (when he was with boys): 'I am slightly I have to say because it's like - male nature for boys, for girls it's just like sweet stuff and all that.' Thus he defined himself *both* in opposition to girls, constructed as less overtly sexual and more romantic, and other less mature and more perverted boys.

Like Zac, a number of boys spoke about how to 'work' girls, as if there were skills which *they* had and most boys still needed to acquire:

Lance   *You've got to try and be sensitive ... and sensible as well ... if they tell you something like maybe it's hurt them don't start laughing.*

Pervaiz   *Some boys they like a girl and they start pushing her, they think she'll like him as well but they've just got some sad ways of impressing a girl. 'Cause they don't know how to do it ... they think that by pushing them people are liking them and then the girls just get away more.*

They were indicating that boys needed to act in appropriate ways with girls, not like they did with other boys. Pervaiz described impressing girls by talking with them and 'not making fun of them' or pushing them as 'playing it cool'; it was a relaxed and mature way of being a boy, and it attracted girls. He mentioned, with some pride, being hugged by girls for being like this.

Some boys who praised girls criticised other boys for being obsessed with football, and by doing so constructed themselves as more individualised, 'less hyper in class' and better with girls than other boys. For example Mike, who liked girls because they 'kinda listen more and they're not just, I dunno they're more sensitive really', described how talking with girls provided him with relief from the tedium of playing football with boys: 'When everyone was playing football I was always like talking to the girls and stuff - then I'd go and play a bit of football and then I got a bit bored I'd go back and talk to them.' He made it clear, when asked if he thought he was more like a girl, that he mixed mainly with boys and that he spoke to girls 'only for 10 minutes'. He did not identify with girls, but saw himself as unique, an individual, as the only boy who broke off football to speak to girls and as their 'favourite'.

Differentiating themselves from other boys in relation to girls, these boys were not seeing themselves as 'less masculine', but as still tough, silly or dirty in the all-male peer group, if perhaps less 'obsessively' so than other boys, and different from girls even when talking in a serious and mature way with them. Like other boys, they described feeling 'awkward', 'working' with girls, trying to be 'sensitive' and 'sensible', placating them and 'playing it cool'. They positioned themselves as more mature than other boys, and less dominated by peer pressure. Lance, for example, described himself not as more like a girl than other boys, but as an '*older boy*' who knew how to treat girls. Much as Wetherell and Edley (1999), interviewing men, found that 'demonstrating one's distance from macho stereotypes' was a common discursive strategy and was often used as a way of enacting the valued 'masculine' attributes of autonomy and independence, so these boys identified themselves as autonomous (in relation to other boys) while distancing themselves from girls.

Talking about girls in different kinds of interview

It was usually in individual interviews rather than in single-sex group interviews that boys praised girls for being different from boys in general. As Leroy, Zac, Lance and many other boys indicated, they were more 'silly' and 'dirty' in groups of boys than they were on their own. In group interviews with boys, but rarely individual interviews, boys ridiculed girls for imagining they were more mature or more clever than boys, for being favoured by teachers (cf. Prendergast and Forrest 1997), for liking 'girl power' and for wanting to play football with boys. As we argued in

Chapter 1, boys enacted gender differently in the group and individual interviews. To illustrate this, we shall compare how boys spoke about girls in a particular single-sex group interview, and how the same boys, interviewed individually, spoke about girls. It was striking, as the following extracts illustrate, how boys were not only more 'funny' and loud but also more misogynistic in group interviews.

Talking about girls in a single-sex group

In this interview with seven 13–14-year-olds at a single-sex school, some of the boys clearly saw themselves as quiet and subordinate whilst others were loud, dominant and witty. Dominic was much smaller than the others and seemed younger – his voice had not broken and he had babyish features. He was dwarfed by Carl and John who were sitting next to him so that he had to lean forward and peer over to 'enter' the circle. Sadip said that of the boys in the group he only went round with Mo because he spoke Arabic, and he did not seem at ease with the other boys. By contrast, Carl had a powerful presence, commanding everyone's attention when he spoke. Through their opposition to girls, these boys seemed to forge a sense of common identity. They resented the ways teachers constantly reminded them of how girls in the neighbouring school were 'outperforming' them, and also how they were positioned as potential harassers of these girls. They mocked these girls for their assumed maturity. They were asked if they saw them at lunchtime and replied in mocking tones:

Carl	*We see girls (1) but (1) like we don't talk to them. Girls are i:diots man*
Mo	*They think of themselves too much. They think that they're betta …*
Carl	*They think they're women.*
John	*They think they're all big.*
Mo	*= like you walk past and they start gigglin'.*
Norman	*And you don't know what they're gigglin' about or whisperin' about.*
Carl	*And they're cowards, they can't even say it to your face.*

Though these boys, like many others, presented themselves as jokey in opposition to serious girls, they clearly resented being the butt of girls' humour, defining girls as weak, pathetic and immature. Smoking was presented as a key way in which these girls (falsely) presented themselves as 'mature'. Later, Mo referred to what was clearly a well-known incident about a boy who tried to assert his authority over a girl who was smoking:

Mo   *One of them smokes and some boy goes, put that shit away, and she comes over and slaps him. The girl comes and slaps the boy.*

Carl   *Dirty big mouth.*

Andrew *…And he shouted it out in the next room and the girl just turned round and slapped him in the face =*

Norman *= 'Cos girls can hit boys, but if a boy hits a girl then there's a court case against him, but if a girl hits a boy and a boy brings a court case up everyone's gonna think he's like really weak.*

Andrew *Women want to be equal to men.*

Norman *But they're not.*

Not being supposed to fight girls was mentioned by boys in other interviews (14 individual and five single-sex groups) and was clearly significant in the way they positioned themselves in relation to girls. In the group interviews, boys redefined themselves as victims rather than aggressors, despising girls for getting them into trouble and/or for provoking them, even hitting them in the knowledge that boys could not retaliate. Only one boy interviewed individually expressed similar sentiments; the others spoke about boys who hit girls as wimpish. Like the boys in the group interviews, they were identifying as strong in relation to girls. However, when seen individually, boys were less likely to express anger towards girls or to revile them for being too assertive. They seemed less intent on showing the 'superiority' of girls to be hollow and invoking masculinity as 'real' or biologically grounded superiority.

Talking about girls individually

Mo, John and Carl, who had been members of the above group, were much less angry about girls when interviewed individually. They spoke about girls quite positively, and were even critical of boys for being immature, messing around and 'acting hard', as the following three examples indicate.

*Mo: Girls as good examples for boys and presenting himself
as a mature boy*

In the individual interview Mo criticised boys, not girls, who smoked for
'showing off' and 'acting older than their age', identifying himself and
his friends, in contrast, as boys who could 'just be themselves' and were
able to reject peer pressure. When it was put to him that in the group
interview only girls were criticised for smoking, he 'blamed' other boys
for this:

> *I think it's like that because - maybe, some of the boys who were in the group
> interview, maybe they smoked, and they didn't want to say it, that boys who
> smoked were bad and stuff.*

In the individual interview, Mo spoke of girls as exemplary students,
pointing the way forward for lazy, football-mad boys. Here, he appeared
to identify with the teachers they had so despised in the group interview
for comparing boys less favourably to girls: 'Us boys like to play more
football, watch TV, waste our time and stuff, but girls like to go home read
stuff, do the work.' Speaking about girls' superior exam results, he said, 'I
hope we boys beat the girls ... are good and stop playing football as much
as we do.' In the individual interview he was distancing himself from other
boys by praising girls while still holding on to his identity as a generally
sporty, lazy boy. His self-deprecation contrasted not only with his defence
of boys against girls in the group interview but also with the way he positioned himself, in the individual interview, in opposition to 'inauthentic'
boys who act hard and are impolite and disrespectful to teachers. This was
reflected in the way he behaved towards the interviewer: very friendly,
slightly deferential and ingratiating, as if as an adult the interviewer would
like him for being, in his words, a 'mature' boy.

John: Idealising girls and becoming 'softer' in the interview

Though John was quieter in the group interview than Mo, and especially
Carl, he had criticised girls for cussing and shouting, and had been keen
to construct men as biologically stronger. He was a tall boy who hardly
smiled during the individual interview, described himself as 'tough' and
spoke about his passion for violence, his temper, his lack of self-control
when fighting and his involvement with a group of white boys harassing
Asian shopkeepers. Yet he became quite critical of a macho culture in the
individual interview, and, as we have seen, spoke idealistically about
girls. In the individual interview he seemed much 'softer' (in the sense

defined in Chapter 1), speaking movingly about his anxieties about his father who was separated from his mother and had stopped visiting him. He said he could talk about this with girls but not boys because they would joke about his 'old man':

> *... my dad, I don't see 'im that much an' [**RP**: Mm] there's (1) like, money problems an' stuff like that, then girls will (2), they'll say 'Oh it doesn't matter. 'Cos you'll see your dad again sometime' an'. (1) An' then a boy could sort of - boy could (2) make a joke out of it an' say oh, um (5), saying stuff. Just stuff (1) to really annoy you and saying, 'Oh you'll see your old man again some, sometime.' And an old man, that's like making a joke. But if you say your dad or your father, stuff like that [**RP**: Mm] it's more comforting than saying your old man.*

John said he preferred being interviewed individually because he could talk seriously about himself and his relationships without being interrupted or laughed at. Paradoxically, he also claimed that as someone who was 'hard' he could say or do what he wanted without fear of others' reactions.

Carl: Constructing girls as just different and sustaining his 'hardness' in the interview

In the group interview Carl's presence had been very noticeable. He was big, muscular and 'funny'. While he spoke, people looked at him and did not interrupt. At one point someone mentioned Carl was the 'hardest' in the year. In the individual interview he was much more subdued. He never smiled, leaned forward, looked at the ground and was reluctant to talk except about fighting. He was asked if he thought boys and girls were similar or different and he said 'quite different'. When he was asked to elaborate he said:

Carl *Girls can like - can express their feelings, like they can talk better an' stuff like that. Um (2), they can things like talk about their personal, personal business and stuff like that.*

RP *OK. do you find it quite difficult to express your feelings?*

Carl *Um (5), not really, me personally. It depends if I - if I want to express them or not.*

This seemed like a commentary on his position in the interview: he was not 'expressing his feelings' not because he could not do so, but because he did not want to. It was not because he was vulnerable, but because he was independent and strong. He was, it seemed, trying to cling on to his identity as a hard boy which he felt was undermined by questions about feelings and relations.

Whereas in the group interview girls' emotions had been infantilised and contrasted with the mature image they tried to adopt, in the individual interview Carl indicated that being emotional over stupid things was what constituted being female and because of this was not good or bad:

RP   *So do you think they're stupid for doing that then?*
Carl *No 'cos like all girls do it. Like all girls do it.*
RP   *So you don't (1) kind of look down on them for doing it?*
Carl *Just think they're stupid. Don't really look down on them. Just like seems a bit stupid like.*

He was positing essential differences between girls and boys and was almost taking a non-pejorative view of these rather than utilising them, as in the group interview, to aggressively assert male superiority. In the group interview, he had also ridiculed girls for acting mature, but in the individual interview he said he acted mature with girls. Rather than being angry with girls for positioning boys as less mature, he presented himself as a precocious heterosexual boy who tended to 'get' older girls:

Carl *Well, if like I'm with girls, I would act like, more mature. Just naturally. More mature, so.*
RP   *Yeah what do you mean by that? More mature?*
Carl *Um (2) act, just like say, act older. Just like say the girls like I usually get are sort of like older than me.*

The three boys described here thus varied their accounts of girls to enact gender differently in group and individual interviews, producing different versions of themselves. In the individual interviews they were 'softer', more serious and much less invested in asserting themselves against girls. As we discussed in Chapter 1, we do not want to suggest that because they tended to be more serous in the individual interviews, the boys were revealing their 'real selves' there and 'acting' more in the group interviews. Our view is rather that the identities the boys were constructing in relation to the ways they were talking about girls were flexible and dependent on the situation they were in.

Girlfriends

In establishing their identities as particular kinds of boys, the boys did not position themselves in opposition to a homogeneous femininity, but differentiated girls by liking and desiring some and not others. They also placed themselves in different ways – as boyfriends or potential boyfriends, as opposed to just as tough and active boys – by evaluating some aspects of 'femininity' differently at different times. The same supposed 'feminine' characteristics of girls which boys spoke about in patronising ways under some conditions, seemed to become virtues when boys were sexualising girls. Wight (1994) noted, in his study of 14–16-year-old Glasgow boys, that some girls (called 'neds') were considered 'unfeminine' and were disliked. In our study, boys also described certain girls as lacking femininity, with 13 of our sample of 78 speaking critically about 'tomboys' and 'geezerbirds'. Six boys indicated that these girls were too much like boys to be sexually desirable. Yet these boys also characterised girls in general negatively, as emotionally fragile, obsessed with their appearance and boy bands, easily offended and lacking a sense of humour.

One of these boys, Georgi, when asked if he thought girls should have a better sense of humour, said that this was 'what makes them interesting … that's what makes girls different'. 'Nobody', he said, 'would be interested in a tomboy'. Yet he had already said he preferred mixing with boys rather than girls because of their different interests. When the interviewer reminded him of this, he distinguished between girls with whom he might mix with similar interests – tomboys – and potential girlfriends. 'I wouldn't mind hanging around with them but I wouldn't like going out with them.' Like Georgi, Donald indicated that he preferred mixing with boys than girls, describing those boys who mixed more with girls as 'woosies', 'who should get to play football, get to know boys'. However, he also constructed himself as a heterosexual boy by eroticising difference. Though girls, as we have seen, were sometimes mocked for their concern about getting dirty, Donald made this a virtue by contrasting them with tomboys whom he desexualised for enjoying football and the banter after, and who did get dirty:

> … *It's more like fun when they go to the pictures and stuff and give you cuddles. Tomboy might be really dirty and stuff and they might go 'good match' and pat you and then you might have a bit mud patch there, where she's gone like that. Girls that listen to music and stuff don't really get that dirty. They*

might occasionally fall over and graze their knee and that, and get a bit dirty
on their hands, but girls quickly go to their house and wash their hands.

Heterosexual desire was often spoken of by boys as developing around
the time they entered secondary school. In some of these accounts this
was associated with an exacerbation of gender difference, with football as
a prominent marker of this process. Alan likened girls in primary school
to boys, mainly because they played football, whereas in secondary
school they became more 'feminine':

But now … the girls would usually sit down and talk about make-up and the
boys would usually play football … and the boys would say like 'You look nice,
what make-up is it?' and the girl would say 'Oh yeah this and this. You're a
good football player' or something like that. We'd meet each other half-way,
yeah. It's nice to know that you can talk about something and she would talk
about you as well.

'Meeting each other half way' meant constructing each other as different and expressing their pleasure in the other's difference. When asked
about what they liked about their girlfriends, or what kind of girlfriends
they would like, eleven boys eulogised about girlfriends being different
from boys, idealising their looks, including their dress, their seriousness
and concern, and their capacity as conversationalists, or more specifically, good and sympathetic listeners. 'She listens and doesn't laugh at
me' (Sadam); 'You can express the way you feel with her, tell her if a relative dies' (Jack). Alan liked girlfriends because 'Girls are different from
boys, can't say to your mates "Do you reckon a French cut [haircut]
would look good on me?"'

A few boys mentioned wanting girlfriends with a sense of humour, but
not if they were funny like other boys; rather they wanted them to appreci-
ate *their* humour, to 'laugh at things which are funny to me not her' (Keith).
They did not want girlfriends to be loud like boys, but neither to be too
quiet and timorous and different from them. As we suggest in Chapter 5,
these differences were sometimes racialised with black girls being named
as '*feisty*' and Asian girls as quiet. Some boys imagined themselves as 'pro-
tectors' and desired girlfriends who wanted to be protected and liked their
boyfriends for being tough and hard. As we have seen, however, the belief
that boys should 'act hard' to impress girls was seen by some boys to be a
popular fallacy, and many boys referred to girls as a civilising influence on
boys, causing them to 'act mature' and to refrain from fighting.

It was unusual for boys to want girlfriends as 'friends'. Indeed, usually friends were other boys who were described as people with whom they could not talk freely about their emotions for fear of ridicule, but, also, paradoxically, with whom they could 'have a laugh' and feel free. It was precisely because girlfriends were opposed to 'active' and funny boys that they were often seen as constraining. Nineteen boys expressed reservations about girlfriends for being too demanding and preventing them from doing 'boys' things' – being with their mates, playing football and having a laugh. They 'keep you from your mates ... my last girlfriend cried when I went to play football' (Chris); 'It's annoying if I want to play football she says, "come here give me a cuddle" ' (Mike); 'Some girls are just too mature for me and too serious and I want to relax and take it easy ... I like having a laugh' (Reg); 'Boys don't really have time for girlfriends 'cause they're usually out doing things or, um, fishing or playing football and riding bikes and things' (Rob).

Like 11 other boys, Rob said he imagined having a girlfriend in the future, and when he was asked how this might come about if boys had no time for girlfriends, he mentioned the possibility of a holiday romance. For on holiday 'you're not doing anything'. 'You've been doing it for the rest of the year ... playing football ... doing all different kinds of sport that it don't seem like fun anymore.' Rob was here presenting football and sport as hard work in which boys were constantly engaged, with holidays providing a break from this and an opportunity, therefore, for having a girlfriend. When he was asked if he thought he might have a long term relationship with a girl, he said yes, and, after considerable reflection, imagined himself as different in the future, as less 'active' and engaged in football. 'Cause you stop playing football as you get older - you start going out and doing different things.' The possibility of a girlfriend depended on him becoming less involved with football, perhaps needing to do less 'work' on this aspect of gendered difference.

A distinction was sometimes drawn by boys between the girls they encountered at school who were denigrated as ugly, feisty, annoying, boring, inactive and arrogant, and girls outside school who were seen as potential girlfriends. Very few of the boys we interviewed had or could imagine having a girlfriend in their school – and certainly not in their class. It was usually in relation to girls in their school (or the neighbouring school), that boys contrasted and asserted themselves as active, funny, and easy going, and these were constructed as familiar, everyday ways of being boys. Potential girlfriends were imagined as unfamiliar, in relation to whom boys 'acted totally different'. In the following example, a group of 13–14-year-old boys from a mixed school, who had said that they did not mix with girls, were asked, in view of this, about the possibility of having girlfriends:

Archie *When you meet - you meet girls out of school - you don't know them, it's better that way, 'cos they don't - know much about you, they don't know what's happened in school or whatever.*

Ollie *Get me like, if you have a girl in school - every day you see her man - you get bored of her =*

Archie *= Start getting bored 'cos you don't want to keep on seeing her and seeing her =*

Sean *= And hearing that voice =*

Archie *You need space. [general laughter]*

Sean *Just hear her walking home from school.*

RP *Yeah.*

Sean *You hear her screeches.*

Denzel *In school yeah - the girls go on all silly and - hyper active and, you just, you can't talk to them like you would, meet someone on the street and just, relate to them differently.*

RP *Mm.*

Denzel *Like - when - you could almost say that when you meet a girl on the street you put on a kind of an act - you don't act like you would normally act, you put on an act for them ...*

RP *Oh right. So how do you put on an act - when - with a girlfriend outside?*

Archie *It's different innit?*

Kim *You don't muck about an all that.*

RP *Yeah.*

Kim *At least - you don't hit them.*

Archie *Yeah, you don't act stupid ... A bit more mature =*

Sean *You don't like - muck around - play football an all that.*

Archie *You do play football but =*

Sean *= Yeah you do play football but like if like you and your girl-friend are out and you got your girlfriend sitting there - you don't just go and leave her and play football. [laughter]*

Girlfriends were possible, according to these boys, only as *outsiders* who were not already positioned as the *everyday* gendered other in relation to football-loving, tough, unemotional and jokey boys. These boys complained about girls at school because they were so familiar – they were 'bored' with them, they 'needed space', they hated their 'screeches'. They were also constructing what they were really like as boys in opposition to these familiar versions of femininity; thus Denzel spoke about 'putting on an act' with girls outside school, as if mucking about and teasing girls and playing (boys only) football were the natural things boys did. It was not that they envisaged relinquishing their 'natural' identities as boys when they had a girlfriend; more that they saw themselves as compromising, acting 'a bit more mature', playing some football, but not 'leaving her' for the boys.

The notion that boys 'put on an act' with their girlfriends seemed to conflict, however, with popular idealised constructions of girlfriends as people they could speak to about their anxieties. Indeed some of these same boys, when describing the sorts of things they said to their girlfriends, mentioned being able to 'pour your heart to her', 'just talk to her normally', precisely because they did not 'treat her like a boy' (nor denigrate her like a 'familiar' girl). Perhaps the fact that they were being interviewed with other boys made them more inclined to present the different ways they were or would be with girlfriends as 'putting on an act'.

Being capable of 'acting' seriously with girls and not teasing, offending or ignoring them as they 'normally' did when they were with other boys at school was, as we have seen, a way in which some boys constructed themselves as more mature and individualised than others. This was presented as a key moment in their developmental trajectories and was associated with heterosexual desire. For example, the following 13–14-year-old boys, interviewed in a single-sex group, spoke about how they now wanted a 'relationship' with 'physical contact' with girls, in contrast to the past when they 'just messed around' with them. Even though these boys did not actually have girlfriends, they were very articulate regarding what boys were obliged to do or not do in order to have such a relationship:

Phil   *You gotta concentrate on what you say more and that, act - more mature and things like that.*

RP   *What does it mean to act more mature then?*

Phil   *It's like, I dunno, you just like, you can't talk about silly things. You have to talk about stuff that she's interested in.*

RP   *Like what?*

Phil   *I dunno [**Gary:** Make-up] music, make-up [**Gary:** Hair], whatever. You have to talk about her as well, you have to compliment her [**Alistair:** Say like you've got your] and stuff.*

Gary   *Ask her like what's your favourite colour, what's you, what's brand name, like designer, stuff like that.*

What is striking about this is how these boys see themselves not only as having to make the girl and her interests the centre of attention, but also how they construct themselves as the prime movers in forging heterosexual relationships. This became particularly apparent when the interviewer asked them if the girl was obliged to focus in the same way on the boy:

Phil   *Actually you don't find the girls do that as much.*
Gary   *It's right for the boy to make the first move normally.*
Phil   *Normally like you compliment her but she won't compliment you back. She'll just like smile and be happy sort of thing.*

The construction of boys as initiators of heterosexual relationships was a familiar one, and was often associated with acting 'mature' and not being (too much) like popular boys were with their male peers (funny, sporty and tough). Some boys, as in the following extract from an interview with a group of 12–13-year-old boys, presented girls as 'playing hard to get', cussing boys they actually desired for being football mad:

Shane   *If a girl likes a boy they don't usually tell them.*
Peter   *Exactly, they just flirt with them.*
Jim   *Wait for the boy to say it.*
Shane   *Yeah exactly … she's all like tearing his face … but inside she's all like 'Oh my love, I love you' [laughter] she's like 'football head, get out of my way'.*

By characterising girls in this way boys could, of course, reassure themselves that girls found them attractive even when apparently rejecting them.

Conclusion

Our focus has been on the ways boys *construct* the gendered 'other' and how this reflects back on their own identities. Thus, we have addressed boys' accounts of gendered relations not just as descriptions but as ways of positioning themselves amongst the array of possible masculinities – an activity which was often full of highly charged emotion. We found that though girls and boys were commonly differentiated and homogenised in particular ways around activity and passivity, hardness and softness, humour and seriousness, our interviewees differentiated between girls. Among the types of girl that boys identified were tomboys, girlfriends/potential girlfriends, quiet girls, loud girls, medium girls and girls who could have a laugh. These distinctions, however, were only made possible by constructing girls and boys, in the first place, as polarised and homogenised opposites, with tomboys, loud girls and girls who could have a laugh being seen as exceptional. The construction of heterosexual desire seemed to involve for many boys a positive affirmation of differences between boys and girls *'in general'*, as illustrated in the desexualisation of tomboys. They identified as heterosexual by desiring aspects of 'femininity' they denigrated when identifying as tough and active.

Carol Gilligan (1983) argues that once adolescence is reached, girls' styles of identifying and behaving are 'relational' and limited by the centrality of their relationships. Their morality becomes structured around an 'ethic of care' in which they are afraid to say anything that might adversely affect their relationships with other people. In contrast, separation and individuation are the predominant styles of adolescence for boys. Most of the boys we interviewed experienced girls as more 'relational', in this sense, than themselves. While the work of Gilligan, Lyn Mikel Brown and others (e.g. Brown, 1995) demonstrates that relationality is hard work, the boys we interviewed considered that girls just naturally talked and that they 'hang around' to do so. They did not see it as work in the form of social cementing or emotional labour.

As we indicated in Chapter 1, some teachers expressed the view that in the single-sex group interviews boys would be influenced by peer pressure, and how they presented themselves in these would therefore be a distortion of what they were really like. When the interviewer remarked on how misogynistic the boys tended to be in these interviews, he was told they were 'just performing', as if how they presented themselves and what they said in individual interviews constituted a much truer reflection of who they were. But boys were neither more nor less authentic in one kind of interview than another; rather, they enacted gender differently. The fact that these versions were so strikingly different and opposed indicated, however, that popular ways of being boys bore major pressures and costs. Dissatisfaction with 'hardness' and messing around was expressed by a number of boys in individual interviews, albeit in ways which reproduced these as essential features of collective masculinity in opposition to a different, positive, sometimes idealised femininity. Though boys commonly saw themselves and other boys as active, funny, physically and emotionally strong and academically lazy in opposition to passive, weak, emotionally brittle, obsessive and unfunny girls, a great deal of unhappiness was expressed by boys with these popular ways of being. Girls were idealised, in contrast, as friendly and sympathetic and good conversationalists. Some boys presented themselves as more individualised than other boys by praising girls (and, also, in some cases denigrating girls who did not live up to their high expectations for girls) and caricaturing other boys as football mad and obsessed with sex. Finally, the fact that the idealisation of girls was almost always in individual interviews implied that boys' identities were not fixed in relation to an unchanging version of the feminine 'other', but were variable, depending on social context.

5

Girls about boys

Introduction

Recent research has indicated that boys and girls in the early teenage years are reluctant to mix in groups (Prendergast and Forrest, 1997; Wight, 1994; Walker and Kushner, 1997). As Prendergast and Forrest observed in their school-based ethnography of 12–15-year-olds, 'If asked to form small groups in class the effect was rather like holding a magnet over iron filings ... a series of single-sex groups would draw together and become defined' (p. 184). In our study, as we saw in the previous chapter, there was much evidence of gender segregation. Some boys were teased for mixing with girls rather than playing football with boys, and when boys did talk about relationships with girls, usually they were with specific individuals – girlfriends and friends outside school.

We conducted nine mixed-gender group interviews, loosely structured around the topic of boys and gendered relationships; later on in this chapter we examine how boys and girls interacted in these. We also interviewed 24 11–14-year-old girls individually about boys so that we could compare these with boys' accounts of themselves and their gendered relations. These girls were from some of the same mixed schools as boys in our sample. They were interviewed by a woman (Ruksana Patel), who asked them a range of questions about their perceptions of, and relationships with, boys: for example, about whether they thought girls and boys were different or similar and if there were different kinds of boys; about mixing with boys and what this was like; and about boyfriends and boys as friends. They were also asked about whether they preferred being girls than boys or would like to be boys. The girls' accounts provide a different perspective on boys and also give some insight into the resources girls draw upon in constituting their own identities. As with the boys, we also want to consider the sorts of positions girls were taking up in the mixed-gender interviews in the light of the views they expressed in the individual interviews, seeing these different sessions as exposing different facets of their experiences of themselves in the context of boys. It is with the individual interviews that we begin.

'Disgusting ... horrible': girls talking about boys in individual interviews

In the individual interviews with girls, it was striking how boys were problematised for being immature, irresponsible, undisciplined and troublesome. This was apparent even in the definitions some girls gave of boys:

Claire   *Unorganised, premature (1) unfocused and listening skills - bad and fighting poorly, they forget their bags at home - they expect to borrow pens from others and don't return them.*

Pauline   *I'd say they're OK, a bit immature ... but I'm talking from my point of view 'cause I like football and stuff, but if you asked another girl it would be completely different. 'Oh boys are horrible, they're nasty, they take the mick', they would say.*

Angie   *Disgusting ... horrible.*

Almost all the girls spoke about nasty and silly things boys did. Some of these were directed against girls, while many related to disrupting lessons and, sometimes, undermining the authority of the teacher. Girls viewed themselves, in contrast, as polite, mature, focused, conscientious, in control, responsible, sensible, and willing to think about the future.

Boys and peer pressure

These constructions of boys were usually qualified in ways which preclude simple and straightforward divisions between good girls and bad boys. Kenway *et al.* (1998) found that Australian girls in secondary schools were 'perplexed and frustrated by the differences between boys alone and boys together' (p. 141), and this was borne out in our study. When girls were accounting for boys' bad behaviour, often they attributed this to peer pressure with the implication that when they were 'on their own', boys were not bad. Constructing boys as being susceptible to peer pressure was a common way in which girls asserted themselves as more mature; it was also often a way of praising specific boys, by emphasising how different they were 'on their own' than when they were with their mates (a notion which links with the claim of some boys to have more 'individuality' than their peer-conforming friends). The ways the girls described these differences – more 'serious', 'nicer' (to girls) on their own – was also how boys tended to be in the individual, compared with the single sex group interviews:

Judy   *When he's alone he's all - he's really quite nice to, they're really nice if they're alone but if they're not - they're all like - have you ever seen Grease?*

RuP   *Grease?*

Judy   *... he's really nice on his own when he gets with his friends he's got to be cool.*

...

Janice   *When they're [some boys] in a group they don't want to sound like they're listening to what we're saying or taking it seriously and they're afraid they're gonna loose their credit, their coolness, but if they're on their own ... they can be more serious.*

...

Christina   *Sometimes they [boys] want to be kind and other people try and stop them to do work at school and things like that ... and they just mess about ... and do things really bad what they don't want to do.*

Not only were boys on their own seen as much better, they were also regarded as more authentic, as if when they were with their mates they were putting on an act, trying to be cool, hard or attention seeking, and doing what they did not really want to do. The implication was that boys' bad behaviour was not the expression of 'hard' tough and aggressive impulses, but derived from weaknesses and anxieties – an interestingly 'psychological' reading of traditional masculinity.

Nice boys

The characterisation of boys as bad, annoying and stupid was also qualified, in many of the interviews, by singling out some boys as *nice*. Boys were described as this for saying 'hi in the morning, bye at home time', being 'caring and loving', 'mature', 'sensible', 'work hard', 'respecting teachers', 'brainy', 'the ones who're going to be lawyers and doctors while the others work in Sainsbury's, would help you with your homework whereas the silly ones would call you boffin'. Often, these boys were described in terms of what they were not, for example 'non-disruptive', 'not rude', 'won't giggle', 'don't talk about girls', 'don't get into fights', as if the norm was for boys to do or be those things. Dawn, for instance, tried to describe what these boys liked doing, but found herself focusing initially on things they did not do:

> *Some boys are like (1) they like to - they don't like playing football, they don't like climbing walls - don't like rolling around the floor, they like to be neat and tidy, gel their hair back, do their homework, do their class work, obey the teachers. That's good yeah but like [laugh] most boys don't.*

Wanting boys to control their wild nature

When girls were asked what kind of boys they liked, however, they did not usually choose 'nice' boys in the sense described above. Some girls liked the 'naughty' and loud ones because they were 'fun', 'easy to talk to' and 'cute' in contrast to the 'nice' ones who were 'quiet', 'boring' and 'ugly'. It seemed the 'nice' ones were not boyish enough. When asked if she preferred nice boys, Dawn said no, because 'that's not how boys are meant to be - boys are meant to be rough and ready.' Most girls agreed with this, even though they claimed to despise boys for being loud, immature and irresponsible. About a third of the girls said they wanted boys to be 'nice' in the sense of not being silly, not shouting in class and showing 'sensitivity' and 'affection', while retaining what were regarded as masculine characteristics – being 'strong', 'lively' and 'funny'. That the 'nice' boys were constructed as not masculine was apparent in Janice's 'slip of the tongue' when talking about them: 'There are boys I know who are just like girls, well not like girls but they act, you know, with respect towards the teachers.' As Dawn implied, football was a key signifier of masculinity, and when girls were talking about the kind of boyfriends they wanted, several specified boys who liked football, but were still able to be 'nice':

Rosa   ... *a normal boy like other boys like - interest in - football ... but I would like them to be smart, have a nice personality like - all - funny, but not too silly, know when to control themselves and I don't think I'd like to go out with someone younger than me ... cause boys aren't as mature.*

Rosa here made it clear that she wanted as a boyfriend a boy who was like other boys (and different from girls) for liking football. The 'but' coming after 'football' seems to be a qualifier: the boy she wanted would be able to 'control' his wild nature, yet still be a boy. Having an attractive personality was associated not with being more like a girl, for example being able to talk like girls, but with being funny in a controlled way, as opposed to being silly, with the implication that this was usually what boys were like. Rosa wanted (like most girls) her boyfriend to be older than herself because she viewed boys as generally 'immature' and hence needing more time to become sensible, and this image of the gradual calming of boys' wildness through the slow achievement of self-control seemed to be a common aspect of girls' constructions of the developmental trajectory of young masculinities.

Ethel also wanted a boyfriend to combine playing football with a 'nice personality':

> *They have to have a nice personality (2) and don't like, not telling me to go away when they're playing football or something, give me some time or something. But not all the time to be together, because it's not going to be that good so just a little bit of time to see them...*

She wanted a boyfriend who was 'nice' enough to prioritise seeing her over playing football for a short time, the implication being that other boys would be too obsessed to see her at all. It may be, also, that Ethel was positioning a potential boyfriend as someone who would be able to resist peer pressure by showing he could subordinate football to her. However, what is very noticeable in these extracts from girls is they do not demand of boys that they become more like girls, only that they sometimes show some interest and keep themselves a little bit under control. The 'nice' boys mentioned earlier are desexualised and hence not attractive as potential boyfriends, so the girls appear on the whole to have rather traditional images of the desirable man – funny, physical, with his potential wildness tempered by self-control and some interest or sensitivity to the girls' needs.

Nice boys, tough boys and 'race'

Sometimes differences between naughty and nice boys seemed to be racialised, with Asian boys, because of their religious commitments, being admired for being responsible, mature, not dirty and rude to girls, and black boys being liked for 'taking notice of girls' (Rosa) and giving girls 'time' (Ethel) but also criticised for being 'bad' and 'thinking they're the best' (Jane). Janice said she admired Hindus and especially Hindu boys for resisting peer pressure when fasting:

> *They might not feel comfortable if their friends say, 'Do you want a piece of chocolate' and they say, 'I can't 'cause I'm fasting', then perhaps they get teased for that and admire boys especially ... because their friends are more likely to say, 'Oh you believe in all that'.*

Dawn (white) admired Muslim boys for being 'strict' and doing 'more work ... they make sure they look alright and that, their shoe laces are done and everything', but also thought 'some of them are too strict ... it just don't seem right for a boy of our age to be having to pray five time a day'. Yet she said she admired them precisely because 'they are strict enough to follow their religion'. They were being constructed as exceptional boys, and both admired and viewed as odd for not being like 'ordinary' boys. Angie, a black girl, respected Muslim boys for having a 'strict religion ... they won't call girls boobless and stuff like that', but while constructing them as 'mature' 'because they don't talk dirty' also seemed to problematise them by saying 'the others [other boys] are so much more free'.

As discussed more fully in Chapter 6, African Caribbean boys tended to be constructed as caricatures of boys in opposition to girls – hard, tough, athletic, rebellious and sexually attractive – while Asian boys were often seen as weak and effeminate and poor at sport. Angie, a black person herself, delighted in telling a story about some black boys being beaten by Bengali boys in a school mini-World Cup football competition. Her story played on these racialised constructions of power and masculinities; it was about black boys receiving their come-uppance:

> *When I tell you the Bengali boys wupped ... erm, the black boys and the black boys started sulking, the game wasn't even half-way through and they started sitting on the floor like this, 'we're not playing' like little nursery children you know but - they got beaten, I think it was about ten nil or something like that, all because the black boys thought they were too bad you know, 'Oh this is simple we don't have to practice you know, we're gonna beat them.'*

Their sense of invincibility as powerful boys was shown to be ill founded and they were redefined as weak, 'like little nursery children'. Angie went on to generalise from their failure to practice to boys' lack of conscientiousness in school work, and claimed that boys would not work for their exams and then would sulk when they failed. Perhaps reflecting her own ethnicity, though probably also popular constructions of black boys as particularly masculine, it was the black rather than the Bengali boys in the story who symbolised for Angie what boys in general were like. She could, for example, have generalised from the Bengali boys' victory against the odds, to boys' determination to succeed; instead, she used the black boys' attitudes to stereotype all boys as lazy, complacent, arrogant and immature. In her mind, the more 'feminine' Asian boys had beaten the supposedly hard, 'masculine' black boys at their own game, a signal again of the way black masculinities often become constructed (and constricted) along the lines of classical 'hegemonic' ideals.

Girls on football

In the interviews with girls, sport and football were constantly mentioned when elaborating on the differences between them and boys, with some girls giving the same kinds of account as the boys. For instance, four girls used the opposition between boys playing football and girls 'just' talking, 'just' walking around or 'just' sitting, with the same connotations of passivity. Angie said football was a 'rough' game and that 'girls just want a quiet time'. Nasha, elaborating on how being with boys was different from being with girls, said, 'when you're with boys then you will start playing more football and all that but girls they just wanna sit down do their hair'. Like many of the boys, Felicity spoke about boys' physical toughness equipping them for football – 'their bodies are built up more so if they get hit they feel it but not so much as girls', not only contrasting tough masculine bodies with feminine bodies but also with girls' dislike of 'getting dirty'.

Some girls seemed to accept this view of femininity in general, whilst exempting themselves from it, using football actively in this process. For instance, Dawn said, 'I'm not like a little girl that sits there and polishes her nails and does her hair. I like to play football and that.' Others, more radically, inverted the terms to which the qualifier 'just' could be applied. Thus, Sarah said that boys were 'just sporty' and 'won't sort of walk around talking to each other that much'. This seemed to imply that real activity is relational talking, whereas all that boys can manage is sport – a reversal of the boys' accounts. Rosa also referred to boys 'just' playing football and spoke about this as an all-consuming obsession which stopped them from doing ordinary things and made them unapproachable. 'They don't bother about eating or nuffing like that, just play and if you go up to them they just ignore.' Ethel, like many of the boys, opposed emotionality and sensitivity against football as a gendered opposition, but associated the latter, not the former with weakness: 'Girls are more sensitive… and more emotional, and they go like bye and hug', whereas boys 'can be sensitive but they try to be more masculine… like they go around with their basketball and football and try to act bad'. Felicity spoke about girls as active (doing dance, while boys 'mucked about') and focused on describing what girls did to occupy themselves – having talent shows with singing and comedy, when the boys 'go off and play football'. Explaining why boys did not sing, she spoke of their 'lack of confidence'. What seems to be going on here is that these girls were opposing the boys' view that girls generally did nothing, by filling in the content of their activity, concomitantly redefining boys' own obsession with football and sport as evidence of their limited horizons and capabilities.

Talking

Like the boys, the girls focused on talk as an important marker of gender difference. They reported feeling uncomfortable talking to boys and feeling more relaxed and engaged when speaking to girls. This was partly attributed to what were understood as mutually exclusive gendered interests and concerns. Girls said they talked about shopping, dancing, singing, boys, home, sisters, friends, periods and clothes. For boys (according to girls), the topic of conversation was, simply and solely, football. Many girls complained about the difficulties they had engaging with boys, saying they felt excluded by boys' talk which was dominated by football, and indicating how restrictive this kind of talk was:

Christina   *They just talk about football and we just stand there and listen… afterwards if they stop talking we make up something and start with it, but in the middle they stop talking with us and they start playing football again.*

It was boys talking about football, not girls, who were seen to be 'just talking', the contrast being with the serious content of girls' talk.

Girls reported feeling freer talking with other girls not just because of shared interests and concerns and because boys were obsessed with football, but also because of not trusting boys and being afraid they would laugh at them and spread their secrets. Girls, in contrast, were spoken about as trustworthy, understanding and sympathetic in much the same way as those boys who said they preferred girls had described them:

Dawn *With a girl you can say more personal things ... you can't say everything with boys 'cause like otherwise they start joking about ... not everything can be a joke ... if you have a family problem or if you've got a problem at school.*

However, as well as suggesting that girls were sympathetic conversationalists, Dawn, who had distinguished herself from the stereotype of the passive girl obsessed with her looks, criticised girls for being easily offended. She was the only girl who did so. Because of this, she reported feeling freer with boys, reproducing a stereotyped version of femininity as over-sensitive and touchy. 'With a boy ... if they're wearing something that you don't like and you give your opinion, then they just take it but if you give your opinion to a girl ... they take it the wrong way.'

Liking being girls and not boys

The feeling that boys were one-dimensional and dull, that girls had a much wider range of interests and were more engaging and understanding, as well as more mature and sensible, was reflected in the overwhelmingly positive responses when girls were asked if they preferred being a girl to being a boy. Twenty-two of the 24 girls replied yes. Eight of these spoke about things they could do and ways they could be which were unavailable to boys. Some girls specified, also, that while girls could do 'boys' things', like wearing trousers and playing football, boys could not be like girls:

Rosa *You can go shopping ... and they like to dress and it's OK and they can be like boys they can do sports and everything ... but boys can't really act like girls and go shopping and everything.*

Five girls liked being girls because girls were better behaved, more mature and conscientious:

Angie *If I was a boy and I grew up and looked back on myself I'd think, 'Oh that's a disgrace you know, the way I behaved.'*

...

Christine *There's no way I want to be a boy... I can do as much work in PE as the boys and I'm really clever and some boys are jealous but I don't care 'cos I know I'll end up with maybe a good job and maybe they won't, but I don't say this to people.*

Three girls preferred being girls because girls could share emotional problems, whereas boys, as Janice said, were expected to be 'harder'. When 'hardness' was spoken about by both boys and girls, it was commonly associated with 'putting on an act'. Janice implied girls could be more open about themselves:

Janice *If I was a boy and I had an emotional problem I couldn't say that to a boy... if you're a boy they expect you to be harder... you feel that you have to fight because you're a boy and you're meant to be hard. When you're a girl you can say, 'Don't be immature', you know, and they just leave it at that.*

Two girls liked being girls because girls, they claimed, had it easier with teachers and parents because they were perceived as more responsible and mature. However, some girls also complained that because parents and teachers had higher expectations for girls, it was boys whose bad behaviour was tolerated and who were more likely to be praised for being good.

Two girls had mixed feelings:

Felicity *It's better being a boy 'cos they don't have to go through as much as a girl, but I'd have chosen to be a girl 'cos they act really good.*

...

Judy *It's unfair how girls have periods and how they have to have the baby... but really I think it's much better [being a girl], like you can tell people much more.*

Periods were not just understood as bad things which girls had to put up with, but as some girls in the mixed-gender interviews implied, they were also seen as making girls more mature and thoughtful than boys. One of these girls said boys had it 'easier' without specifying how; when she was asked to say more, the girls in the group all laughed. When a boy intervened and said 'periods and having to give birth and all that lot', they went on to contrast having to put up with periods with 'the worst problem boys have to cope with' namely, 'losing a football match'.

One of the two girls who definitely would have preferred to be a boy, Diana, used the same contrast between 'active' boys and 'passive' girls as the boys often held to. 'They do more things than the girls do, we just sit there and talk.' The other girl, Susan, wanted to be a boy because 'You get treated better by boys.'

Being like boys

That girls could be 'like boys' was, of course, apparent in the label 'tomboy' which some of the girls used to describe other girls, as well as themselves. As with the boys, liking football was presented as the most salient feature of tomboys. But, unlike the boys, girls expressed little animosity towards them. Five girls mentioned currently liking playing football, Dawn, as we have seen, preferring football to stereotypical girls' interests. Two of these girls called themselves tomboys. Nasha, though describing herself as 'sort of' a tomboy and saying she was 'more football and all', felt it necessary to add 'but - I am a girl - I do - girl things'. Susan described herself, without qualification, as a tomboy for liking 'boys' stuff':

Susan *Like me and Yvette, like, tomboys 'cause we like boys' stuff.*
RuP *What is boys' stuff, what sort of things?*
Susan *Like football, riding a bike (3) playing games like football, bas-ketball, stuff like that.*

The fact that she identified with another girl who was also a tomboy may have enabled her to position herself so enthusiastically as one.

For some girls, being a tomboy was a past identity, and many of the girls spoke about playing football as something they used to do in pri-mary school but did not do now. These memories seemed to help the girls construct their present identities as not passive and fragile, yet they were also reluctant to be treated, notably it seemed by boys, as not really girls. Remembering primary school as a time when they were tomboys was quite acceptable, something which is supported by the finding that tomboys in primary school are not problematised by boys but accorded male friendships and male respect (Reay, 1999).

Consistently with findings from the longitudinal study by Blatchford (1998), some of the girls in our study, recalling primary school as a time when they used to play football, affirmed a view of themselves as much less 'active' now than they were in the past and in relation to boys. But these memories also undermined the assumption that girls were essentially different from boys – inactive and fragile. A number of girls recalled how good they were at football. Claire recalled being 'the best goalkeeper' and Iona said she was 'the best one in my class', before moving to a seemingly unrelated topic, criticising some girls for their obsession with their hair which they brushed in lessons. What she seemed to be doing was to present girls as not necessarily very different from boys, as if the growing separation of the sexes was due to an active choice by girls to act more classically 'feminine'. As we have seen, girls' 'obsession' with their appearance was commonly opposed to boys being tough and not afraid of getting dirty playing football. It seemed that most girls were invested in constructing themselves as more different from the boys in secondary school than they had been in primary, while some retained a strong sense of their abilities and perhaps nostalgically referred back to a period when difference seemed less crucial.

Mixed-gender interviews

We turn now to the nine mixed-gender interviews about boys which we conducted, focusing on how boys and girls interacted with each other in these. As indicated in Chapter 1, many boys were surprised at how engaged they had been in the mixed-gender interviews. One boy who had expected relations between boys and girls to be tense, identified a specific girl as being responsible for the surprisingly relaxed relations between boys and girls. This was because, as in some other mixed-gender interviews, she unexpectedly 'started sticking up for the boys' by agreeing that boys were discriminated against by teachers. But this girl was perhaps particularly important in making the boys feel relaxed because she was the focus of their teasing, to which she reacted strongly but which she also seemed to enjoy. At one stage, to the amusement of everyone, she chased a boy round the room who asked to see her 'football socks'. Having a girl whom they could tease like this enabled the boys to feel unexpectedly relaxed and to be loud and funny.

In another interview where the boys were loud and funny, two of the girls, though laughing, were very quiet, and the third, Elspeth, like the girl in the interview above, spoke much more and was teased by the boys. While she seemed to enjoy this, she was unable to speak seriously without being interrupted by the boys. The boys' 'humour' took the form, at times, of sexual explicitness, which made Elspeth laugh. For example, Danny, complaining about how boys were treated less fairly than girls, said:

Danny	*Say, erm, she was to put, erm, she was to pinch my penis right, and then I was, I was about to squeeze her tits, right, but I would get into trouble more than she would.*
Elspeth	*He just comes out with it [giggle].*
Stuart	*It's true.*
Elspeth	*The way he just comes out with it though [giggle].*
Stuart	*It's true. Look at girls, yeah, and because we can't really touch girls, can we right? Girls can go up and pinch boys but when they go, 'let me feel you, let me touch your bum' [**Elspeth** giggle] they're like 'MISS'. [laughing and giggling from boys and girls]*

This may have been an issue the boys felt strongly about, but they were also constructed by Elspeth as funny and outrageous for being so explicit, and they laughed at themselves for the same reason. Talking like this with girls around (and in an interview with an adult) made them seem funny and was consistent with certain received gender roles, in which girls were constructed as more sensitive and less jokey than boys, but also as potentially appreciative of boys' humour. Elspeth thus seemed to act as a catalyst enabling and encouraging the boys to be funny.

In the third 'jokey' interview, a boy was teased by the girls in a warm way for his arrogance and immaturity. This boy was popular, sporty, good looking, loud and amusing. He was not sitting with the other boys, but in the centre, halfway between them and the girls, with his legs stretched out. His physical position signified extreme confidence and ease. In teasing him about his following among girls and his concern to prove himself the best athlete, the girls were not only highlighting his popularity as a boy, but making him the centre of attention. While he denied he was arrogant, he did so, it seemed, with his tongue in his cheek and he clearly revelled in the attention.

Difficult and hostile interviews

Only two of the mixed-gender interviews we conducted turned out as one might have expected on the basis of girls' and boys' descriptions of the difficulties they had in talking to each other. In one, there was no discussion at all between the boys and girls; not only did they appear to have little in common, but they seemed to inhibit each other. The girls were very quiet; the boys spoke more than the girls but were just responding to the interviewer; there was little interaction or eye contact between the boys, and none between the boys and girls. In the other interview, the girls described the boys as troublesome and immature and the boys showed anger towards the girls for 'acting' mature. In this interview, football was constructed by both the boys and girls as a prominent marker of gender differences. Terry, for example, complained that girls did 'nothing', while boys played football, and demanded to know what girls did at break time:

Terry   *What do you do good at break time? - Stand around?*
Nancy   *No, talk.*
Terry   *Yeah exactly, talk.*

As we saw in the individual interviews with girls, football was invoked to signify boys' immaturity, which was associated with a lack of commitment to schoolwork, a trivial focus on winning and losing, and boys' pathetic and unrealistic aspirations. Asked for an example of boys' immaturity, Nancy said, 'Still thinking *at this age* that you're gonna be a football player, most of them "I'm gonna be a football player"'. Nancy and Louise complained about boys being obsessed with girls' bodies, which they also took as symptomatic of boys' immaturity:

Nancy   *Even if girls are talkin about boys yeah, we leave it till after class. All boys are sayin', 'Oh she's got big tits', and like it's we're here to learn we're not here to talk about.*
Terry   *So what, so what?*
Louise *That just proves the point innit you're saying 'so what'.*
Nancy   *You're being ignorant, it's not - it's boys they do [**Paul**: Yeah, girls do that as well] most of the time. 95% of the boys in my class are like that and they don't get on with their work=*

Paul retorted by ridiculing girls for idolising male pop stars in magazines like *Smash Hits*; as he did so, he satirised girls by putting on a pathetic, drooling tone, implying that it was girls who were really immature:

Paul   =*yeah 95% of the girls in my class are like that they just bring in a magazine Smash Hits or whatever, they bring it and sit there, just starin' at some poster of some breh [boy] just going [silly girly voice] 'Ahhh ahhh' [slight laugh].*

Here it was in relation to their potential as good, conscientious pupils that they were contesting maturity. The boys went on to reject the assumption that they were less mature than girls by defining themselves as 'active' in class (as well as the playground):

Paul   *In class by - like if the teacher asks a question, all the boys will put up their hands of [**Terry**: Yeah], even if they don't know the answer, they'll still put their hands up [laughter and giggling from the girls] just to try, just to try they will not be sure of the answer but they'll still put their hand up just to try [**RP**: So you're saying] and NO girls put their hands up, they up and they all wait until Miss says 'Come on, come on girls like all the boys have been asked and still no girl has been asked' and Miss has to scream at them, 'Come on put your hand up.'*

Paul was presenting boys as ideal pupils and satirising girls for their passivity, using an example in interesting contrast to the complaint commonly expressed in single-sex group interviews with boys that teachers preferred girls and were more lenient with them. As it happens, the youngsters in this group were all black and middle-class, so the specific direction this animated debate took might have been a product of gender assumptions (boys' activity/immaturity; girls' passivity/sensibleness) mediated by specific class based and racialised aspirations.

Girls as more mature than boys

Though girls positioned themselves as more mature than boys in five of the nine mixed-gender interviews, it was only in the one described immediately above that the boys challenged the girls on this, and that the boys and girls were so angry with each other. What was particularly striking in the other four interviews was the quietness of boys compared to girls, and the absence of boys' talk about girls. This was not because girls were insignificant in relation to the ways these boys were positioning themselves. On the contrary, the girls tended to set the agenda about boys, and the boys, in part, agreed with them, accepting, most crucially, that boys were more immature than girls and that this was problematic. We want now to focus on the kinds of gendered relations and identities being forged in these four interviews.

Contesting boys' constructions of football

In one of these interviews, football again featured prominently when the girls were criticising the boys. Here the girls complained about the ways boys asserted themselves through football, monopolising football and playground space and being so serious and competitive. Under the conditions of this group discussion, however, the boys became quite thoughtful and critical of boys' football practices. Two boys who had mentioned liking football when introducing themselves supported the girls and blamed some boys for being 'obsessed' with football. The third boy, Boris, who was rather fat and quiet and was sitting on the periphery of the group, outside a girl, had not mentioned liking football. Without any prompting, he said, 'I don't like people who take it seriously 'cause if you do something wrong they'll go tell you "Oh yeah, why did you do that?"' The other boys then said, 'In P.E. they always put Boris into goal', which 'he doesn't really like' and 'they start shouting if he lets it in'. In this sequence, the other boys took Boris' side against more powerful boys, referring to them as 'they' and not 'we'; as the discussion went on and it became clear how miserable Boris was, an atmosphere of considerable sympathy pervaded the group.

'Girls', one girl said in this interview, 'take turns if everyone doesn't want to play in goal'. Another girl said it was all right playing with other girls but 'with boys they want us to play in goal' and they were only able to convince them to take turns if they were playing with smaller boys. Playing with girls, she said, was 'more fair' and 'just for fun'. The boys agreed that 'it's more fun playing with the girls', because it was less competitive. This contrasted with interviews with boys on their own, in which the seriousness of football was emphasised and the ineptitude of girls was spoken about so authoritatively, especially in groups. It did seem that the two boys in this group who were interested in football were trying, in the light of the girls' critique of boys and football, to reposition themselves as boys who played football without needing to prove or assert themselves against other boys. This was possibly because, rather than constructing football as a boys' game and rubbishing it, the girls spoke about enjoying it and criticised the ways it was competitively organised by boys and how they were excluded. This opened up a space for a more concerned mode of masculinity, more capable of recognising the pain caused by the macho footballing culture of the school, to many boys as well as to girls.

Constructing boys as being susceptible to peer pressure

The girls in these interviews sometimes expressed agreeable surprise at how quiet, thoughtful and mature the boys were, though they also implied that this was not what they were really like. As one girl said 'You wait when we're back in class', as if the boys would suddenly revert to their normal selves and become noisy again. Another girl disputed whether one of the boys would be as positive about girls playing football if he was with his mates in the playground. While boys needed to be 'reminded' of this, the effect of 'exposing' boys in these interviews for what they were 'really' like was to make them quiet and defensive. Constructing boys as being susceptible to 'peer pressure' as many girls and some boys did, was one way of accounting for the differences between boys in groups of boys and on their own. But this carried the implication that they were more authentic on their own, reproducing anti-social behaviour as a feature of collective masculinity with which girls (and boys) had to put up.

In one mixed-gender interview, the girls took over the interviewing role and invented moral dilemmas for the boys in which male peer pressure was counterposed to being independent, true to one's feelings and judging others by their inner worth or personality. Instead of posing similar sorts of dilemmas for the girls and positioning them, too, as susceptible to peer pressure, the boys looked uncomfortable and unsure how to respond:

Rebecca   *Say if a girl was your best friend, you see her in the corner crying and you really want to go over to her and ask what's the matter but you're =*

Andrew   *Your mates would go =*

Rebecca   *= You're scared of what your mates would think. Would you like go over to her and see what's the matter? - But you* *really cared about her, she's like your best friend and she was crying [**Toby**: You really cared about her] but you were scared of what your mates might think.*

Tom   *(3) Mm, I'd probably go over there (2), I don't know (1), I might do.*

Alice   *Because I mean, a girl would do that with a boy definitely, any girl that we hang around with would definitely go up to a boy if it was her best friend and see what the matter is, but just because it's a girl and they see a boy go up to a girl they call him woosy or something.*

Other dilemmas the girls invented for the boys also concerned their relationships with girls and the reactions of their (male) peers; for example, whether to go out with a girl, 'all your mates fancy her, she's good looking but she's got a really bad personality', or what to do if 'you fancied' a girl who had 'a nice personality' though 'your mates think she's fat and ugly'. The boys' responses, when confronted with these dilemmas, were marked by long pauses and tentativeness, and this was taken by girls as evidence of boys' susceptibility to peer pressure. It was also noticeable that the boys did not support each other, but rather helped to construct the dilemmas. None of the boys questioned what the girls would have done in similar circumstances. The girls delighted in the discomfort and reticence the boys showed when choosing between their peers and 'feelings' in the dilemmas they had invented for them, reflecting, perhaps, their opposition to the ways 'boys together' dominated the playground or disrupted lessons, and how they were re-positioning themselves in the interview as powerful.

In this group the girls placed themselves almost like teachers in relation to boys. In another interview where the girls had complained about boys laughing in class and 'drawing attention' to themselves because they were bored, one of the girls unexpectedly criticised some girls for 'showing off' in class. But this was in a way which reinforced constructions of girls as mature and boys immature. She was more critical of them than noisy boys because girls can 'put themselves in the teachers' place ... but sometimes the boys just take no notice at all'. The identification of girls with teachers in relation to 'childish' boys has been observed by a number of feminist researchers (e.g. Berlotti, 1975; Walkerdine, 1990; Francis, 1999) who have examined how these positions result in girls and boys being, in class, respectively, 'sensible-selfless' and 'silly-selfish' (Francis, 1999).

Girls blurring gender boundaries and encouraging boys to be critical of popular masculinities

How boys appeared – hard, naughty, funny – was frequently contrasted by the girls in these interviews to what they were really like – shy, unsure what to say, insecure. They were thus deconstructing popular versions of masculinity, but implying that, in contrast to boys, girls were true to themselves and did not need to put on an act. Ironically, however, it was not boys who questioned girls' claims to be authentic, strong and sensitive, but the girls themselves, even when they presented boys as immature in relation to them. These girls often described boys as being less likely to 'bitch', 'bear grudges' and 'talk behind people's backs' than girls. Being 'bitchy' was usually spoken about in connection with girls competing sexually. Like hardness for boys, sexuality for girls appeared to be particularly significant in hierarchically organising identities. A number of girls distinguished themselves from 'popular girls' who were 'really bitchy', 'always combing' and wore 'short skirts'. They were despised for showing off and positioning other girls as less attractive. The same girls who identified as 'teachers' in relation to irresponsible boys, expressed a preference for boys' company over competitive relations with girls, re-positioning boys as friends. In this context, boys' fighting was taken as evidence not of their immaturity but of their 'directness', their lack of 'bitchiness', a way of immediately resolving a conflict which girls would, in contrast, pursue endlessly and indirectly.

How did these girls reconcile their contempt for boys' 'immaturity', fixation with football and hardness and inauthenticity with their preference for boys over bitchy girls? When this was put to the girls by the interviewer, the familiar distinction was drawn between what boys were like in groups and boys on their own, when they were 'really sensitive'. In a group they would laugh at girls because they did not want to seem soft, but on their own they would 'listen to you'. Some girls mentioned finding it easier to tell 'personal' problems to boys on their own than to girls because they feared girls would spread these around. Yet, these same girls had eulogised about how girls were able to talk about intimate things with other girls and how this made them different from boys. When the interviewer remarked on this, one girl distinguished between 'personal things' which she preferred speaking about to boys, and 'personal, personal things' like periods, about which she only spoke to girls.

Sometimes the girls in these interviews were resisting popular forms of masculinity by counterposing a superior essential feminine identity. They were also, however, deconstructing popular forms of masculinity and indicating alternative, empathetic and non-competitive masculine identities even though these could only be lived by boys in isolation from other boys. While the boys may have felt they were being put on the spot by the girls and being called to account for being immature and inauthentic when they were with their mates, they were able to talk critically in these interviews about hardness and competition between boys in ways which were not possible in single-sex group interviews. Popular masculinities were being challenged not only by girls but by boys and it would be wrong to interpret the boys as just defending themselves by tending to withdraw and letting the girls set the agenda; they were also producing 'softer' masculinities. Taking the lead from girls, boys in these interviews were much more critical of the way boys exclude girls from football, are loud and naughty in class, and bully and marginalise other boys. The girls were making attractive the critique of popular masculine ideals partly because they were more powerful and 'setting the agenda', but also because they were undermining, paradoxically, how girls and boys were differentiated in terms of maturity/immaturity, passivity/activity.

Rather than invoking football as a signifier of boys' immaturity, some girls contested the ways it was used to assert male hierarchies. Though positioning themselves as more mature, the girls were critical of 'bitchy' girls and, in contrast, spoke about boys as trustworthy friends. Though invoking periods as markers of essential differences between (flippant) boys and (responsible) girls, the girls seemed to want boys and girls to be similar, telling stories about how they were 'tomboys' and distancing themselves from 'popular girls' for accentuating their 'femininity'. Being a tomboy 'when I was younger' was, as we have seen, an acceptable identity for girls, and some of these girls talked, with a sense of defiance, about how they refused to wear bridesmaids' dresses and dress up for parties when they were younger. They were positioning boys not as irreconcilably different, but as in principle similar to them. Sometimes, indeed, the girls 'took the side' of boys. Although critical of boys messing around, they spoke about teachers picking on boys more than girls for being noisy; in one interview a black girl claimed teachers discriminated most against black boys. The effect of girls saying this, as one of the boys remarked at the end of an interview, was to make the boys see the girls as less hostile and less of a threat.

Conclusion

In almost all the individual interviews we conducted with girls about boys, the girls were extremely animated and engaged. Talking about boys for an hour with an adult female interviewer was something the girls seemed to enjoy and found easy to do. Most boys, as we saw in Chapter 4, were also keen to speak about girls (though this comprised only parts of the hour-long interviews). Some, however, seemed indifferent to girls, and many were rather vague about what girls did and what they spoke about. In four of the mixed gender interviews the girls spoke more about boys than the boys themselves, and set the agenda about boys. Boys' vagueness about girls no doubt stemmed from constructions of girls as passive and doing nothing and hence invisible. Boys in contrast, at least in groups, were extremely visible to girls and were constantly spoken about as troublesome and annoying, dominating space, disrupting lessons and so on (see Spender, 1982; Mahony, 1985). Girls could not ignore them in the way boys could girls.

In an interview-based study with 13–23-year-olds about their experiences of sex education, Barbara Walker (Walker and Kushner, 1997) found that whereas the boys referred to girls as a 'different species', the girls felt that they understood the boys. Walker attributed this not to the (problematic) visibility of boys in relation to girls, but to the tendency of boys to 'confide' in girls. As we saw in Chapter 4, girls were indeed regarded by some boys in individual interviews as people in whom they could confide. This, in part, reflected dissatisfaction with popular ways of being boys. The girls we interviewed (individually and in mixed groups) not only complained about boys, they also spoke in an affectionate and sympathetic way about them. Their hostility to boys in general was usually qualified, with some boys being singled out as 'nice', and boys 'on their own' being seen as 'sensitive'.

In the individual interviews, the girls constructed similar kinds of gendered dichotomies as the boys, though attaching quite different meanings to these and evaluating the 'feminine' and 'masculine' components differently. As with the boys, football was an important signifier of these differences, and therefore was as significant in the construction of the identities of girls as it was for boys. Football is not an expression of inbuilt differences between boys and girls – though this was how it was constructed by many of the boys we interviewed, who juxtaposed 'active' boys letting off steam in football with 'passive' or 'gentler' girls 'just' talking. Although some girls accepted this, others reconstructed or challenged it by positioning themselves in relation to boys, through the mediation of football, as mature, not obsessed, friendly, interesting, engaging and uncompetitive – that is, active in more constructive ways than boys. A few girls said they enjoyed football and were good at it, though were also critical of boys for letting football take them over.

The familiar gendered dichotomies in the boys' and girls' accounts which seemed to preclude the possibility of friendships between boys and girls, had another element to them: they were also understood as making heterosexual relationships possible. 'Difference' was eroticised. While both boys and girls spoke about how little they had in common with each other, how boring, for example, girls thought 'football-mad' boys, or how suffocating and constraining boys found girls who 'just talked', most boys wanted as potential girlfriends girls who were not 'tomboys', but were, in contrast, 'inactive', 'fragile' and concerned about their appearance, while girls wanted as potential boyfriends boys who were sporty, though not 'obsessively' so, and funny, though not 'immature' and 'disruptive'. 'Nice' boys were less attractive to girls of this age, perhaps because they were seen as having given up the essence of their 'masculinity'; the tension between gendered difference and the challenge of socialising a boy – a classical stereotypical view of hetero-sexual relations – seemed to carry much more of an erotic charge.

Many boys were surprised that the girls and boys interacted, in most of the mixed-gender interviews, in ways which enabled them to engage with each other without hostility. For, as we have seen, in the single-sex interviews both boys and girls tended to argue that they had little or nothing in common with the other. In the mixed-gender interviews, the boys and girls usually occupied quite different positions, both physically, with the boys and girls not sitting between each other, and discursively, with the girls constructing themselves as more mature than the boys, criticising or teasing them or acting as catalysts for boys' humour and being teased themselves. Nevertheless, in most interviews antagonism was at a minimum and the discussions were characterised by a thought-ful search for communication, even if this was often expressed in puz-zlement about why boys act the way they do.

The problematisation of boys as being influenced by peer pressure in a way which made them inauthentic and insensitive was put forward in a number of mixed-gender interviews where the girls positioned them-selves as mature in relation to the boys. As in the individual interviews with girls (and some boys), boys' presumed susceptibility to peer pres-sure was seen both as confirmation of their immaturity and as making them immature. At times the girls seemed quite elitist, acting like teachers and portraying the boys as rather slow and stupid pupils. While constructing essentialist and opposed versions of masculinity and femininity, however, they also seemed to be keen to break down polarised gendered identities, for instance to relate to boys in ways other than as non-footballers to footballers, or to be close to boys as friends and not just girlfriends. As with some of the girls we interviewed individually, a number of these girls defined themselves as similar to boys in being ex-tomboys.

Our view is that boys in these interviews were not, as in many single-sex interviews we conducted (notably group ones), constructing girls as different and patronising or attacking them for being 'soft', but, to some extent at least, identifying with their concerns. That is, given the sincere and rather penetrating questioning of 'hegemonic' masculinity instituted by some of these girls, boys were sometimes able to take a step back and acknowledge the difficulties involved in sustaining this mode of masculinity, this way of 'doing boy'. In the course of this, some alternative masculinities – more sensitive, more contained, less bullying and obsessed – came into view.

6
Ethnic identity, 'race' and young masculinities

People should just be happy for what colour they are an'. I am. I'm perfectly happy being English. I'm perfectly happy being white. (John, 13, white)

In contemporary society, the construction of gendered identities involves a narrowing of choices which takes place in the context of other, over-lapping layers of identity construction, most notably and obviously those of class and, especially, 'race' (e.g. Back, 1995; Cohen, 1997). This is not, however, a process whereby pre-existing essential differences between ethnic groups automatically produce different kinds of young masculinities. Rather, as will become apparent in the course of this chapter, a process of 'racialisation' occurs whereby images or discourses of 'whiteness', 'Asianness' and 'blackness' become vitally embroiled and invested in the ways in which masculinities are experienced. That is, eth-nicities and racialised 'difference' are powerfully intertwined with emer-gent masculinities not because of pre-existing and immutable differences between cultures, but because constructions of cultural diversity are cru-cial elements in the social contexts out of which masculinities emerge. This makes readings of 'race' and ethnicity central to the process of gen-erating masculinities. Since cultural practices are racialised and gendered as well as classed, racialised masculinities are both culturally produced and productive of cultural practices.

Amongst the various areas of discussion promoted by the interviewer in our study, all the boys were asked about their thoughts on issues of 'ethnicity' – how they saw themselves in terms of ethnic identity, whether they had friends from 'other' ethnic groups, what their experience was of racism and so on. At one level, we were interested simply in document-ing the views and experiences these boys have of ethnicity, 'race' and racism as expressed to our white, male interviewer. Additionally, how-ever, we were attempting to understand the way these young people con-struct 'racialised' identities for themselves and to examine how these

146

identities intersect with their positions as young men. This involves recognising that ethnicity and 'race' are plural, dynamic and socially constructed concepts, which are frequently used in overlapping ways – an idea conveyed in the terms 'racialisation' and 'ethnicisation' (Anthias and Yuval-Davis, 1992. There is not some global essence of 'whiteness' or 'blackness' giving rise to particular forms of masculinity; rather, racialised differences are taken up in many different ways to inform and generate a highly variegated structure of identity. In many of our interviews, this process can be seen in action.

'It doesn't matter what race you are'

Many of the boys we interviewed would not have agreed with the introduction to this chapter. They presented an account of ethnic difference as something which is somehow unnecessary or irrelevant to good personal relationships. Adopting the language of multiculturalism, they regularly told us that race differences are trivial and that everyone, of whatever colour or creed, should accept everyone else as equals:

> It's what you are inside that counts really. (Arthur, 12, white)

> It doesn't matter, you know, what your skin colour is, what it matters is who you are, and what's in here (2) that's it. (Keith, 11, black)

> It's the inside that counts, it ain't skin. I don't mind if I was pink, purple, any colour. It's nothing to be ashamed of. (Donald, 12, white)

Twenty-four boys interviewed on their own said something of this sort, about a third of our sample, reflecting a substantial tendency to claim in the interview a fair-minded attitude towards ethnicity (particularly 'colour') that might make one think that it is not a very significant issue for them. For some boys, this did indeed seem to be the case; for example Arthur, the first boy quoted above, presented a very consistent picture of antagonism to racism and interest in 'other' cultures, matched by an account of his friendships which were very multicultural. This does not, however, mean that his perceptions were not at all *racialised*: for instance, he told us of the benefits involved in learning from 'other cultures' and clearly identified himself as 'English' and liking English things ('famous monuments and London') suggesting that his egalitarian values are not the same as a lack of racial awareness. Donald also could see the difference whilst denying it significance: having told us that black boys like to wear Nike gear, he said:

> You get the occasion where the black person who's going, 'Oh, you're trying to act like us, you're trying to act like us', and saying , 'You shouldn't be wearing that 'cause you're white'. But that's being racist. But all my friends round my area, they don't care what I wear. I've had a pair of Nike trainers before. And they don't mind. They said, 'Oh they're nice'... I was just wearing them because it was the latest trend around.

Graham, a 12-year-old white boy, was perhaps the strongest in denying the importance of ethnic and 'race' differences, so much so that he could not even see them as an important part of his own identity. 'Being white is not important to me,' he said, 'I wouldn't mind if I was, say, black.'

A few of the other boys who told us that race is unimportant were more contradictory, going on to express not just racialised perceptions, but sometimes quite racist ones. Chris, for example, an 11-year-old white boy, said it did not matter where people were from, but he also talked antagonistically about the Turkish boys in his school, describing ritualised racist name-calling, even though he denied it had significance. 'Most like, Turkish boys, two Turkish boys in my class, mostly cuss us for no reason, like me and this boy, Mark, and some other people. They cuss us for no reason so we cuss them back.' Michael, a 12-year-old half-French, half-English white boy, said that 'race doesn't matter', but he also essentialised differences by suggesting that 'most black people are quite loud, they can be quite loud, and white people, white boys, they probably follow after them and try and be like them.'

While many boys denied the existence or significance of 'race', several of these same boys, and many others, identified a lot of differences. Some of this came to light in their accounts of the limits of their cross-race friendships. Two-thirds of the boys told us about such friendships, many of them claiming to mix easily with all types of people ('Most of my friends aren't coloured', said Sam, a 14-year-old Asian boy; 'One of my best friends in my last school was ethnic', said Charles, an 11-year-old white boy), although some made clear distinctions between the groups they would mix with and those they would not. Thus, Scott (12, white) explained why he did mix with blacks but not Asians:

> Asian boys aren't that loud, I'm quite talky and I can talk for ages so I go out with people who talk. Most of the Asian kids in the cricket team don't talk that

much. It's come to school, do your lesson and then go home. With the white kids all the black kids come to school have a laugh play cricket and have a laugh on the way back to the coach.

However, two-thirds of the boys (not identical, but obviously overlapping, with those who said they had mixed-race friendships) described a culture of relationships amongst the young people they knew in which ethnic groups kept largely to themselves. This was explained in terms of geographical location of different groups, language and cultural preferences, or – occasionally – either a sense of superiority or a response to racism:

Turkish people in our school seem to hang around together talking Turkish. (Mark, 15, white)

He'll [a Caribbean boy] go to his other friends from his country and like muck about with them for a while, go and talk with them...he knows he's got friends there. He'll go and like talk to them, like talk to them in his own sort of like accent. (Benny, 14, white)

I think, er, a few Asian people, a few white people, few black people do stick around with each other. But most of the people tend to mix in a group, in, you know, the people who do stick around in groups, when they do, you know, greet each other, it's not as if they're hostile to each other. I think they just like to stay with each other because they've got more in common with each other. So, um, they feel more easy about being with people from the same race or something like that. When people tease you they always pick up on one thing and tease you about that. If you're staying around with people who are more like you, they're not likely to tease you about it. (Colin, 14, mixed parentage)

What all this suggests is that the boys in our London sample are very aware of ethnic differences and groupings, that for many of them their social world is genuinely 'multicultural', but this is not the same as saying that everyone is the same.

'There's very little difference between people of different races, only the way they've been brought up'

Boys had very strong and diverse views on the nature of ethnic differences. Some of these were explicitly racist, although they commonly included a disavowal of the significance of this:

I'm not racist, no, but, like, (2) you know like - black people, (1) yeah, they kiss their teeth and that, and like - move their head and stuff... black girls are mouthy. (Terry, 14, white)

There are no differences between black and white boys although around the area which I live, well most of the crime is being done by black boys. (Keith, 11, black)

Everyone like hates Kurdish people, I don't know why. They think like they're really dirty and - disgusting and all that... they [Kurdish boys] stick together. They go around with weapons all the time a bit like gangsters...It's like they haven't been brought up properly like. (Zac, 13, Asian)

Many of the differences talked about by the boys in our sample, however, were not so much obviously racist, as organised around a number of discourses through which black and Asian boys were produced as having masculine identities contrasting in significant ways with those of white boys. As noted in Chapter 2, British and US research with young people suggests that black young men of African Caribbean descent are viewed in some ways as 'super-masculine'. They are seen as possessing the attributes that are constructed by young men as indicative of the most popular forms of masculinity – toughness and authentically male style in talk and dress. Paradoxically, while they are feared and discriminated against because of those features, they are also respected, admired and gain power through taking on characteristics which militate against good classroom performance (Mac an Ghaill, 1988; Back, 1996). Sewell (1997) found that many of the 15-year-old black boys he studied were both positioned by others, and positioned themselves, as superior to white and Asian students in terms of their sexual attractiveness, style, creativity and 'hardness'. They are, 'Angels and Devils in British (and American) schools. They are heroes of a street fashion culture that dominates most of our inner cities' (Sewell, 1997: ix). At the same time, however, they are the group of pupils most likely to be excluded from schools.

In Sewell's study, boys' accounts indicated that masculinities were racialised in two ways: through differential treatment from teachers and others; and because black, white and Asian boys were considered to be differentially positioned in terms of 'popular' masculinity. This was also the case in our study, where it was clear that part of the dynamism of culture in British multiethnic schools revolves around the expression of a range of cultural repertoires. The following example is notable not only for the positioning of black boys as popular, but for the differential production of

Asian boys as not popular – a racialisation that was common among the boys we interviewed, as also in Sewell's group. The context is a group interview with four white boys from school year 8 (12–13-year-olds):

Des   *Don't know, I think the black boys are more popular.*
RP   *Are they?*
Des   *Hmhm*
RP   *Why's that?*
Des   *Don't know it's just - black boys seem to get friends easier - and they're more popular I suppose.*
RP   *Yeah - they get friends more easy yeh.*
Des   *Mm. (3)*
RP   *But I was just wondering 'cos you said that black boys tend to be quite popular and I was wondering if it was the same with Asian boys (3). What about in your class, are Asian boys as popular as black boys?*
Des   *No, I shouldn't think so.*
Jason   *No.*
RP   *They're not, no.*
Des   *No. (2)*
RP   *Why's that? (3)*
Des   *Don't really know (sigh). (3) Black boys and Asian boys just go round with - like who they want - but they don't, they don't go out picking, they wait for them come to them (1) they've only got a few friends.*

Black boys were commonly constructed as more likely than other boys to embody the characteristics of popular masculinity, particularly sporting ability, coolness and toughness. Nine white boys, for example, explicitly stated that black boys were tougher and harder than boys from other ethnic backgrounds:

RP   *So they tend to be more interested in football then?*
David   *Well, black people are good at athletics, they're very good at running and everything, and high jump.*
          ...
          Black boys are good at sport, look at the Olympics and things, they're 100 metre champion ... I think speed games they're good at but not necessarily other athletically things like rugby ... all the people who do the last leg of the 4 × 100 for the houses for sports day are all coloured kids. They're the quickest in the year. (Scott, 12, white)

This familiar notion of the in-built superior physicality of black people, which coincides with visions of 'ideal' masculinity but which is also racist in its strong connotations of 'animality', recurs frequently in the descriptions of racialised difference given by young white boys. These descriptions racialise both black boys' bodies and their cultural practices. Although these accounts often leave whiteness unmarked, they also implicitly racialise it in opposition to blackness. The following extract, from an interview with a group of six 12–14-year-old white boys, demonstrates their contestation of black boys' perceived cultural dominance and their explicit normalising of 'white style' in comparison with 'black style'. In this extract Somalis are constructed as 'black wannabes', for it is primarily African Caribbean boys who are seen as smart and tough (much to the consternation of these white boys), and not other black boys:

Jamie = *White people have their own styles so do black people - sometimes Moroccans have theirs (1), but Somalis just copy.*

RP *What's the white style then?*

Dorin *Kind of normal in't it [**Bill**: Tracksuit] - normal clothes (2), no flashness no nothing.*

RP *No flashness?*

Bill *Casual clothes.*

RP *So black boys are more flash are they than white boys?*

Bill *Yeah, they like showing off.*

RP *Why do the Somalis and Moroccans try and copy the black boys and not the white boys? (3)*

Jamie *It's just that (1) they learn that - the clothes that look (1) the - top in'it?*

Bill *I - I wouldn't wear them =*

Dorin *= Black people they wear like, like design designer wear (2).*

RP *Right.*

Dorin *And like they [**Lenny**: More expensive], yeah, much more expensive.*

RP *More expensive, yeh?*

Bill *= Yeh*

Jamie *= Doesn't mean they've got more money or nothing, it's just that - they like - they like to show what they've got and everything but (1) [**RP**: Right], they're just spending their money just on clothes.*

As will be seen in the next quotation, the racialisation of black boys' bodies and cultural practices is often hedged around with uncertainties, reflected in the verbal formula that 'people say' that black people are characterisable in certain ways, while nuancing that account by recognising that some white boys are also tough. It also links with the ambivalent way in which some white youngsters want to 'be' black in order to achieve the cultural trappings of 'cool pose':

RP   *Right. Does, does it make a difference being, being white, d'you think?*

Paul   *No. People that 'finks like black people might be stronger, like, most black people are better than white people at basketball 'cos (1) they like - play it a lot.*

RP   *Right (2) D'you think, d'you think black people are stronger than white people?*

Paul   *Don't know like, people like say - like boxers, most boxers are black. [RP: Yeah, yeah] 'Cos people say like - black people's bones are harder an' that. [RP: Right] But (1) ... the strongest boy in our year's (1) somebody I don't like, there's a boy called Sam. He's white but, like (1) there's four strongest boys, three of them are black, one of them are white. [RP: Mmm, mmm] But most people they're just like (1), mixed, who's the hardest an' that.*

RP   *D'you think some white boys then envy black boys (1) 'cos they think they're stronger?*

Paul   *Yeah like, they wanna like, some people wanna be black 'cos (1) they might, like, be more popular. Like, black people like, don't like really cool. Black people have like black slang don't they an' they call people - bro an' that. Like white people don't call each other - names like that, an' black people call some people some. And sometimes people wanna be black an' that. (11-year-old white boy)*

This did not mean that all boys, black or white, accepted that it is the case that black boys automatically are more 'hegemonically' masculine. It was, however, a pervasive narrative which partially defined cultures of masculinity and against which boys positioned themselves as they attempted to embody, appropriate or repudiate it. Many boys in our study expended a great deal of energy in this racialised 'jockeying for position' (Edley and Wetherell, 1997). For this reason, some white boys were reported to be adopting the cultural practices they considered central to 'black masculinity'. In accounts such as the one below, it is always other white boys, not the speaker, who is reported to want to be black:

RP   *Do you think of yourself as being English, or white?*

Bob   *Um, I do think of myself as a British person, a British citizen but I, I don't think of myself as any other race because I was born in England, which makes me English, so I'm not nothing else, I wouldn't try and be nothing else.*

RP   *Right. Do you think some boys do they want to be something else?*

Bob   *Yeah. Yeah, try and act hard or try and talk in a, like some people like try talkin' like a Jamaican accent or =*

RP   *= Do they?*

Bob   *Yeah and like kiss their teeth like Africans, like Afro-Caribbean do, try and copy them.*

RP   *This is English boys tryin' to be like that. White English boys?*

Bob   *Yeah. Some do. Yeah.*

RP   *So why is that then? Why do they try and be like that?*

Bob   *Dunno because they look as … quite hard people and if they try and, if they act like that then they're gonna, people are gonna think oh look they look hard. Don't look at them else they're gonna start trouble. So that's probably why.* (14-year-old white boy)

The idea of black boys as *attractively* hard in comparison with Asian boys, whose cultural difference was marked more by their language and sense of togetherness, was a very central one in much of the material from the boys in our study. It seems only to be African Caribbeans that white boys might want to emulate, never Asians:

> *I don't really get on well with Asian boys... I get on when I go abroad and things, I get on with the person who is Asian. I wouldn't deliberately be friends with an Asian person, I don't know it's their - it's their character or something. It's not the type of person I'm friends with. Asian boys are quiet. They don't usually say that much as there isn't many of them.* (Scott, 12, white)

> *They're [black boys] more aggressive and they lead more ... because the people sort of look up to them and things - and so they sort of - kind of fear them.'* (Matthew, 14, white)

The ambivalence felt towards these 'hard' black boys in comparison with the relative disdain or lack of interest felt for Asians (although some boys also see Bengalis as 'hard') is very striking, and connects with the sense of admirable strength and 'style' associated with black masculinities.

This idea of black style is a hotly disputed topic, but clearly recognised by boys of all ethnic groups:

> *Most of my [white] friends from my old school, most of us didn't even know what Addidas and Reebok was and they [black boys] used to pick on us.* (Alan, 12, white)

> *Some people bowl ... If you're really hard you sort walk with a kind of limp thing...it's what all the gangsta rappers do on television and things and people are bound to do it ... It's probably mainly black people. I don't know. Quite a lot of white people.* (Norman, 13, white)

Finally, *girls* from different ethnic groups are also seen as different, with black girls in particular being viewed as aggressive and assertive. Five boys referred to black girls as loud:

> *As Joe was saying yesterday, black girls are quite mouthy, they're all know-alls, they don't mind saying anything.* (Scott, 12, white)

> *Where there's a, you see a big gang of black girls or anything, they are really racist to white girls and all that ... You see more white boys being racist to black and more black girls being racist to whites.* (Billy, 14, white)

> *Black girls act like black boys, know more black boys, act tough. It's stupid they should have white friends as well.* (Greg, 11, black)

As the following discussion between some black 13–14-year-old boys in a mixed group shows, this idea that black girls are more aggressive can lead to them being both admired and disparaged at the same time, and is not confined to white boys' racist perceptions. They are also seen as more likely than boys to stick to their own-race groups and to actively exclude others:

Anthony   *= I think black girls - definitely stick to their own colour more.*

Lawrence   *Yeah, yeah, yeah, yeah.*

Marcus   *Mm.*

Anthony   *And they do - 'cos you'll see a lot of - you'll see a black girl - they're always in groups of black.*

Marcus   *Yeah.*

Anthony   *And you'll see white girls - [**RP** Right] in the groups of white.*

RP   *Yeah...*

Anthony   *But with girls it's a bit worser - if you see a group of black girls - or - a group of white girls - like say you see a group of black girls with a - white girl with it then she'll be called a tag-a-long (1), or - a idiot.*

RP   *The white girl would be called tag-a-long?*

Anthony Yeah.

RP   *Oh really, yeah.*

Anthony 'Cos, that's what it's like.

RP   *Who - who's she called a tag-a-long by, who calls her that?*

Anthony There's - people - by both colours to be fair - 'cos, - white people could say, 'Oh look at her she's from [inaudible] black following them about' - black people say, 'Wow what a idiot, why's she just following around black people, why can't she follow her own colour?'

Lawrence That's wrong. You shouldn't say that.

Anthony Well you shouldn't but some people are like.

RP   *Is it - is it - is it black and white boys that say that or girls say that as well?*

Anthony It's a bit different with boys - girls are a bit bitchier - they're =

Marcus Laughs

Anthony Girls are a bit bitchier.

Lawrence No, it's true, man. That's why they say that as well.

Anthony Yeah, the girls are ignorant man. They'll be quick to cuss and - they're bitches.

RP   *So - it's okay for a white boy to go along with a group of black boys then is it?*

Anthony Well, yeah, it's more easier - than - a white girl going with a group of black girls.

Our findings on the positioning of black and Asian boys are to a considerable degree borne out by those of other studies, such as those by Back (1996) and Cohen (1997) described in Chapter 2. Awareness of the ambivalent ways in which white boys perceived blackness was also very strong amongst the black boys interviewed in our study. In the following example, four black 12–13-year-olds, Kwesi, Dennis, Mike and Joe, are discussing differences between white and black boys:

RP   *Could I just ask you finally, um, do you think that - there are differences, between black boys and white boys and Asian boys?*

Mike Mm.

RP   *You do?*

Mike Black boys get in trouble more [**Dennis**: More] get, they get suspended more from school.

RP   *Yeah.*

Mike   *Yeah.*

RP   *And why's that?*

Mike   *They've got bad [inaudible] I don't really know why (2), I don't really know why ...*

Joe   *Way life is.*

RP   *Right (3) Is it because, because people pick on you or, or, or what or is it because black boys are different?*

Mike   *Well I reckon sometimes =*

Joe   *They don't - they don't [impassioned tone] really understand us basically like we do different things - so like they - don't really understand - us - they get jealous [**Mike**: Sometimes; **RP**: They get jealous?]. The only way they get at us is just - by doing something.*

RP   *Why do they get jealous, jealous of what?*

Joe   *I don't know(2), they want to be as good as you like (2) Dennis - can like do something that - a white person or Asian person that can't, they can't do.*

RP   *Mm.*

Joe   *And like they'll think - 'A::h he's betta than me so I wanna do something which I'm - better than him.'*

RP   *Right.*

Joe   *So they just take the mickey out of him basically.*

        ...

Mike   *So (2) it's like [inaudible] sometimes like one of my friends in our class wants to be black in't?*

Joe   *Mm.*

Mike   *He wishes he was black.*

Joe   *He'd rather be black than white because [**Dennis**: Is that what he says? (surprised tone)] he says there's a lot of - racism - and he hates it.*

RP   *Yeah, yeah how do you feel about that? (1)*

Joe   *I understand it basically - I understand what he's saying.*

RP   *Yeah - so do you do you like white boys who want to be black? (1)*

Mike   *They're OK yeah [unsure tone] (1) just the same really.*

Joe   *Sometimes you just - get fed up with it (2) but*

RP   *You get fed up with it?*

Joe   *Yeah.*

RP   *Why's that?*

Joe   *'Cos you always find - a lot of whites out there - that - act black [**Dennis:** Act black] fink - 'A::h yeah I'm going to act black' and all this.*

Dennis   *And they're not.*

Joe   *Just gets on [**Dennis:** Just the fact that they're not] your nerves.*

RP   *How do, how do they try and act black then?*

Joe   *Like start talking black and start kissing their teeth something like that.*

RP   *Yeah.*

Dennis   *Doing things that - mostly black people do.*

RP   *Yeah, yeah (3) and that, and you find that annoying do you yeah?*

Joe   *Sometimes yeah.*

Dennis   *If they're white they're white they should just accept it [**Joe:** Exactly] not try and act like a black person. (1)*

Mike   *Sometimes some people might find it offensive as well - that they're trying, er, um=*

Dennis   *=Imitate a black person.*

Mike   *Yeah - some people might find it offensive (1) some black people.*

Interestingly, none of the white boys we spoke to admitted to trying to copy black styles, although five mentioned other white and Asian boys who did. These black boys, however, in common with many others we interviewed, saw it happening and recognised it as a mixture of envy and antagonism, making their own response to it uncertain. On the whole, like most white boys, they tended to draw on a discourse in which it was morally reprehensible not to be at ease with one's own ethnic identity ('*If they're white they're white they should just accept it*' – an exact parallel of the quotation from a white boy with which this chapter begins) rather than to feel flattered by others wanting to be black. Certainly, the racialisation of attitudes and behaviour was something which they were aware permeated their lives.

Ethnic identities

The racialisation of masculinities discussed above, particularly the positive value placed on certain kinds of 'cool, hard' black masculinities, produced ambivalence in those white boys who resented exclusion from cultural practices which many boys saw as a condensation of 'popular' masculinity. Among white boys, this resulted in both attraction and aversion to black masculine cultural practices which sometimes generalised to all black people, as in the following example:

RP *Is there any reason why you have Asian friends but not black friends?*

Luke *Um (4), 'cos I suppose because most of the - black boys (2) again are like (1) think they're like sort of (1) rude boys and well, hard and they like - music I don't like, I don't know they just - I don't get on with them.*

RP *Do they tend to stick together, the black boys, or do they mix?*

Luke *They mix with other people as well but*

RP *With similar kinds of interests?*

Luke *Yes (1) it's just - it's not - I don't think it's 'cos they're black, it's just 'cos - they're - not the type of people I'd get on with most of them - relate to other groups.*

RP *Have you ever thought you'd rather not be white?*

Luke *Um (2), nah actually um (6) 'cos (3) I don't like most of the black women, not 'cos they're black - but just not 'cos (1) they relate to the group that I don't like so I wouldn't want (1), NO I've never wanted to be black actually.*

RP *Are there any things that you admire about black people?*

Luke *Um (8), they seem more confident in a way they're sort of (5), they act sort of bigger and louder and more confident - and I sort of admire that.*

RP *Do you wish you were more like that then?*

Luke *Sometimes (1) but not like (2) [inaudible]. It's not like, I don't think about it a lot - I don't think, 'Oh I really want to be black' - or, 'I really want to be like that'.* (14-year-old white boy)

Alongside the ambivalent positioning of black masculinities described above, a variety of racisms appear in our participants' material, particularly amongst the white boys. Straightforward assumptions of racist identities are resisted by the boys – racist discourses are currently recognised to be socially proscribed amongst British people and in British schools (Back, 1996; Billig, 1991; Tizard and Phoenix, 1993; Troyna and Hatcher, 1992), and some boys explicitly claimed that if they made certain kinds of comments they would be unfairly labelled as racists. But this did not prevent numerous long-established racist ideologies appearing in their narratives, in many instances connected to exactly the same elements of 'coolness' and physicality which also excited envy and admiration. The account below ascribes black boys' concern with style and appearance to their having 'a chip on their shoulder'. The white speaker told to 'go home' by black boys flips the meaning from what is presumably the dismissive admonition that he should go away, to a discourse of racialised exclusion from the nation – a discourse he is afraid to voice to the black boys who antagonise him:

Alan *Seems to be all black boys have a chip on their shoulder. Er, you do get white bullies - I'm not sayin' that, but half of the school here, erm, half the black boys - all of them walk around walkin' like that, brand names, lookin' down at people, like Year Seven's, the little girls. They look at you and stare at you as if you're lower than them. And the worst bit is and then they say 'What you doin' ruckin' up my clothes' and you're like, 'Pardon? Ruckin up your clothes - what's that?' And they say, 'You're juggin' my clothes, you're ripping them, you're touchin' them' and you're like, 'Sorry, we're in a corridor' and you're bound to bump into them, especially when they're walkin' in a line. And they're lookin' at you as if to say, 'What you doin' here? Why are you here?'*

RP *Mmm.*

Alan *Not being racist, but they come over here. Mean I have no problem with black people. Most of my friends are coloured and foreign but sometimes it really annoys me especially when they say, 'What are you doin' - why are you here. Go home' and all of this. I'm like, I am home, this is England. And I say in my mind, why have I got to go home - I live here? This is my home. Sometimes I feel like sayin' 'Go back to your home, Jamaica' - somewhere like that, and then think about sayin' most of my friends are coloured, be upsettin' them as well.*

For this boy, Alan, an element of his construction of his everyday experience of school is of the black boys swaggering and looking down on him, as if to say to him, 'What you doin' here? Why are you here?' They take up all the space and in so doing push him out: it is literally the case, in his account, that there is no room for him. His interpretation of this corridor jostling is a racialised perception of contestation of space and cultural practices. Black boys are constructed as 'coloured and foreign' outsiders who usurp what is rightfully his – they tell him to go home.

In his vision, the black boys are constantly asserting their superiority and hence pose a cogent threat which is based on their capacity to undermine his sense of location and identity: they treat the place as home, when he sees it as his home – 'I live here. This is my home'. His wish is that all of them, from wherever they might have come, should go back to their home, which he calls 'Jamaica – somewhere like that'.

Alan's immediate association, 'my home England, their home Jamaica' demonstrates how both black and white boys are racialised (and reproduce racialisation) in relation to each other. As described above, many of the boys we have interviewed share Alan's conviction that African Caribbean boys are 'hard', stylish and to be admired, but also carry an image of aggression and disdain for others. Importantly for understanding contemporary racism, they are not constructed as inferior, but as belonging elsewhere. Their reported airs – superiority, disdain, and 'lookin' down at people', their '[staring] at you as if you are lower than them' – are markers of cultural as well as racialised otherness and are deeply resented. For Alan, it is as if his home has been invaded and taken from him.

In keeping with the findings of a number of studies, however, many of the boys we interviewed saw black and white boys as being more like one another than they are like Asians, who were disparaged for differences marked out by their tight culture, strong family ties, and – particularly – their language (Back, 1996; Boulton and Smith, 1992; Cohen, 1997):

Billy   *That's what most people don't like about (3) the Bengali people 'cos they speak in their own language and you can't really understand what they are saying, but when you are speaking in English you can, you can understand what they are saying [**RP**: Yeah] right and …*

RP   *Is that something you don't like about them?*

Billy   *Yeah, 'cos you don't even have to say anything about you [**RP**: Right] (2)* (White 14-year-old)

Extracted from the uncertainties of 'you' and 'they' in this boy's talk, the theme again seems to be the way the white boy feels excluded, with this exclusion carrying a paranoid charge. The Bengali-speaking boys could be saying anything to one another and this is automatically excluding because it is hidden in their own language. Very centrally for this boy and many others, 'culture' becomes something bound up with envy, in all the ambivalent senses of the word. An explicit bond, expressed through shared language and 'sticking together', is something very noteworthy; it is also antisocial, dangerous, promoting antagonism and a wish to destroy. In this quotation, power relations are evident in contestation about the intersection of cultural practices, inclusion and exclusion. This boy and the others from whom we have quoted clearly demonstrate how their identities are constructed in relation to who or what they are *not* – in this case they are racialised as white in contradistinction from black and Asian people. What perhaps can be seen here are the seeds of an attitude towards 'culture' which is deeply emotional: the strong investment that these boys have in placing themselves inside or outside particular 'ethnic' or racialised masculine cultures suggests that racialised constructions of difference are central to the production of identity positions.

Black and Asian boys in our sample were often very aware of their ethnicity, usually proudly but sometimes even when they said either that it was not important to them or that they did not think it *should* be important:

> *To be coloured means you are different, but nothing's going to happen, you've just got to be careful ... You know you're black, different to other people 'cos there's so many white people ... sometimes people say are you Indian. I'm not, I'm Mauritian. Don't like this 'cos I don't like India... I want friends to know I'm not Indian I'm Mauritian.* (Tariq, 11, Asian)
>
> *Being black is important 'cos you stick up for other black people if there's racism.* (Olu, 11, black)
>
> *I love my colour, well I don't mind what colour I am...as long as I'm happy.* (Dean, 13, mixed parentage)
>
> ...

RP *Is being Jamaican - is that important to you?*

Sol *Yeah, it is important to me because - I don't really wanna lose where I come from - d'you get me? - Well I'll never really lose it anyway because, I go back every year, I can adapt to there [**RP**: Yeah], and then I come back I'm in Englan' now it's different I'm - you have to say I'm in Englan' now, I'm English right - [**RP**: Mm] I'm in Jamaica now, this is where I come from, I'm Jamaican - talk the same with them - act the same, go where you used to go with your old friends everything but once you're back here you're back here.*

RP *So how, how is it different - how do you feel different in Jamaica than - you feel in England? =*

Sol *= I feel more at home in Jamaica.* (Black 13-year-old)

White boys, on the other hand, commonly seemed not to have thought about their ethnicity ('ethnic' means 'other' to many whites), but when they did so in the course of the interview their routine assertion was that they were happy with their whiteness and – despite the instances of 'black wannabe's' – that they would not ever want to change:

> *I'm proud I'm white ... I don't think it gives me any extra advantages or nothing like that ... I ain't ashamed to be white ... and if I was any other colour I wouldn't be ashamed to be any other colour, I'm just me in't.* (Andy, 13, white)
> ...

RP *How would you, how would you identify your own ethnic background. What would you say you were?*

John *(4) (I dunno) I'm (2) just English. Um (1) My ancestors could be (2) German for all I know but I am English. I'm (1) I'm all English. My mum, my dad's English. My nan an' granddad are English. And so basically I'm English.*

RP *Do you think of yourself as white? Is that ...?*

John *Yeah, but um I don't try and mix in with the blacks. I don't start listening to the (1) like, swing. I like a bit of swing, yeah, but I don't try and fit in with the like, the backwards hat, the baggy trousers an' stuff like that. I just wear what I wanna wear. [RP: Right] Rather than trying to fit in. I just wanna wear what I think looks good on me.*

RP *Yeah. Do, do some white boys, do they try and be like blacks then, or ... ?*

John *Not that I know of. But I mean, maybe in different schools, boys could be doing that. But I haven't really noticed that.*

RP *No, I was just interested in why, why you were saying that you don't (1) try and =*

John *Because then I'd be saying (1) I'd be told that I would be a black wannabe. [RP: OK, yeah] Which I'm not. [RP: Yeah] An' I don't wanna be a black person. [RP: Yeah] I'm perfectly, I'm perfectly happy with being white.* (White 13-year-old)

Although a very few white boys did express some interest in ethnic identity, the contrast given in these last quotations between the black, Asian and mixed-parentage boys' consciousness of their ethnicities and the white boys relative inarticulateness on the subject is much more characteristic of our data. On the whole, like John, when asked to say something about their ethnicity they struggled to understand the question, then developed a version of themselves as 'white and happy with it' which they also attempted to present as different from a white-supremacist position. This produced some convoluted language and, as with John, several instances in which a boy seemed to be uncertain about what his racialised identity might mean.

Interestingly, boys of all ethnic backgrounds were largely (though not completely) in agreement that they would only go out seriously with girls from similar backgrounds to their own. Occasionally, the reasons for this were given as racial preference, but often it was to do with what kind of girl they found attractive, what parents might say, and what peers, culture and religion dictate:

Terry   *That's (3), that's - like, (1) there was a boy, (1) you know, 'e went out wiv, um, (2), you know, an Indian girl at my last school and they called 'im - a Paki-lover for that. 'Cos 'e =*

RP   *= 'This a white boy?*

Terry   *Yeah.*

RP   *Was it, yeah? Yeah.*

Terry   *They called 'im a Paki-lover - For yea:rs. [nervous laugh]*

RP   *Really?*

Terry   *You know. It's bad.*

RP   *Yeah.*

Terry   *So then I thought, I'll just stay clear of them - I don't wanna be, like, called names.*

RP   *Yeah. (1) So you - stay clear of them - because of that?*

Terry   *Er, I stay, - I wouldn't go out with a black person 'cos I didn't wanna be called names.*

RP   *Oh, I see. Yeah. Yeah. (1) D'you still feel like that?*

Terry   *I still know the same people. But, no, I (5), I'm not - racist or anything. I just, I don't find them as - good-lookin' - as white girls.* (White 14-year-old)

    ...

RP   *What race would you want your girlfriend to be?*

Jed   *Same as me.*

RP   *Why's that?*

Jed   *I don't know, because my mum and dad would say something, she should be the same as me.* (White 14-year-old)

    ...

Anthony *I've got white friends, that are girls but, it's not a racist thing but - I just [inaudible] to stick to my own colour to be fair, when it comes to that.* (Black 14-year-old)

Racism

The experience of racism is itself a major marker of racialised identities in boys' lives. Of the 34 boys we interviewed who were black, Asian or had mixed parentage, 23 spoke about having experienced, observed or heard about racism in or outside school. Of the 44 white boys we interviewed, this figure was 11. For many boys, it is an issue about which they have strong feelings. Predictably, these are more ambiguous amongst white boys than black, because white boys have to find ways of positioning themselves as either racist or not, and this positioning can be very complex. However, black boys too find themselves having to work hard to account for their experience of racism, even though they mostly agree that this experience is powerful and real. The following long example, from the discussion with the group of 12–13-year-old boys mentioned earlier (Kwesi, Dennis, Mike and Joe), shows just how awkward it can be for them to know how best to locate themselves:

RP *You said that, that y'know you're proud, to be black and proud to be African and, and do some people (1) do you feel that some people, think that it's, think that it's, y'know that it's not something to be proud of then?*

Dennis *Mm, some people try, put, mostly Africa down and they're always taking the mickey out of their [**Mike**: Yeah], language and everything [inaudible] speech, but (1)*

RP *Some people do that do they yeah?*

Mike *Yeah.*

Dennis *Yeah.*

RP *Like, like who? (3) Is it people in this school do that?*

Dennis *I [**Mike**: Yeah] don't don't - I don't [**RP**: Are there?] know people in this school. I know, I know people that do it.*

RP *Right.*

Mike *And teachers that put you down as well. (1)*

Joe *Yeah.*

RP *How do they do that?*

Joe *All different things.*

Mike   *Like say your work [cough] like you're like a you're asking for help [inaudible], you just stuck there you're saying, 'Sir can you come and help me please?' and they just ignore you.*

Joe   *And then at the end of the lesson they say you haven't done your work.*

Mike   *Yeah.*

Joe   *And you get in trouble for it.*

RP   *Right - and you think that's because, because you're black then?*

Joe   *Yeah.*

RP   *They do that, yeah (1) So with, with white boys th - they pay more attention to them [**Dennis**: Yes] do they? (2) Do you ever do you talk about that much?*

Joe   *We had a discussion - during break bout it.*

RP   *Mm.*

Joe   *With, er, Barbadian teacher.*

RP   *Oh did you, wh- what did - was it a man, this teacher [**Mike**: A woman] a woman, what did she say?*

Mike   *She said=*

Joe   *She's basically talking about our education.*

Mike   *Saying that we need to have a good - solid education* behind *us.*

RP   *Yeah, and what and what - yeah?*

Mike   *In order to get somewhere in life.*

RP   *Oh right - and she was talking to, to all - to black boys was she?*

Mike   *Yeah.*

RP   *Yeah (1), were there black girls there as well?*

Joe   *No.*

RP   *Why was she talking to black boys in particular?*

Mike   *Because what [**Joe**: Because] happened, right, a couple of weeks ago, we were doing our work, and then she says [inaudible] 'It's most it's mostly black boys that get low grades' - so like all of us felt offended by that 'cos like, it's not really something you should be saying to, another, um, somebody else who are (1) same colour as you, so we went we went up to her and then we started like question her as to why she said that.*

RP   *Mm.*

Mike   *She sat us down started talking to us as about why she said that - and how, it evolve, it evolves, around racism and how black boys get suspended more and all that.*

RP   *Mm.*

Mike	'Cos they're (2), more, their behaviour's more bad and all that - so that's how it started really.
RP	And, um, wh what do you think of that then?
Mike	I reckon in some ways yes she was right, but the way she said it, it didn't really I didn't really like it but she was right, in a way.
RP	Wh- when you were discussing, with her, just recently what did she say then, and, I mean you, you told her about, um, teachers discriminating against you?
Mike	Mm.
RP	How did, what did she say to that?
Joe	Mm, just put it behind us basically (1) get on with our work.
RP	Do you think that's good advice or wha=
Joe	=Yeah.
Mike	Yeah.

Here, the encounter with the black teacher who makes them think about their response to racist attitudes on the part of other teachers (itself something several boys and girls told us about) is experienced both as challenging and (in the end) supportive by these black boys. Accepting the reality of racism and suggesting they should *'just put it behind us basically'* makes it part of the work to find ways of resisting racism which are not, at least in school terms, self-destructive and confirming of racist prejudices about black masculinities. Many other black and Asian boys recounted stories about racism which showed both its prevalence amongst young people and also how commonly they felt the victims of racism on the part of adults. In the next example, from a mixed group interview dominated by some black boys, there is no black teacher available to mediate their experience and make it into something from which they might be able to draw strength:

Lawrence	Some teacher said like, white people do, better on results than black people - it might be true or noth- or something but, there's no reason to say it, and then when she tried, when we told her, right, she like, tried to say, 'It's true, it's true, it's true', and everything. It might be true but there's no reason to say it. Shouldn't be putting down black people like that.
RP	She, do you think she was putting down black people, yeah?
Lawrence	Yeah.
Marcus	Yeah. Mmhmm.
RP	Yeah. Do, do other teachers do that as well?

Marcus	*Yeah…*
RP	*Yeah…Why do you think it is that, that some teachers do pick on, on black, boys?*
Lawrence	*Because*
Anthony	*Got a grudge against them, prejudiced.*
	…
RP	*Do, do other boys here, think that teachers pick on black boys?*
Jonathan	*Sometimes.*
Nigel	*Yeah, some.*
RP	*Do they, yeah?*
Jonathan	*No but, that has happened, I've seen it happen to kids.*
RP	*Have you?*
Jonathan	*Black people, yeah.*
RP	*Like what - can you give me an example?*
Jonathan	*Like, er, when, em, the boy hasn't done anything, he's sitting down, and say like a white boy an he, an he threw something, and the black boy gets the blame for it.* (Jonathan 14-year-old Asian, other boys 13–14-year-old black)

In several instances, particularly in groups, great bitterness was expressed at experiences of this kind; there was also quite considerable agreement from black, Asian and white boys and girls that it is black boys in particular who suffer from some teachers' racism.

Experiences of racist attacks and abuse from other boys are also very widespread. Some of this, as in the next extended example from a 12-year-old Asian boy, Sadam, requires a subtle set of discriminations of signs to make full sense of the situation:

RP	*Could you define, tell me what, what your own race is, how would you find your own race?*
Sadam	*My race, um, I would simply call it a Paki race [laughs here].*
RP	*That's… Yeah.*
Sadam	*Yeah and, um, that's it and, um.*
RP	*That's, that's, that's, that's what you call yourself?*
Sadam	*Yeah.*
RP	*What, Paki?*
Sadam	*Yeah.*
RP	*You would, yeah?*
Sadam	*Yeah.*

RP   *'Cos Paki is ofte =*

Sadam   *= Pakistani*

RP   *Yeah, I'm just interested because it's often used as a term of abuse isn't it?*

Sadam   *Yeah = [**RP**: Paki] but like you know you get used to it 'cos they are gonna call you anyway [**RP**: Yeah] from wherever, whatever you say they gonna call you anyway so you get used to it.*

RP   *Right. And you don't mind calling yourself will you call yourself that?*

Sadam   *Yup.*

RP   *Yeah.*

Sadam   *But um if, if someone else like said it, um, abusedly, yeah then*

RP   *Right.*

Sadam   *I'd do something about it.*

RP   *OK so, so you think some boys or some people said in a joking way = [**Sadam**: yeah] whereas some people =*

Sadam   *Yeah, 'cos my mates they, they say it all the time and I know they are mucking [**RP**: Um] about 'cos you know, um, they're Bengali themselves [**RP**: Mm] so doesn't matter. (9)*

RP   *Does that does that happen quite a lot then?*

Sadam   *My mates or - other people?*

RP   *Your, your mates doing that?*

Sadam   *Yeah they, they are just mucking about, it's just that it's just a laugh calling you a Paki stuff like that [**RP**: Yeah] you know that's a laugh but when someone when a white person or a black person says it and means it like you know, yeah, then you know that he's being racist.*

RP   *Right. How, how do you know when someone means it?*

Sadam   *Well he's, he's gonna put on a serious face like he's, he's seriously you know, say it like, um, he'll just say 'Paki' and me and my mates they like, they just smiling at the same time saying Paki so.*

RP   *Does that happen sometimes that people say it to you seriously?*

Sadam   *Yeah, um [inaudible] I live around Kings Cross so it's not that, um they're quite racist down there.*

RP   *Are they yeah? Yeah*

Sadam   *So the bus stop if you're waiting there, in there 'Oi you Pakis' and stuff like that, 'Go home, we want a white Britain' and stuff like that.*

The interviewer has clearly struggled to stay abreast of a lot of this material, particularly the distinction between 'Paki' as racial abuse and 'Paki' as friendly cussing. His sympathy for the plight of Sadam and his friends is interestingly juxtaposed against the matter-of-fact way in which Sadam tells his tale.

Colin, a 14-year-old of mixed parentage, adds further subtlety to this distinction between racism (and sexism) and ordinary cussing:

Colin   *Because one Asian boy won't go to another Asian boy something like you chink or something like that. As they'll be more alike. But if you mix around with a group of more people, there is a lot more teasing in the big groups. But usually I don't think there's anyone here right now who really, really hate each other.*

RP   *Just joking, teasing and yet you were saying that Asian boys don't like it.*

Colin   *You know it's joking, sometimes they won't like it, but they won't say it, say something like that, they just stay around with each other because=*

RP   *=Asian boys won't say they don't like it?*

Colin   *Or whoever say, won't say they don't like it, because, um, they'll say you're a girl or something like that, you know.*

RP   *They'll say you're a girl?*

Colin   *Yeah, you're a girlie or something like that. You can't stand up for yourself or something like that.*

This same boy then goes on immediately to draw on the stereotypes of black versus Asian masculinities to explain how certain racist words are suppressed, whereas others, like the ubiquitous 'Paki', are allowed through and have to be negotiated with the subtlety described above:

RP   *In the group interview people were saying that Paki was a term that was used quite a lot whereas nigger wasn't.*

Colin   *I think that's usually because the group of black, because black people are quite big in this school, something like nearly six foot now, but usually the Asian people are quite small. Some people use it, like a lot of African people, like Ugandan or Kenyans, they look quite Indian, but people think they're Indian, because they look it, so they misuse it sometimes.*

RP   *Black people are quite big?*

Colin   *Yeah, that's why it's used less. I think a lot of people think even though it's not really, Paki is less you know not strong as saying something like nigger or something like that.*

RP   *Why do you think that?*

Colin   *I'm not sure, but, I think some people think it's okay for black people to call each other nigger and things like that, but it's not good for other people to call it them, but I think it's different with the word Paki but I'm not sure why.*

RP   *Do you ever use the word Paki?*

Colin   *No, no, not really, because I think it's too racist.*

The complexities of distinguishing between different kinds of racist words and how they can be employed within or across racialised groups are very great, but are attested to in many of our group and individual interviews. It seems as though these terms are both used as abuse and also drawn on as part of the culture of jokey 'cussing' which is so characteristic of boys' communications with one another. This does not, however, mean that there is no pain attached. For example, Zac, another 13-year old-Asian boy, had developed a self-protective, psychological or moral account of the sources of racist abuse, but was still clear about his distress at experiencing racist attacks:

Zac   *I'm proud of being a Hindu because most people, to be racist to you, they'll call you a Paki, yeah. And I think, I find that quite offensive really but - and I used to like, you know, swear back at them when I was slightly younger. Now I understood that they're only being stupid and racist. They're racist idiots who need to sort themselves out really. And I've learnt to just avoid them and ignore them really. And they'll, they'll soon realise how stupid they've been when they grown out of that and they'll really kick themselves in the butt. They'll say 'Why did I say that, why did I say that?' [inaudible] They're really stupid.*

RP   *Does that happen now at all that you're called Paki?*

Zac   *Um, um, no, not, it doesn't happen as often as it used to. Yeah, because, um, like say if I was to be on the street, it'll still happen because if they see, if you're brown, they'll assume that, they'll call you a Paki yeah and they'll start pickin' on you because - I was up the park wiv my mate yeah, he was Pakistan or Muslim, I dunno what really. And these kids just came up to him and they knew I was Hindu and they tried to pick on him 'cos they thought he was a*

Paki. And he was like a slightly darker skin colour. And I said 'Stop it man. What are you lot doin'?'

RP   *Who were these kids who picked on him?*

Zac   *Um, they were like, really any kids, white kids really.*

RP   *White kids, yeah. Boys?*

Zac   *Boys yeah. And I was so angry at them. I said 'Get lost the lot of you.' And they just went and I felt so sorry for him. I was thinking how do they live, you know? And I see all these programmes about racism and kids getting beaten up so badly and having it seen right, being in front of you, you feel so bad and guilty you wanna do something, you know, but you can't.*

RP   *You can't?*

Zac   *Yeah, because those kids could have well, have beaten [inaudible] three of them and I couldn't do nuffin to stop them and I feel so bad you know. And I think why should he getting beaten up? And I felt so bad. Yeah. It's really, really stupid.*

Many white boys we interviewed were clear in their denunciation of racism, but a few gave explicitly racist accounts of relationships, although these were rarely unequivocal in terms of their attitudes. Chris, a 12-year-old white boy, is here trying to pin the blame for racism on migrants; in so doing, he reveals some classic racist attitudes:

Chris   *I think there's more brown people in this world [**RP**: Do you?] 'cos they all come over here 'cos they don't like their own country [**RP**: Yeah] and the English really get fed up with it, and so you get those racist wars and everything.*

RP   *Right, what, what do you think about that?*

Chris   *I think people should just stick to their own country really.*

        ...

RP   *What about in this country do you think this caused conflict people coming over?*

Chris   *(3) Yeah definitely. There were these Somalians who lived across the road from me, they got petrol bombed through their letter box by these racist people [**RP**: Right] and their house got burnt down.*

RP   *So who do you think is to blame for that?*

Chris   *Racist people.*

RP: *Do you think 'cos you said that, that you thought it was wrong for people to come over.*

Chris   *It is, they should just stay in their own country [inaudible] any*
            way.
RP   *So do you blame, do you blame the Somalians for coming over*
            here?
Chris   *Yeah, 'cos they started war over there. 'Cos they haven't got any*
            food or water its 'cos they haven't got enough intelligence to
            build you know their villages near the water where there's a
            river, near where there's trees with fruit on em and things. You
            know they're not intelligent enough they go and build out in the
            desert somewhere.

But mostly, when white boys described racist acts or actions it was in the
context of an immediate disavowal of their significance as racism:

John   *Yeah. But it's racism I really hate. [RP: Do you, yeah?] Yeah,*
           I hate racism. Think it's just out of order. It's wrong.
RP   *Do you ever come across racism?*
John   *Not as much as I thought in this world would be. No. Not at all.*
           Um (4), But there are quite racial things like (1), say if we go to
           a shop an' it's run by Asians [RP: Mmm] and, um, they can't
           speak very good English (2) and, um, (3) so people go in there
           and they get (3), and they get cussed because of their race an'
           then they said stuff like 'You shouldn't be over here. You should go
           back to your own country.' And stuff like this.
RP   *Who says that?*
John   *Some boys round my area. I didn't like - I didn't wanna say that*
           but I mean (1), round my area if you go into a shop, the (2), um,
           they want something an' they can't afford it an' then they say 'Put
           it back. You can't afford it.' An' then they start cussing 'em because
           of what their race are. [RP: Mmm] I've never really taken part in
           that. [RP: Yeah] Yeah. I've just always stepped away from racism.
           I hate racism. It's not, it's not a good thing to do really. (White
           13-year-old)

John hates racism but spends his time in gangs abusing Asian shopkeepers. We have discussed the subtle dynamics of this elsewhere (Frosh *et al.*,
2000); the point here is simply to note that the activities of this boys' gang
are organised around racism in a way which looks closely entwined with
their masculine displays. For John, it is apparent that his own personal
identity conflict is partially structured around presenting a non-racist

identity to the interviewer whilst participating in the racialised masculinities of his immediate environment. This is similar to the dynamic for several other white boys in our sample; black boys tend to be clearer about the existence of racism and where the responsibility for it lies.

Conclusion

In this chapter, we have tried to draw out the many ways in which young masculinities are entwined with racialised identities in our London boys. It seems very apparent that race and ethnicity are very prominent in the thinking of these boys: their discussions in groups on the topic are animated and rich, and there is ample evidence both of a pool of racialised experiences and of racialised thinking in their individual discussions with our interviewer. Their concern with ethnicity, 'race' and racism was deeply emotional; for many of them, particularly black and Asian but also for white boys, establishing a sense of an 'ethnic identity' was a significant personal concern, whilst direct and indirect experiences of racism were very painful. In this context, the boys' emergent masculinities were heavily marked by ethnicity and 'race', directing their interpersonal relationships and inflecting their personal accounts of their lives; so much so, that to talk about masculinities without reference to these 'racialising' forces would make little sense. Masculinities, we argue throughout this book, are multiple and variegated, constructed anew by each particular boy in relation to the positions made available by the wider culture. In the context at least of 'multicultural' Britain – and probably everywhere else as well – these positions are heavily imbued with 'race', ethnicity and racism. This means that the masculinities we see emerging in these London youngsters are themselves deeply racialised: full of the tension and drama, and the pain, of belonging and not-belonging, including and excluding, that the dimensions of difference encoded in 'race' produce.

7

Policing young masculinities

Introduction

Recent ethnographic and qualitative research in schools has noted the ubiquity of homophobia among boys and young men, and has begun to address the significance of this not only as it concerns those boys derided and vilified as gay, but also as it impacts on the identities and experiences of boys in general (e.g. Epstein, 1997; Mac an Ghaill, 1994; Nayak and Kehily, 1996; Redman, 1998). Why are boys so homophobic and what are the effects of this on their identities? Drawing on the work of Judith Butler (1997), among others, this research has suggested that popular masculine identities are produced through homophobic performances. For example, working within this framework, Nayak and Kehily (1996) analyse boys' homophobia as performances through which boys give substance to masculinity as well as constructing themselves as masculine. That is, boys' homophobia is seen as a set of activities through which they publicly and repetitively assert their 'normal' masculinity through heterosexuality. Concomitantly, because of its status as 'not masculine', homosexuality is associated with femininity and the construction of masculinity is partially underpinned by projecting this 'femininity' onto particular boys who are singled out as gay or not sufficiently masculine. Nayak and Kehily suggest that the compulsive and repetitive way in which boys assert their masculinities through homophobia implies just how fragile and precarious these identities are. As Butler (1997: 237) observes, 'crafting a sexual position ... always involves becoming haunted by what's excluded. And the more rigid the position the greater the ghost, and the more threatening it is in some way.' Boys' homophobic performances may thus be understood as ways of shoring up their masculinities by constructing the feminine other as an ever-present threat.

Although we did not introduce the topic of homophobia ourselves, about a third of the 78 boys we interviewed individually mentioned boys

175

being called gay, as well as 'woosie' and 'girl'. The boys labelled as gay were seen as possessing the same characteristics that were denigrated in girls. Hence, homophobia was intertwined with misogyny. As Epstein (1997: 109) found interviewing gay men about their experiences and identities at school, homophobia was expressed 'towards non-macho boys and was in terms of their similarity to girls'. Like the research we have cited, we found in our own work that boys had to be careful about what they did or said for fear of being called gay, effeminate and so on; in this sense their identities were 'policed', scrutinised for lack of conformity to a core, heterosexual notion of appropriate masculinity. In this chapter, we focus on how this occurred, how boys policed themselves and others by repudiating versions of femininity. The material from the boys we interviewed also indicates some of the costs of this policing, not only to boys ridiculed as gay or to girls, but to boys in general. Our interest is in how this kind of 'policing' constitutes and regulates particular kinds of relationships between all boys. Our suggestion is that there is a variety of practices involved in policing, including not just blatant homophobia, but also more subtle strategies for constructing 'non-hegemonic' masculinities as 'feminine', and that these have the dual effect of alienating boys who transgress the hegemonic norm too obviously, and confirming the received boundaries of 'masculinity' for those who do not. We start, once again, with football.

Being with girls and transgressing gender boundaries

As described in the previous chapters, boys' behaviour and appearance was powerfully regulated by a set of gendered contrasts. Boys were seen, by boys themselves and to some extent by girls, as 'naturally' active and energetic, physically tough, easy-going, funny, brave and sporty, while girls were passive, fragile, obsessed with their appearance, easily offended, emotionally weak and academic. These contrasts were taken as *defining* masculinity and femininity and as present in all activities; as a consequence, the performance of boys and girls – the way they related to these different activities and ways of being – was constantly examined by their peers for signs of gender conformity or deviance.

As the previous chapters have shown, one very powerful site for the exploration of masculine identities in our London sample was that of the football pitch, and football is a particularly good example of how behavioural nonconformity amongst boys could become constructed not just as gender nonconformity, but as something pathological in gender terms – something girlish. From here to the attribution of homosexuality was, for most boys, no step at all. Football was constructed as a masculine activity: boys played it because they were boys, while girls did what were seen as feminine things like standing together and talking. The fact that these sorts of divisions were so familiar and taken for granted meant that little overt policing was necessary. Most boys did not need to be dragooned by other boys into playing football. However, aptitude and liking for football was not only something which distinguished boys from girls, it also discriminated between tough, active, 'real' boys and others – who might find themselves being called girls or 'woosies' for not playing or liking football. We begin by focusing on one of these boys, Oliver, and the antagonism he experienced from other boys. We have selected him because he was the only boy in our study who reported choosing to go around with girls rather than play football; according to his own account, this move made his gender position very complex.

Unlike the other boys, Oliver went to an area during break which had been officially allocated to girls because the main playground space was dominated by boys playing football. His narrative was that this choice was based on his own superior knowledge of what was and was not worth doing – with football being very much in the latter category. Oliver constructed an account of boys in general as lacking in sense because of their obsession with football; his choice to go with the girls was therefore, in his version of things, not because of any inadequacy on his part, but because he was one of the few boys who could do what was necessary to be successful at school and, by implication, in life. This meant that despite repudiating football, Oliver could still give an account of himself as possessing a real, sensible masculine identity. Thus, when asked how other boys saw him as different, he focused specifically on football, forging a positive identity for himself as a boy who was not obsessed by it, and, as a result, was liked by teachers as well as by girls:

> *I don't play football ... I hate football. What's the point, of 11 men running up and down a bit a gre-, a bit a grass, kickin' a ball? There's no point a that. A::n' everyone teases, everyone goes 'Oh, you can't play football' an' that, when I'm talkin' about interesting stuff with the girls. An' goin' I.T. Club wiv my friends, an' that. (1) And, (5) boys just, (1) ah, what can I say? (2) Boys (2) are just, ah, what is it? (2) Idle. Boys are just too idle.*

Like some boys we referred to in Chapter 4, he was critical of boys for their preoccupation with football, but went much further. For Oliver, football was an obsession with trivia, which made boys unable to concentrate in class or to develop friendships with girls. He was also convinced that his girl friends would be shocked if he started showing an interest in football; this conviction enabled him to construct himself as better than other boys in the eyes of girls:

> *If (1) I go up to a girl now and go, 'Did you watch the Man United game last night, or the Arsenal?' They go, 'Oliver!' [shocked tone], and walk off. And they won't speak to me for the rest of [**RP**: Yeah], the year.*

Constructing himself as different from and better than boys in general for not liking football and being liked by girls, Oliver played with and reproduced familiar gendered polarities.

The price Oliver paid for this set of attitudes and behaviours was high. He was generally seen as transgressing normal gender boundaries, and the other boys taunted him with this as a masculine insufficiency, calling him 'girl':

Oliver   *All the girls around the girls' area, treat me like if I am a girl. But the boys, nah, they don't treat like if I'm a boy, they treat me exactly as how I'm girl. Goin' around pushin'... makin' sexist comments an' that.*

RP   *They make sexist comments to you?*

Oliver   *Yeah. They go [mocking tone], 'All right, girls?'*

RP   *How d'you feel about that?*

Oliver   *It (3) it really (1) irritates me, 'cos - I'm a boy like any other boy ... It feels really rotten to be called a girl.*

Oliver enjoyed being treated as one of their own by the girls, but he assuredly did not like being teased and devalued through being called 'girl' by the boys. Moreover, these two identities as 'girl' were mutually reinforcing: being teased and called 'girl' by other boys reinforced his estrangement from them and his investment in being singled out as a friend by girls. He spoke, for example, about how the girls supported him when he mentioned being teased, by making him special and one of them: mimicking them, he said, 'Don't worry, Oliver ... as far as we're concerned, you're one of us. And the boys can go an' mmn themselves.'

Part of the constraint placed on Oliver by his self-claimed voluntary exile from hegemonic masculinity was around sexuality. Identifying with girls, in part, through a rejection of football, also meant for Oliver not relating to them sexually, and indeed differentiating himself from other boys who did so. He was critical of other boys for whistling when girls who wore mini-skirts bent over and showed their knickers, for not appreciating what he idealised as the 'inner beauty' of girls and 'taking the mickey' out of him for liking 'ugly' girls. Though idealising girls in opposition to boys, he was not friendly with the girls who wore mini-skirts – a shorthand for those whose main interest was thought to be flirting and sex. Indeed, they saw him as intruding in the girls' area and would say to him, 'Get out, boy'. Unlike other boys whom he described as 'flash', he declared that he wore clothes for functional reasons and defined himself with great relish as the most popular with girls, precisely for not focusing on his looks:

> *Last time I went round the girls' area one of my friends was talking [high voice] 'Look how the boys wear* perfect *trousers* perfect *shoes. Why can't they all dress like Oliver for he's the smartest. Baggy trousers for more room and to get some air in there'... If I come in with really tight trousers so I got no room in them, Kickers and all that, I go round the girls' area, all the girls would tell me to get out.*

It may be that there was an element of teasing here which Oliver did not recognise; it also seems clear that Oliver was allowed to be 'one of the girls' only under the strict condition that he did not introduce boys' culture, whether through football or sexual display. Despite his attestations about his special status with the girls and the enjoyment he derived from this, Oliver's story suggests that he was tolerated rather than welcomed, and that his superior airs were the product of considerable uncertainty about where he might belong. This was no doubt fuelled by concerns about being subordinated, constructed as girlish (by other boys) and incapable of heterosexual desire. He mentioned acting as a mediator, asking girls out for other boys (this was a role almost always performed by girls for boys – see also Wight, 1994), yet when questioned about whether he would ask girls out for himself, he seemed shocked and said, 'They'd think that I'd be joking', and 'just doesn't feel right'. When asked whether he would like to be able to ask them out, he said he would, and seemed unhappy. Not being able to relate to these girls as potential girlfriends was experienced by him as a cost incurred by being friendly with them. The implication, for Oliver at least, is that gender relations are eroticised by emphasising gender difference; 'crossing over' can only be achieved at the expense of sexuality.

This idea that gender difference and sexual desire run together was a popular assumption among the boys we interviewed. Thus, for being seen to mix with girls rather than boys, boys were commonly constructed not only as girlish but also as gay. (When asked if he was called gay, Oliver paused, looked uncomfortable and said 'No' in an uncharacteristically low voice. Whether or not he was labelled gay, he clearly found the idea worrying.) Their reputation, indeed, could be salvaged by having a girlfriend. For example, in the following extract Olu appears to redefine a boy who 'hangs around with a lot of girls' and 'acts like a girl' as 'normal' for having a girlfriend:

Olu   *I've got this friend, we call him gay because he hangs around with*
        a lot of girls and he acts like a girl but he's not gay. His name is
        Jonathan - he is half Italian.
RP   *How does he act like a girl then?*
Olu   *He screams and laughs like a girl, he doesn't walk like a girl. He*
        laughs and screams like a girl.
RP   *What do you think of him?*
Olu   *I just think he's normal. He's got a girlfriend. I don't think he's gay.*
        If he was gay I'd still be his friend because I've known him for quite
        a long time.

Whereas having girlfriends was taken as a sign of masculinity, boys who hung around with girls as friends were liable to be constructed as effeminate, especially if these were subordinated boys, like Oliver, who was fat and who did not play or like football. One boy, Mark, who spent break-time kicking a plastic bottle around on his own, seemed quite anxious when the interviewer asked him if he mixed with girls, as if his masculinity was being questioned. He wanted to know, 'How are you asking me questions about mixing with girls? I'm just asking.' He described himself as 'not tough'. 'I haven't been brought up to be tough really ... I can't really put on a tough look very much. I haven't really got the right haircut, I haven't got the right - personality or the right face.' He went to a private school and fantasised about not being able to survive what he perceived as the much harder macho culture of state schools. Yet having constructed himself as a soft boy, he was clearly anxious not to be seen as girlish, which he presumed the interviewer had concluded when asking if he mixed with girls.

For most boys, friendships with girls were presented as exceptional and longstanding, and not as signalling a preference for the company of girls over boys. Eight boys spoke about their girl friends in this way. One of these, Donald, claimed that he had 'known her since nursery and we're like good friends' when accused by some of his boy friends of being 'a woosie hanging out with a girl'. Donald enjoyed being with girls, but he spoke about his affection for them in a way which confirmed his identity as a heterosexual boy. Even though he did not construe any of them as girlfriends he spoke enthusiastically about 'getting a kiss and a hug' from them. He was highly critical of boys like Oliver for hanging around with girls because they preferred being with girls than boys, describing them as 'woosies':

Donald   *You're silly for hanging around with a girl. You should be hang-*
ing around with big boys, you should be part of us playing foot-
ball, not walking around with girls speaking about 911[US
teenage programme] and all that, stuff like that.
RP   *If boys have girlfriends are they called woosies then?*
Donald   *Not really ... if one of us went out with a girl that was 14 or 12*
our age, and good looking and stuff, they'd say 'Oh nice girl-
friend', and then they'd go when people touch like that [demon-
strates by patting himself on the shoulder] they pat you on the
back and stuff like that.

For having 'nice girlfriends' boys were patted on the back, but boys who went round with girls as friends were constructed as 'woosies' who engaged in 'girly' conversations about boys' bands rather than playing football with 'big' boys.

In contrast to the 'girly' boys, some boys who spent much time around girls were high status because they were seen as strongly heterosexual. Interestingly, there was some evidence that this was racialised, and in at least one case that teachers disparaged the overtly sexual behaviour of black boys as a way of dealing with the threat they felt under from them. In the following extract, Mervyn describes being criticised for 'being with girls', but this was by teachers, not other boys, who appeared to consider him too heterosexually active. Whereas Oliver indicated that he liked girls as friends in an asexual way, Mervyn emphasised that he liked girls because he was sexually attracted to them. Some teachers neverthe-less tried to make out that he was transgressing gender boundaries; it is clear from the response of Stewart, another black boy, that the scenario

Mervyn describes is a familiar one:

Mervyn   *Some teachers say to me if I like being with girls so much why don't I join them? I think what's the point of saying that? I'm not going to be gay when I grow up...*

RP   *What do the teachers mean by that?*

Stewart   *That means why don't you be a girl if you enjoy being around them so much?*

RP   *Meaning what?*

Stewart   *They're trying to say if you're with the girls, if you like a girl, yeah, why don't you join them, that means go and talk to them on the table, they mean why don't you be a girl so you can associate with them?*

Mervyn   *One teacher called me a male whore. I find that term abusive.*

Unlike Oliver, Mervyn was a tall, powerful and popular boy. He described himself as strong which he elaborated upon in relation to being black. He was 'not just any black boy' but a 'strong black boy' who was confident, articulate and outspoken about racism. Because of this, he said he was perceived as a threat by some teachers: 'When they get a strong black boy like me, it's like a challenge to them.' Recent ethnographic research (Sewell, 1997; Connolly, 1998; Gillborn, 1990) confirms the view that teachers tend to construct black boys as more rebellious and threatening, often linking this with perceptions of them as physically large and as heterosexually mature and attractive. Sewell found that for some African Caribbean boys, the knowledge that teachers were afraid of their appearance, 'style' and 'gesture' was a source of power and acted as an incentive to perform in these 'threatening' ways. Mervyn was proud of being a 'strong black boy' who could stand up to teachers, but was also highly critical of teachers for constructing him as a threat and picking on him in class. He was keen to present himself as a boy who was popular with girls, but was angry with teachers for harassing him for being like this. If he is to be believed, the disparaging discourse of homophobia was called upon by teachers as well as by boys, when they felt it might be useful.

Mixing too much with boys

Boys might be called gay not only for mixing too much with girls, but also for mixing too much with other boys. When asked whether they would prefer to be at a single-sex or mixed school, all the boys from mixed schools, including those who had belittled girls, said they were glad their schools were mixed. This was for 'positive' reasons – they liked 'variety' or they learnt how to 'act' with girls – as well as because they did not want to become gay. In group interviews in two of the four single-sex schools in our study, some boys expressed resentment at being caricatured as gay by boys from mixed schools. Very few boys also mentioned this in individual interviews; it was embarrassing for them and an issue which they found easier to talk about in a group. When asked, as a group, about the prospect of having girls at their school, some 13–14-year-old boys from a single-sex private school initially spoke about the problems this would cause with boys 'trying to impress girls' and a few being 'shy'. Then one boy reflected on the reaction of boys from mixed schools to them:

Colin   *Well, most most of my friends out of school [several giggle] they go to mixed schools [**RP**: Mm] so they take the piss - about that you know.*

Hicham   *That you're gay.*

Leroy   *Gay, yeah.*

Richard   *Say you're gay 'cause you go to a boys' school.*

RP   *Oh really, how do you feel about that then?*

Richard   *It's out of order innit? [several: yeah] It's so stupid because you go to a boys' school they reckon you're gay [giggle] like you want to go to a boys' school because you don't like girls or something.*

RP   *How do you respond when you're [**Hicham**: Just cuss them back] called that?*

Several   *[Loud laugh] yeah.*

As soon as Colin referred to his friends outside school, the others knew he was alluding to how they were seen as gay, as reflected in their embarrassed laughter. He did not even mention the word gay, though the others seized upon this. Clearly this was a familiar and contentious issue, the airing of which was facilitated, as we see here, by the presence and the support of other boys. These boys were also aware of being positioned by state school boys as snobbish and 'wimpish', and it may be that they associated this with being seen as gay by boys from mixed schools.

The viewpoints of boys mocked as gay

Only two boys we interviewed said they were called gay for being unpopular, though many more boys described themselves as unpopular and non-sporty, and some, like Oliver, spoke about being bullied. These two boys, Pete and Alan, were both extremely open about themselves, fluent and emotional, and treated the interviews partly as opportunities for thinking through how and why they were unpopular. Both of them said they found the interviews therapeutic and particularly liked the second one because they were no longer 'nervous' and had established a relationship with the interviewer which enabled them to talk about themselves and their anxieties. It was at the beginning of the second interview, when asked what he would want to investigate if he was researching boys, that Pete mentioned homophobia as a key preoccupation for boys, and also revealed that he was called gay:

Pete   *I had one in my mind earlier, (5) I think it's something in this school, er, like everyone makes fun of people, pretending that they're gay or something like and then it's almost like everyone's homophobic. Well people always call me gay, well I know I'm not, and I know that is very true and they just say it to wind me up. Like some people do and I just completely ignore, and they, they know I'm not they just say it to annoy me. They're like kind of the horrible people I don't really know them, that's really all the words that I hear from them, 'Oh you're gay' and I'm like yeah, I know I'm not, and you've probably never kissed a girl in your life before that's what I'm saying, it's probably true because the person that always says that is really ugly, I can't see how any woman would like him.*

RP   *Why do you think he says that to you then?*

Pete   *Because I'm not very popular, that's for a start and I'm with a very, very sad friend.*

Though admitting he was called gay, Pete was quick to deny he actually was gay, a position reinforced by characterising his abusers as people who did not know him and undermining them as heterosexually inexperienced and unattractive. It was his abusers whom he constructed as *really* the subordinate ones, compensating for their lack of potential as heterosexual males by picking on him. He also implied that it was not even for being 'sad' that he was called gay, rather for having a 'sad friend'. When elaborating on his relationship with this boy, he denied having any physical contact with him, and indicated it was unfair he was called gay, especially as girls could hug other girls without being called lesbian. Later he mentioned that weak boys were called gay, but denied that he was weak.

Being called gay clearly caused Pete much consternation. When talking
about a different topic (his relations with girls), he mentioned once having a girlfriend, and when asked what it was like having one, he praised
its effect in stopping other boys calling him gay.

Alan introduced the topic of boys' homophobia near the end of the first
interview. He had been talking idealistically about girls, constructing
girls (unlike boys) as people who were 'open to you', as well as trustworthy precisely because they were not homophobic:

> *To your mates, you can't exactly say, erm, 'I'm gettin' my hair cut - do you
> reckon a French crop would look good?' Your mates would probably say it was
> gay, yeah, and you call me gay for the rest of your life. But a girl, they say,
> 'Yeah, it would look good, but curtains [a type of haircut] would look better.'
> Girls are more open to you, but keep it to theirselves in their group, without
> blurting it out.*

Because girls were not homophobic, not only were they more 'open' in
the way he illustrated, but also, he said, 'You can talk to them about being
called gay.' He mentioned that this was 'a big issue in this school', and
said that he was called gay 'all the time'. Like Pete, he explained he was
seen as gay because he and another boy, with whom he was close, were
constructed as 'sad' and quiet. But unlike Pete, he seemed much less
invested in presenting himself as actually or potentially quite 'hard', and
rather than undermining those that called him gay by questioning whether
they were heterosexually attractive and popular, he criticised them for
being bullies:

RP   *Why do you get called gay?*
Alan *'Cos me and my friend, we joke a lot. Me and my best friend
[inaudible] he's Asian. We talk to each over and most of the time
we laugh at each over as well, 'cos he says a joke and you can
drag it on and on and keep laughin' and you're sittin' there tryin'
not to laugh 'cos the teacher's talkin' to you and you might start
[laughs] 'ha, ha, ha!' deliberately to try and get him into trouble
and you're like tryin' to shut up and then they goes, 'Look at 'em
two, gay, laughin' at each over's sad jokes.'*
RP   *But don't boys - don't boys quite often laugh at each other, without being called gay?*
Alan *Erm, it depends who you are, 'cos I'm usually, well, I'm a quiet
boy, yeah, compared to the bullies, where a bully who laughs at
another bully can't go up to them and say, 'You're gay.'*

RP   *Oh I see, yeah.*
Alan   *'Cos they'd punch your head in.*

At the beginning of the second interview Alan expressed much more concern about being seen as soft not only by other boys but by his father (see
Chapter 9), something he said he did not feel able to do in the first interview. He recalled how he broke a boy's fingers with a karate punch when
he was first called gay, and while expressing considerable regret at this
('I'll never do that again') spoke with some satisfaction about his usually
hidden fighting potential. Also, in the second interview he elaborated on
the sorts of things which boys did which caused other boys to call them
gay. There was much contempt in his voice for those boys who called
boys like him gay for doing things which he presented as ordinary and
fun and as having 'nothing wrong' with them:

> *If I was to have a shower, like in P.E., now, me and my friends, and say
> another - the other half of the changin' room come in and say, 'Ooh, look at
> 'em lot, gays in the shower, havin' a shower together' an all of that. And most
> of the time it is coloured people that say that. It hurts, 'cos you jus havin' a
> good time an you're not. It's not gay and there's nothin' wrong with it - you're
> jus showerin'.*

His anger was racialised and perhaps reinforced by identifying the teasing boys as black (or in his words, coloured); for Alan, a white boy, was
highly critical of black boys for asserting themselves in what he viewed
as aggressive ways. Perhaps prompted by the fact that he was talking
openly to an adult male about naked boys in changing rooms, Alan
reflected on how some boys might imagine 'something was happening
between us':

Alan   *I mean, some of my friends - well, not my friends, some people are
outside and they was in 'ere, they'd say somethin' was happenin'
between us.*
RP   *Oh, would they?*
Alan   *Yeah. They think it's strange two men in a room or even two men
and a child in room alone together on their own, so it's stupid,
ridiculous.*

The idea that boys 'outside' might think 'something's going on' was also
raised in another school, a single-sex state school. In that school, boys

passing by banged on the windows and opened the door while the individual interviews were being conducted. When asked why these boys were doing this, the interviewees said, 'They think something's going on' and assured the interviewer they were not serious, they were 'just messing'. For Alan, however, the suspicions of other boys which could be provoked simply by seeing a man interviewing a boy in a room were not to be dismissed as just boys' messing around but highlighted how 'stupid', 'ridiculous' and obsessive was boys' labelling of other boys and men as gay. He was angry about this because he experienced being labelled in this way.

Just cussing

Many boys suggested that homophobia, although extremely common, was insignificant, claiming, for example, that calling a boy gay was 'just' a cuss or 'just' a joke. In the single-sex state school referred to above, the boys said they called other boys gay because this was a cuss, unlike swearing, which did not incur detentions. What was striking about these accounts was the taken for granted and implicit homophobia which allowed boys to assure the interviewer that no-one was actually gay. In the passage quoted below, the boys said they did not know of any gay boys (like all the boys we interviewed) and revealed their intense homophobia. Then when asked if they ever got called gay they said they did and illustrated how this was 'just' a joke:

RP	*Are, are there any boys here who are gay then, d'you think, in this school?*
Several	*I don't know, I don't know [inaudible].*
Neil	*I don't know and I don't wanna know I swear.*
Adam	*They, they, they wouldn't show their faces in this school [laughter] =*
Sadam	*Yeah, come down with pellet guns ain't it.*
Paul	*Especially in this school 'cause if they're gay, erm, people will like, beat 'em up and, bully em.*
RP	*Would they yeah, yeah. [1] Do any of you ever get called gay - at all?*
Several	*Yeah, yeah everyone gets yeah called like =*
Adam	*= like I call these lot gay sometimes =*

Neil   =*like I could be having a cussing match yeah=*
Several   *[inaudible] [RP: Why, why do, do you call them gay?] that's a laugh it's just a joke.*
Tom   *His sss like his surname's Ray and mine is May [**Sadam**: That's right] and sometimes they say Sadam Ray is gay with Tom May. [raucous laughter]*

Simply asking the question whether there were gay boys in their school introduced the possibility that there might be, and caused the boys to distance themselves from gays in emotionally charged ways. The intensity of the homophobia displayed by the boys in the above group contrasted with their relaxed and jokey manner and tone when discussing gay cussing. For this was 'just a joke'. The implication here was that there was no-one near them at school who really was gay, and that if there was, it would certainly not be a laughing matter.

Jokey cussing was common among boys and constitutes, in part, an acceptable way for boys to express affection. But this has costs. As we saw in Chapter 1, while boys reported enjoying having a laugh with other boys, many boys found other boys' laughter inhibiting. In the case of jokey cussing about being gay, this was a term which was not 'just' used in an arbitrary way, like any swear word, but also on occasions when boys and men were seen as being too close to each other and/or as too effeminate. This was in spite of seeing them as not really gay – it was more like they were being warned off going too far along the 'non-masculine' route. Hence the banging on the windows and doors when some boys were being interviewed individually. Some boys in the group interviews spoke with much laughter about teachers who were seen as gay for crossing their legs, winking at boys, taking the choir or being 'too' companionable with other male teachers. When one of the boys in the above group said, in response to a question about how he got on with other youngsters, that he 'liked a few boys', everyone burst out laughing. This boy went to great pains to explain that what he meant was 'like a gang, a gang, a gang where there's girls *and* boys'. This kind of joking may have been significant in relation to the ways many boys bonded with each other, but it also helped to police boys, reminding them of the unacceptability of close relations between boys and men, as well as making it difficult for them to be serious with each other. Furthermore, there was a thin line between jokey and serious cussing, with unpopular boys being cussed aggressively as gay, even though no-one thought they were actually gay; the fact that gay was 'just' a cuss did not help them.

Trying not to show interest in other boys' looks

Many of the boys we interviewed spoke at some length about their own
and other boys' appearances, though they also tended to play down their
interest in their looks when comparing themselves with girls. The question of whether good looks made boys popular was almost always interpreted as being about popularity with girls. While many boys spoke about
wanting to look good in designers, and took style of dress as a key marker
of popularity among boys, and some boys mentioned 'working out' to get
'six packs' and make their bodies look muscular, none said they or other
boys found particular boys good looking. Indeed most boys who were
asked this found the question strange and seemed uncomfortable. For
example George, after talking about girls complimenting him on his
looks, was asked:

RP   *Do you think boys are kind of aware of how other boys look?*
         Do they, do they see some boys as being good looking?
George *(2) I don't think so. Well, (2) hm, dunno. Seems a bit batty, for*
         boys to be about, um, judgin' other boys on how they look. It
         seems wrong.
RP   *It seems wrong. Why's that?*
George *(5) It makes you seem queer or batty or something when you*
         look like, um, sayin' 'He looks nice' or something.

In an interview with year-8 boys at a mixed school, the boys themselves
raised the hypothetical but, in their view, impossible scenario of boys
complimenting other boys on their looks. The passage illustrates the
ubiquity and intensity of fears about being thought of as gay:

Geoff *'Cos if a boy goes, 'You're really good looking' you gonna*
        kinda run off but like.
Sam   *Yeah, I'd knock 'em, I'd give 'em one.*
Arnie *What are you some kind of a sicko or something? [several*
        laughing]
Dan   *There's no way you telling me I'm good looking.*
Geoff *Yeah, he probably goes 'You're very nice looking'. [several*
        laughing]
Sam   *You gay or something boy?*
RP   *So it doesn't, like it doesn't make you popular with boys if you*
        wear good clothes, if you look good?

Several   *Well no, wait, wait.*

Sam   *If you, if you wear good clothes if you wear good clothes that's exactly different ...*

RP   *How's that different?*

Sam   *'Cos like if you wear designers then everybody's like 'Aah right yeah designer'.*

The question about designers caused the boys to change tack. While they were clear that complimenting boys on their physical features and on their clothes were quite different, they were not able to explain how and why, though what seems apparent is that talk about physical features is interpreted sexually.

Idealising girls and homophobia

Boys' talk about behaviour they regarded as 'gay' was, like most of their gendered comparisons, situated in a field of contrasts with girls. Thus, complimenting someone of the same sex on their looks was understood and frequently presented as something which girls did, not boys. A number of boys also referred to girls being much more affectionate towards each other, kissing and hugging, unlike boys. The association of affection with femininity could lead boys not to expect or want similar shows of affection from boys. Like many boys we interviewed, Zac liked girls because he considered them more sociable, talkative and affectionate than boys; he imposed rigid boundaries between these characteristics, construed as feminine, and masculine ones. He described himself as an unusually sensible and sensitive boy with girls who, nevertheless, could be dirty and immature, like any other boy, when he was with his male peers. Asked what he thought of girls hugging each other, he replied:

Zac   *I think it is because that's the female nature really innit?*

RP   *Is it?*

Zac   *Yeah like - y, well you see women givin' each other kisses just like - good luck and all that. If boys did that, they'll call you gay.*

RP   *Yeah. When you say that it's the female nature, do you mean that the boys don't do that=*

Zac   *= It's not, like boys are manly and girls are like - you know, like little puppies really, you know, muck about and all that.*

RP   *Right. Do boys, do you think would you like to hug another boy?*

Zac *[Laughs] No not really.*

RP *You wouldn't? Why not?*

Zac *It's not in my nature really. And, I would never do it in school anyway. I do to my relatives of course because, how can I fancy my relatives anyway? I'd be really stupid. But I would never do it to a friend, one of my friends, mates. I would do it to a girl though, yeah.*

Girls hugged and kissed because this was 'the female nature'. He laughed when asked if he would like to hug a boy, and explained his aversion to this in terms of his 'nature'. While Zac idealised girls, his patronising description of them as 'little puppies' indicated also that he was denigrating them. Being like little puppies implies, here, being immature, lacking emotional control and showing affection in impulsive, untamed ways. He liked girls because they were affectionate and he wanted to hug them, unlike boys. He also positioned himself in relation to them as a 'manly' boy who did not show the same sorts of infantilised emotions as girls did with girls. Yet, when constructing himself as different from his male peers as a mature boy whom girls liked, he characterised girls as mature and boys as immature. Though he liked hugging girls, he was clearly presenting this as not being like a girl, but as indicating his heterosexuality; he implied this when he said he hugged his relatives because, 'How can I fancy them?'. The implication is that he did not hug boys because he was not gay, but hugged girls, instead, because he was straight.

Unlike Zac, who tried to distance himself (at least in relation to girls) from 'hard' and crude boys, John, a tall boy who hardly smiled during the interview, described himself as 'tough' and spoke about his passion for violence, his temper, his lack of self-control when fighting and his involvement with a group of white boys harassing Asian shopkeepers. Yet, constructing rigid boundaries between boys and girls, he also, as we saw in Chapter 4, idealised girls as friendly and emotionally supportive. He said, 'I prefer speaking to girls about my problems than I do to boys, especially to older women.' This view was echoed by a number of boys we interviewed individually who said that they would not tell adult males about problems to do with girlfriends, bullying and work because of being seen as 'wimpish' or because their fathers would joke about it. John mentioned being able to speak to his mum, and not his dad, about 'problems at school' and 'puberty', and he also contrasted the sympathy girls showed when he spoke about his anxieties at not seeing his estranged father with what he imagined would be the jokey and insensitive responses of boys, should he divulge these feelings to them. Though John expressed dissatisfaction with boys and men for being teasing, unsympathetic and unsupportive, he seemed to preclude the possibility of having 'soft', 'serious' and 'tender' relations with boys and men by constructing these types of relations as gay unless they were directed towards girls:

John   *Sometimes when I'm feeling down an' that I don't really wanna see (1) boys. Could just see the girl's face or something like that.*
RP   *Right. D'you want to elaborate on that, why, why's that?*
John   *Um (5) How shall I say, um? (5) 'Cos (1) 'cos say if you're gay an' you come to a boys' school, you would like seeing boys an' stuff like that. But I don't, 'cos I'm not gay.*

John illustrated his 'toughness' or 'hardness' when the interviewer asked him what would happen if a boy, rather than a girl was 'quite tender and comforting towards you':

John   *He'd be pushed aside.*
RP   *By you? Would you push him aside?*
John   *Well, depends if (2), depends if the boys would push him away first or if I don't get to hear him he might just be bugging me or something, so I just push him to the side and then I feel sorry for them because they're trying to help me and then I don't, then I get angry and I'll lose my temper.*

It did seem that he was reluctant here to say that he would 'push him aside' perhaps because he had been so critical of boys for being unsympathetic and emotionally disengaged. He spoke generally – 'he'd be pushed aside' – and when asked whether he would do so, he said he might, though qualified this with '*just*' and went on to express regret. At the same time he mentioned how angry he would be. Interestingly, he switches from 'him' to 'them', referring to pushing 'him to the side and then I feel sorry for them because they're trying to help me'. Perhaps by switching to the third person plural he was trying to make a more general and concluding statement about his (imagined) relations with 'tender' boys. Or may be it was a way of depersonalising such a relationship which seemed threatening. In any event, it seems that John is implying a causal link between pushing away other boys when they show signs of concern and getting angry himself, as if he knows he has missed an opportunity.

Envying and blaming girls

There was evidence in some of the interviews that boys appreciated the ways in which the very narrow lines drawn around acceptable masculinities constricted their lives. As in the example above, this sometimes took the form of regretting the barriers imposed between boys by the fear of appearing gay. However, it also found expression in feelings of resentment about girls 'having it better' than boys, for example for being liked by teachers or for having available to them a wider range of possibilities:

Rob	*Girls think they're so good and everything, but they won't let you do nothing right.*
Andy	*Some of them =*
RP	*= Girls think they're so good?*
Andy	*Yeah.*
RP	*What do you mean?*
Rob	*Like they think they can do everything.*
RP	*Like what?*
Craig	*Like if there's a baby in the family or something yeah =*
Jim	*= You go to pick up the baby and they go, 'No, don't.'*
Craig	*'You're doing it wrong.'*
Jim	*'Don't do it like that.'*
Andy	*There's a boy in my class really, and he says he's like, like [inaudible] likes Barbie dolls.*
RP	*A boy in your class?*
Danny	*Yeah. [Laughter] He said he likes Barbie dolls and then all the girls started laughing and then he said, um, 'What's the difference? An Action Man is a Barbie doll', but it's different, it's different. //*
RP	*And was it just girls that teased him?*
Jim	*No. Girls and boys teased him. 'Oh my God, you play with Barbie dolls!' [noisy laughter]*
Rob	*'You're queer.'*
Danny	*'You're poof.'*
RP	*Is that what happens? Do some boys get called poof then?*
Jim	*Yeah, they get called gay and things like that.*
Rob	*Yeah, if boys do something that girls do, it's considered wrong, but girls are doing everything now, short hair, wearing trousers, everything like that. Playing football. And you don't call 'em nothing.*

Usually, as we saw in Chapter 1, it was in the individual rather than the single-sex group interviews that boys spoke about things they did or liked which might be denigrated in the presence of other boys as soft and effeminate. In the above group interview, the boys were able to talk about doing or wanting to do things which might be constructed as effeminate because they were attacking girls. As well as complaining about girls not letting them care for babies, some of the boys mentioned putting vaseline on their lips and being called poofs by girls for doing that, and one boy recalled dressing up as a Spice Girl in primary school and also being called a poof by the girls. (This boy made it quite clear, however, that Spice Girls were not role models for him, and he was 'mucking around and everyone was laughing and everything'.)

What seems to be going on in this episode is rather mixed. In part, the boys are lamenting the greater flexibility available to girls, who can transgress gender roles with less fear than can boys. On the other hand, it is clear from the mockery directed towards the boy who likes Barbies that they are still mainly exercised by the need to confirm established gender behaviours and would not wish to be thought of themselves as having this peculiar interest. The boys were not really challenging the polarisation of gender identities into active, sporty males and passive, emotional and relational females. Rather, their opposition to girls for colonising things the boys might want to do was motivated by resentment against girls generally. While there are glimpses of the idea that being excluded from nurturing (as in the image of picking up the baby) is a loss, the presentation is not that this is produced by the construction of masculinity, but rather that girls get in the way. When it comes down to it – when dolls and babies are really in the frame – the boys back away, worried about feminisation and the accusation of homosexuality.

Addressing homophobia in schools

We have focused in this chapter on what researchers refer to as the policing of boys' identities, on the limitations this imposes on all boys and the particular anxieties experienced by boys labelled as gay and/or effeminate. We examined ways of constructing girls which underpinned boys' investments in homophobic practices. Recent research on the ways boys police themselves has tended to make links only between misogyny and homophobia, pointing out that those boys who are called gay are constructed as effeminate and consequently denigrated for being weak, unsporty, and so on. We found, however, that homophobia entailed idealisation as well as denigration of femininity. Many boys said that they liked girls precisely because they were construed as close and affectionate in contrast to insensitive, detached boys, yet by splitting girls and boys in this way, they themselves could not experience the closeness, sensitivity and seriousness they attributed to girls. Of course, girls were also denigrated – even by boys who idealised them – as inactive, fragile and boring, and there is no doubt that the opprobrium heaped on boys like Oliver was about his being 'soft', 'weak' and 'inactive'. Unpopular boys were usually constructed as unsporty, small, bookish and effeminate. We saw in Chapters 4 and 5 how gender difference was also eroticised, with boys wanting girls to be weak, inept at football and unlike 'tomboys', and girls wanting boys to like football and be funny, even if in moderation. Tomboys were characterised as rough, as too much like boys, and it may be that for some boys becoming heterosexual entailed eroticising weakness as a feminine attribute and associating this with being affectionate.

Recognising that homophobia is linked to the idealisation and not just the denigration of girls has important implications in relation to anti-homophobic educational practices with boys. As we have seen, this idealisation was linked with dissatisfaction with other boys. Our findings suggest that anti-homophobic practices can be developed which aim at addressing the self-interest of boys, as it were, focusing on the costs to them of being homophobic, rather than simply problematising them for this and for being misogynistic. This does not mean that boys' homophobia, sexism and disruptive behaviour should be tolerated. On the contrary, we would argue for a stronger response to it and less tolerance – including less tolerance of the legitimation of homophobia by teachers, which some boys reported occurring. Some boys at a private school even mentioned teachers calling boys 'poofs' for their perceived lack of commitment to rugby. But simply blaming boys for being homophobic and misogynistic is likely to be counterproductive. Many boys we spoke to were concerned about being seen as less mature, responsible and clever than girls by teachers, parents and girls themselves. This gave rise to much resentment, and seemed to make them more inclined to ridicule and deride attributes which they associated with femininity, asserting their perceived superiority as physically and emotionally tough, hard and active boys. Schools need to address homophobia and boys' investments in this, by helping them to value the sorts of characteristics and ways of relating which they commonly deride (though also idealise) as feminine. This presupposes being less didactic and authoritarian, and developing the sorts of relationships which validate boys and encourage them to feel valued.

8

Boys and schooling

Introduction

In many countries, boys have come to public attention because they are gradually slipping behind girls in terms of the educational qualifications they achieve. Two decades ago, it was girls' educational underperformance which was identified as problematic in many of these countries; currently, however, commentators are concerned that many boys are at risk of social exclusion through poor educational performance. As noted in the Introduction, there is some doubt about the robustness of much of the evidence on which the claims of a growing crisis in boys' schooling are based. For example, it is clear that some boys (who, in Britain, are particularly those from the working classes and those of African Caribbean, Pakistani and Bengali descent) have for a long time done badly at school, while others (particularly from the middle classes) still have high achievements (Epstein *et al.*, 1998; Mac an Ghaill, 1988; Willis *et al.*, 1977). In addition, girls are not uniformly successful at school.

However, it does seem that as educational demands have shifted and increased, boys' ways of expressing masculinities have become less compatible with the gaining of educational qualifications, at a time when it is increasingly important for them to do so because fewer unskilled jobs are available. Many girls' ways of expressing femininities seem more compatible with good educational performance (Arnot, David and Weiner, 1999). In this context, it is salutary to remember that it has traditionally been taken for granted that boys 'naturally' do better educationally than girls and that information that challenges this is easily overlooked or reconstructed as evidence that girls lack innate ability (Murphy and Elwood, 1998; Walkerdine, 1997, Cohen, 1998). Because of this, it is often implied that if boys do badly it is because something has gone wrong with the educational process, and that the solution is to find more suitable ('boy-friendly') methods of teaching. In addition, the assumption that boys naturally do better than girls has continued to affect teachers' perceptions. In a study of girls learning maths, for example, Valerie Walkerdine (1988) found that many teachers believed that girls only did well because they worked hard, whereas many boys did not do so well, but were nevertheless seen as naturally talented. Walkerdine argues that in teachers' constructions, the 'natural child' is implicitly an active and rebellious boy, who does not sit and learn quietly. Michele Cohen (1998) argues that this reflects a discourse of 'a habit of healthy idleness' which is accepted and condoned by some teachers.

This implicit gendering of childhood is likely to play a part in the story of boys' educational attainment. However, the many publications that have addressed themselves to the question of the gender gap in attainment between girls and boys point to various other factors. Noble and Bradford (2000) identify seven possible reasons: boys' 'anti-swot' culture; genetic differences; changes in society; changes in families; the curriculum; school management and classroom management and practices. More generally, several researchers have argued that boys have struggled more than girls to adapt to major changes in contemporary society, especially the shift in traditional patterns of male employment and the skills required to meet new occupational demands (e.g. Arnot *et al.*, 1999). The complexity of these factors makes it extremely difficult to disentangle the relationship between masculinities and schooling (Bleach, 1999). It is clear, however, that the attainments of both boys and girls are affected by social changes as well as by school policies and what teachers and students do (Epstein *et al.*, 1998). This chapter explores what boys have to say on this issue; that is, on how the apparently tricky relationship between school learning and masculinities is negotiated.

Constructed oppositions between popular masculinity and doing schoolwork

It is all too easy for media reports on boys and education either to treat boys as if they are passive recipients of an educational system that is failing them, or as hooligans whose mindless behaviour is responsible for their educational problems. Neither of these positions can be justified if we consider what boys themselves say. In our interviews, many boys explained that they faced contradictions in negotiating both masculine identities and schoolwork. The major reason for this was that popular or 'hegemonic' masculinity (discussed in Chapter 3) is pervasively constructed as antithetical to being seen to work hard academically. This posed problems for some of those boys who wished to attain good qualifications without being labelled by other boys in pejorative terms. Far from being mindless, boys had continually, and actively, to negotiate how to position themselves in relation to popular and unpopular masculinities and, hence, to education. It was, thus, far from a simple matter for them to reconcile educational demands with the constraints imposed by canonical narratives of masculinity.

In a study of boys in a Midlands secondary school, Mac an Ghaill (1994) found that the boys he typified as 'Academic Achievers' (who worked hard because they aspired to professional jobs) were considered effeminate by boys and teachers alike. Similarly, in our study, a pervasive narrative was that being viewed as 'clever' or a 'swot' was not really masculine and was likely to make for unpopularity. Many boys counterposed schoolwork and sport; being good at the former was a marker of unpopularity, whereas sporting prowess often led to high masculine status. The account below demonstrates this clearly, and also exemplifies a narrative device commonly used by many boys: the creation of a hierarchy of popularity with boys at different points in the hierarchy being reported to play different games and to do different amounts of schoolwork:

Sadeem   *We are a less popular group of people. We're not the least popular group of people.*

RP   *So the least popular group of people, could you describe them?*

Sadeem   *Um, (3) I would say it's people who, who do lots of work and things like that and (4) um (7) um, that's mainly it actually, just people who are sort of boffins...We just all play basketball together - and most of the ones the ones at the top they play football (1), and (1), the bottom ones just stay [laughter], stay in the classroom and do homework (2), and play cards or something.*

This account, like many others, indicates clearly that 'jockeying for position' in hegemonic masculinity is not something that stays outside the classroom. Instead, boys' positioning in the hierarchy of popular masculinity created quite specific expectations for how they would behave both in break times and in lessons. Indeed, some boys drew subtle distinctions between different kinds of boys who work hard at school.

RP	*Right (1). But what kind of boys are likely to get called 'geek'?*
Christopher	*[quiet then louder] Boys who work too hard, who really, really work too hard then they study for this test and they've studied and studied and studied and they've got it really good and they've got it perfect in their heads and they fail it.*
RP	*Mm. Yeah, yeah and they fail it?*
Christopher	*'Cos they work too hard. They overwork themselves.*
RP	*Right. So boys who do well in tests but don't work too hard, they're ok, t- they don't get [**Christopher**: Yeah], yeah.*
Christopher	*Yeah. 'Cos people who work too hard they usually get nervous, really nervous.*
RP	*What about boys who work hard and do well in tests, are they called geeks?*
Christopher	*No, they're called boffs.*
RP	*Ah, boffs.*
Christopher	*'Cos they know everything, they're clever.*

The polarisation of popularity and schoolwork had significant consequences. For example, a major obstacle to boys treating school as a place in which to do serious schoolwork is that this could lead to their being bullied:

Thomas	*It's your attitude, but some people are bullied for no reason whatsoever just because other people are jealous of them and I find that quite annoying.*
RP	*How do they get bullied?*
Thomas	*There's a boy in our year called James and he's really clever, and he's basically got no friends and that's really sad because he's such a clever boy and he gets top marks in every test and everyone hates him. I mean I like him, when I see someone bullying him I just tell them to go and get lost, I just find that really annoying.*
RP	*Is it clever boys that get bullied?*
Thomas	*No not always, it's also because he's really shy. Some people are really clever and they get bullied, it's just he's just bullied, I think he's bullied too much and he never answers back so they find it easy to bully him.*

It is interesting to see how, in this extract, Thomas deals with the dilemma of presenting himself as a boy who is nevertheless sympathetic to school achievement. He disclaims the notion that everyone hates the really clever boy in his class by professing that he (Thomas) likes him and defends him from bullying. He thus distances himself from the potentially troubled position of being one of those who bullies a boy just because they are jealous of his academic attainments. Instead, Thomas constructs for himself the position of being kind and morally responsible.

Negotiating the expectations of popular masculinities and the dangers of unpopular masculinities

Thomas' account vividly demonstrates that boys do not necessarily have a free choice to work at school. Part of the policing of boys by other boys described in Chapter 7 involves the policing of classroom practices. However, while this is undoubtedly because of the equation of doing schoolwork and unpopularity, the fact that there seems to be some envy involved ('... just because other people are jealous of them') indicates that most boys do consider that there is merit in doing well at school. It seems possible, for example, that clever boys who are not shy and who 'answer back' can manage to achieve academic success without being bullied. More generally, we found that an important part of being 'cool' and popular entailed the resisting or challenging of adult authority in the classroom. This was part of an oppositional culture around which high status could be constructed. Popular boys were generally expected to 'backchat' teachers. 'Hegemonic' masculinity had to be constantly established by repeated demonstrations of insouciance. Boys who were seen as too conscientious were often derided. But many boys also expressed anxieties about impending examinations and whether they would achieve good grades. This was often because good qualifications were considered important to doing well in employment. In addition, boys sometimes referred to their parents' expectations as putting academic pressure upon them:

RP   *Is that, do you think - does that put added pressure on you - the fact that your brothers, have done well, then?*

Sol   *Yeah.*

RP   *Where does the pre-pressure come from - is it, is it, is it, your parents, or, or, just you?=*

Sol   *=Well not even really my parents - my parents just, don't say, 'Oh you have to get the same amount', but you can feel it. When he* *comes home with his results everyone is happy jumping over the gate, but wh- if I fail, nobody is gonna really, feel sorry for me 'cos they're gonna say, 'If your brother done it, why can't you do it?' [**RP**: Yeah, yeah (1) hmm] They're gonna say, 'We brought you up in the, um, right, right way, same way as your brothers and they done it.' [**RP**: Yeah, yeah]*

Often, as with Sol, boys had to find ways of doing well enough at school to appease their parents or satisfy their own ambitions (or alleviate their fears), whilst not losing credibility as 'masculine'. There were four main ways in which boys dealt with this dilemma raised by the counterposing of popular masculinity and doing schoolwork, which we describe in more detail below. Some claimed a middle position, some managed the demands of popularity by not working as expected in the canonical narrative; some managed to be both popular and to do well at schoolwork and others got on with their work in ways that made them unpopular with other boys.

Negotiating a middle way

When it came to schooling, the most common strategy was for boys to negotiate a middle way for themselves in which they did do schoolwork, but not so single-mindedly that they came to other boys' attention as over-studious. Mustafa offers an example here:

RP   *Yeah yeah - so what, what about you? What, what would you say, that you're, you're, popular or, or what?*
Mustafa *I'm about in the middle.*
RP   *Oh right, how d'you get to be in the middle?*
Mustafa *I wouldn't know.*
RP   *Yeah.*
Mustafa *There's some people you don't even know them. They're always quiet in the class. [**RP**: Yeah] And they're, some people, they talk, an but they don' like, get into trouble. [**RP**: Mm] And then some people get into trouble, but not that much like me. [**RP**: Ok] Sometimes you get into trouble, and then the popular boys, because they're popular they have to like get into trouble. They always, like backchat, backchat the teacher [**RP**: Mm] Get loads of detentions.*

Mustafa's middle position here involves getting into trouble in class, but not as much as do popular boys who, he suggests, 'have to like get into trouble ... because they're popular'. His account reminds us that popularity carries costs. Far from being entirely free to choose how to behave, there are weighty expectations on popular boys that they will satisfy other boys' desire for the spectacle of confrontations with teachers. Why does Mustafa position himself in the middle? It seems that, like many of the boys we studied, he values schooling, but gets bored with what he sees as repetitive work. He does not condemn the behaviour of popular boys who he defines, in rather a restricted way, as being popular simply because they are resistant to authority, but he does argue that 'they're just wasting their time':

RP	*Right - so if you're ... actually quite naughty - then you become popular?*
Mustafa	*Mm*
RP	*Then yeah? - yeah.*
Mustafa	*They'll think you're cool.*
RP	*Right (.) what d'you think of those - those people those boys?*
Mustafa	*Think they're just wasting their time.*
RP	*Do you?*
Mustafa	*Yeah [RP: Right]. 'Cos obviously you're here to learn - not to muck around and show yourself off ...*
RP	*Yeah, but you said that you you, you're a bit naughty as well - you get into trouble?*
Mustafa	*Sometimes I get into trouble. Sometimes I get bored with the work a bi' - I've done my work. [RP: Mm]. I get bored with it. Then I start talking to the person next - next to me sometimes they finished sometimes they haven't, an they start talking back an the teacher says 'Why are you talking?' I say, 'I've finished my work.' [RP: Mm] And then they start and I like [laugh], I back chat them.*
RP	*Right, right, so it's only it's only if you get - so bored you mean - the you do work first of all. [Mustafa: Sometimes like you do yeah, some work] yeah*
Mustafa	*An then you get bored of doing the same thing all over, every time ...*
RP	*The, the boys then, who, who are popular, and, and who, you know who mess about in class they don' do any work then, do they?*

Mustafa   *They do some work like they write um title on the line. Like the first question, like, when, er when everyone was like, on their third sets of questions they were like on their, starting their second, or they haven't never finished the first one yet.*

RP   *Right, right.*

Mustafa   *'Cos they keep on throwing things around the classroom and mucking around.*

The distinction Mustafa draws between himself and the popular boys is, thus, one of degree. He does more work than they do, backchats the teacher less and does not throw things around the room. He makes it clear that he is also different from the quiet boys in the classroom. He avoids experiencing a troubled subject position around the dilemma of school-work and popularity by moving between positions. His way of negotiating a middle position is thus different from that of Thomas, which involves no back chatting and refusing to get involved in any disputes. In the extract below, Reg suggests that the reason he works hard sometimes is that he has to because he has dyslexia. Like Mustafa, he balances periods of working hard with periods of 'naughtiness':

Reg   *I'm a bit more serious in shcool than outside school.*

RP   *Why are you more serious in school?*

Reg   *'Cos I got dyslexia and I need to work a bit more harder than-everyone else, sometimes (1) people say to me 'Ah you're a boffin' but I'm not a bof, in like they're 'Ah boffin now you got to be a bit more naughty as me.' (1) 'Nah that's right for you, you, quite brainy an everything I need to work a bit harder.' 'Oh yeah I s'pose' (1) an that's ma mates saying, 'Oh come you gotta be a bit more naughty 'cos you like getting a bit boffin' [**RP**: Oh really yeah]. I go 'Ah nah I gotta do a bit more work.'*

RP   *Right.*

Reg   *An then they just say no more.*

RP   *Yeah (2) so do they tease you at all then for, being a bit a boffin in school?*

Reg   *Oh no I'm not a boffin's like 'cos, erm, I've bunked a couple lessons an everthing (.) [**RP**: Yeah] like they say to me 'Ah' (1) erm (.) right if I sit down and do er some work in class they like 'Ah boffin come on, av a laugh' an I go, 'Nah' 'cos some lessons I need to work harder an some lessons I don't so [inaudible] naughty in one less-son an hard working in the other lessons then they call me boffin*

*an some times [**RP**: Right] but na (1) they go 'Ah, you being a bit
of a boffin now come on you gotta be naughty a bit more' (1) this
me 'Noa' they go alright then (1) an they leave me. (1) Like some
boy, I'm not the biggest, I'm not even a boffin really (1) [**RP**:
Right] Its just 'cos I do ma work sometimes like they call me a boffin but everyone gets called boffin sometimes [**RP**: Right} (1) even
naughtiest boy if he does his work they call him boffin.*

Maintaining popularity and not working

Again and again boys explained to us that popular boys have to mess about
in class and not do their schoolwork. From such accounts, it appeared popular boys were thought to maintain their popularity through misbehaving.
However, boys who reported that they were popular and that they did very
little schoolwork did not mention that they felt compelled by these expectations, but gave more variegated explanations of their behaviour. The
extract below, from Michael, is reproduced at length because it documents
the many reasons why popular boys said that they did not work in class.
Michael constructs himself as popular because he is both funny – liking to
make people laugh – and tough (although he denies being a bully). He presents a history of short-term exclusions from school, confrontations with
teachers and dislike of doing hard schoolwork:

RP	*Yeah, but you said that you kinda of tell them what to do? [**Michael**: Yeah] and so are you the one that is the kind of leader?=*
Michael	*=Yeah, just, I don't like shout at everyone, tell them what to do. Its just em like when, if I wald somewhere and they enqui-... want to walk with me and stuff like that*
RP	*Why do you think that is?*
Michael	*Dunno, 'cos they like me, think I'm funny.*
RP	*Right, so it's because you're funny that you're popular is it? Any other reason?*
Michael	*Yeah, but I always get in trouble for it.*
RP	*Oh do you yeah? Do you get into trouble quite a bit then?*
Michael	*Hmm, yeah quite, like um, a little while ago I was in art and the teacher like shouts out 'Michael', shouting out my name, and whatever done something and then I didn't even do any-thing wrong and she shouted out my name so I just shouted*

	out her name back at her and I said 'How do you like that?' and she sent me out, and gave me detention…
RP	*Yeah, who are the kind of people that get into trouble then that teachers tend to shout at?*
Michael	*People who, always, are funny, tell jokes and stuff.*
RP	*Yeah?* =
Michael	*= Yeah, I always get into trouble through say talking to other kids, and making jokes and stuff like that.*

Michael's account demonstrates how both the social context and boys' positioning and previous experience all come together in their negotiation of hegemonic masculinity and schoolwork. Michael does not enjoy schoolwork and has not achieved well at in the past. Furthermore, he appears to have difficulty in managing his temper and is neither afraid of confronting teachers nor of attacking other boys. While he does not gain prestige from school achievements, he does gain prestige from making other boys laugh and dominating them even if – as Talonen (1998) argues – this may be because they are afraid of him. For some boys, this strategy of maintaining popularity may provide an excuse for not having to try with schoolwork and, hence, having to face possible failure (Katz and Buchanan, 1999). While no boys in this study gave this explanation for not doing their schoolwork, this may have been a factor in how boys like Michael positioned themselves.

While some boys who were popular clearly did very little work, others who did no work in their classrooms may have been able to keep up with thier classes by working more secretly. In the excerpt below, Greg, who has already indicated that he is very good at maths and works in class, suggests that 'bunking' classes can be a strategy designed to maintain a hegemonic performance. He also demonstrates that racialisation also features in how boys deal with schooling:

Greg	*'Cos, 'cos most black boys in this school. Yeah. Most of them are really bad and they don't really like their subject. They bunk classes and things like that.*
RP	*Why do you think that is?*
Greg	*I don't know. Um, probably they wanna show their friends that they're big or something.*
RP	*Right.*
Greg	*Because there's like this boy in year 11 he's, um, he, like he like thinks he's big. He's really brainy. When it comes to exams he'll*

> *pass all his exams but, but he don't like going to lessons and things like that because he wants to show his friends that he's really big.*

We did not interview the boy referred to by Greg, and since he was four years older than Greg this story may be a cultural myth in his school. However, it may well be that some boys are using a strategy which allows them to maintain hegemony over other boys, but are also able to do well academically – perhaps by working out of school. Such boys share some features in common with the boys typified as 'Real Englishmen' by Mac an Ghaill (1994), who wanted to be seen effortlessly to achieve at school. The distinction between popular boys who do no work and those who do is, therefore, not simple – and it may well not be obvious to other boys. This is paticularly the case since many boys talked about being different out of school from how they are in school and some said that they worked at home and not at school:

RP   *Did you ever get teased for being a boffin?*
Julius *No it wasn't like that… I used to mess about and then at home just study, and now I do both. I can mess about and study at the same time so no I don't get teased… It's completely different. Like in year 7 everyone messes about 'cos it was something completely different from primary school… and we liked – we all enjoyed it we messed about but in the end we were getting older we were maturing… I've grown up I've stopped being silly… just used to always mess about always fight and everything.*

Negotiating popularity and high grades

We saw in Chapter 3 that a few boys (ten) managed to achieve a status accepted by other boys as hegemonic and to do well at school. These boys found ways of demonstrating that they were 'hard' and/or good at sports while getting on with schoolwork and often hiding how important this was to them. There were other boys who managed to retain some degree of popularity and to work hard and do well at school. It was generally easier for boys from the private schools than from the state schools we studied to achieve popularity while maintaining high grades. This was because the whole school accepted that students were there in order to do well and that most parents were paying a great deal to achieve this. In the following extract, Dennis makes sportiness and competitiveness part of the definition of what it is to be a boy, in opposition to doing academic work, including homework, and he makes it plain that he hangs around with the sporty types. Nevertheless, he also includes academic success as something allowed to boys, through the medium of their competitiveness:

RP   *Define a boy?*
Dennis *A young male who likes mainly sport rather than academic work and would prefer to go out instead of going working and stuff, doing homework and stuff. Um always competitive enters competitions and stuff and try and beat each other.*
RP   *What sort of competitions?*
Dennis *In the playground, football and stuff and rugby, always try to be the best of each other… and like at school trying to get the best grades.*
RP   *But I thought you said that boys weren't that very academic?*
Dennis *Um they still try like 'cos it's quite a good school here. They try and get quite good grades to please their parents…*
RP   *So boys are both competitive academically and also in sports?*
Dennis *Yeah. But they're more [inaudible] sports.*
RP   *So that's more important to them than work is it?*
Dennis *Yeah.*

The account above also demonstrates an important difference between the state school boys and the private schools boys we interviewed. Boys at both types of schools defined masculinities and popular masculinities in similar ways. However, boys at private schools gave accounts which indicated that, since they had no choice but to get educational qualifications, they had to do some academic work. This allowed them to avoid the troubled position of constructing themselves as working too hard to be properly masculine while still criticising the most hard working boys in their classes.

Although boys at the state schools generally did not have access to narratives suggesting that they had no choice but to work hard, some managed to do well academically and to be sufficiently popular to be comfortable in class. Andy, the 13 year old quoted below, suggests that he has had to learn how to take teasing about being clever and that he makes a distinction between what he does in school and out of school. It is notable that, right at the start of his interview, when asked to introduce himself to the interviewer, he mentions football and fun (elements that make for popularity among boys in school) as well as saying that he enjoys school:

RP   *Right. Okay (1). Perhaps I, I could start off, by asking you urm
        (1) if you were to introduce yourself (1) and say three things
        about yourself (2) urm (1) which would help me to understand
        who you are, what (.) what would they be?*
Andy   *Ahhhhh I dunno, urrr, I play football =*
RP   *= Yeah*
Andy   *A lot. (3) Urm (1) I like to have (1) fun with my mates (2) and (1)
        just laughter, urm (2) just en-(1) joy school.*

Later in the interview, Andy explains that he is in the top group for maths and is very good generally at schoolwork. He describes how he has learned to deal with the teasing that comes from this. However, although he says that he now laughs himself when he is teased about working too hard, this is a point in the interview when he becomes quieter and more halting, as if it is a difficult topic for him:

RP   *Right. (1) Would, would you say that you're quite (1), good (1), at
        (1) work compared to other boys?*
Andy   *Yeah, I would.*
RP   *Okay, yeah.*
Andy   *'Cos like everyone in my class (1), they think that I work too hard.
        (1)*
RP   *Do they?*
Andy   *Yeah (2) and they say that my brain's gonna blow up. [laugh]*
RP   *Right, when you say everyone, do, do you mean boys, other boys
        like that =*
Andy   *It's just, yeah. But they're only messing around (1) so, er that,
        they don't really bother me.*
RP   *They're only messing around?*
Andy   *Yeah.*
RP   *Yeah. (4) Do, do, do they kind of tease you for that then a bit?*
Andy   *Yea::h (1), they tea:se me but (1) it don't really bother me (1) 'cos
        (1), I'd - 'cos I've got hyped up before (2), and they've just told
        me it's a joke, so like (1), now I've realised (1) that when [laugh]
        they do tease me I just have a laugh a bit myself.*
RP   *You (1), you laugh, yourself, yeah?*
Andy   *Yeah.*

RP   *Right.*
Andy   *Which (1) is quite funny really. [low tone]*

From the quote above, Andy faces difficulties in being perhaps the only boy doing so well in his class and in balancing this with maintaining some popularity by engaging in activities accepted as indisputably masculine – laughing at himself and by also playing football. However, Andy is clearly committed both to working hard in class and to showing that he can have fun without getting into trouble:

RP   *You said, urm (2), that (1) there are a lot of boys (1) you muck around and, have a laugh and, urm, that came out in the group interview. (1) Urm (1), does that mean that y- tend not to do that, that y-, because you're =*
Andy   *I, I =*
RP   *= Because you're hard working?*
Andy   *Sometimes I have a laugh in class but, not too often.*
RP   *Yeah.*
Andy   *But, like outside the class I will have a laugh, I'm different outside the class.*
RP   *Oh, you're different?*
Andy   *Yeah. I think I am.*
RP   *Right. So how, how are you different?*
Andy   *I dunno, I have a laugh (1) I, I'm the same in class someways like - I won't get in trouble in class, I won't get in trouble outside a school outside class (1), and (1) I just - I'll ave a laugh though.*
RP   *Yeah. Right, sometimes you have a laugh, so, wha-, what sort of things?...*
Andy   *I dunno amusing, laugh just (1) making, fun, out of everything (1), like finding everything funny.*

We have already seen in previous chapters that 'having a laugh' is central to being acceptable as masculine. This has been found not only in this study, but in most studies of boys and masculinities (e.g. Back, 1995; Hewitt, 1986; Kehily and Nayak, 1996; Mac an Ghaill, 1994). It is not surprising, therefore, that boys can sometimes escape bullying if they are able to 'have a laugh' at their own expense and appear not to mind being teased. For some boys, being able to use this strategy appeared to save them from being in the category of doing well at schoolwork, but being deeply unpopular with peers. While Andy's position seems more tenuous than those of boys discussed as 'having it all' in Chapter 3, his account demonstrates well how popularity has to be worked at and that being good at schoolwork is only tolerated by other boys if there are mitigating factors such as being good at sport, being able to laugh at oneself and accept others laughing at one. As Andy's example demonstrates, boys can laugh mercilessly at high achieving boys if they make mistakes in class:

Andy   *'Cos when I do things wrong [Umm] people laugh at me a lot.*
RP   *Oh do they?*
Andy   *Yeah 'cos (1), and like when Nicola gets things wrong 'cos like we're quite clever [RP: Yeah] and getting things wrong is quite rare, so that they say ,'I can't believe the brainy boy got it wrong' [excitedly]=*
RP   *= Yeah so that's really=*
Andy   *=And someone'll get it right and they'll go 'Arr look, arr, he's better than you, arr, I'm better than you' [RP: laughs] (1) so it's really, really funny if [RP: Yeah] you get something wrong [RP: Yeah? Yeah.] especially when [inaudible] gets something wrong.*
RP   *Right (1) Do you get, I mean you talked about boys being popular for playing football but I wonder, if you become popular because you are clever and you help boys who make mistakes?*
Andy   *Not as much as playing football or messing around.*
RP   *Right (3), but helping people, does that make you quite popular?*
Andy   *Nah.*

One of the advantages of seeing boys often in three interview situations (one group and two individual interviews) was that we gained a good sense of how boys worked at their narratives in different contexts and, hence, at how they positioned themselves as masculine and in relation to schooling. This was invaluable in vividly demonstrating what some boys had to struggle with in order to maintain their constructions of themselves as both popular and clever. For example, when asked about being 'cussed' for being 'quite clever', Bob (in the excerpt below) starts from a potentially troubled position in that his friends have already said in the group interview that he is cussed for being clever. To recuperate from that position, Bob produces several different refutations in a few minutes of interview. He argues that he sometimes does not work; that the only people who get cussed are two kids who sit in the front and work; that he does not sit in the front, but sits with his friends; that he likes to have a joke with his friends and that some of them had been joking in the interview; that he does not know whether he is sometimes called 'nerd' for getting high marks; that some people are jealous of him and that they are dumb because they will not do well when they leave school. The fact that he interjects an expletive as soon as he is asked whether he is cussed for being clever may be seen as his performance of not being someone who only works and never answers back when cussed. Bob's account gives us some idea of how uncomfortable it is to be constructed as a 'nerd' and how much effort it takes for boys who do well at school to construct themselves outside that definition:

RP   *It's - they also said, um, that you that you are quite clever in, in class and in a group interview.*

Bob   *Yeah.*

RP   *And, and did you - you do well, you do quite well in work do you?*

Bob   *Yeah. [RP: Right]*

RP   *Do you get, do you get cussed for that? = [inaudible] =*

Bob   *It's like, like - 'cos in my - like in classes I don't do [inaudible], sometimes I just like do nothing and, um, the only cuss is like people always sitting in front like these two kids - they also sit in the front. They always do their work whatever [RP: Um] and when someone cusses then they just um they do not give a fuck about it ... they just let people walk all over them.*

RP   *Yeah, you don't, you don't sit in the front then ... in class?*

Bob   *No, I sit with my friends [RP: Yeah] and like have a joke and stuff.*

RP   *Right. So people, people don't cuss you then ... about being clever?*

Bob   *No, not really ...*

RP   *'Cos some people said that in the group interview that you, that you were cussed a bit.*

Bob   *No, they are only joking and would some of us, would like joke in that interview.*

RP   *Oh, you were joking yeah?*

Bob   *Some ... yeah some parts.*

RP   *Y..Did that ? So was that a joke or when, when people said that you were called nerds sometimes [Bob: Uh], was that a joke when people said you were call nerds sometimes for getting =*

Bob   *= I don't know =*

RP   *High marks, but does that happen?*

Bob   *Some, sometimes like people jealous or something 'cos like, um, if they call me nerd [inaudible] they are dumb or stuff like that.*

RP   *Right. Do you think, do you think they are jealous then, of you, some people?*

Bob   *I don't, I don't know, because 'cos, um, they are probably not going to do well when they leave the school and don't want to do nothing.*

There are other ways in which boys may be able to maintain constructions of themselves as popular, but to do well academically. In their research in Oslo schools, Harriet Bjerrum Nielsen, Kari Vik Kleven and Monica Rudberg identified a group of 18–19-year-old boys who called themselves 'The Clan' and dominated their class through their artistic intellectualism (Rudberg, 1999). This group of boys may well share some features with the group of boys in the Midlands typified by Mac an Ghaill (1994) as 'The Real Englishmen', who wanted to be seen to attain well without making effort, but who considered themselves an intellectual, masculine élite. In our study, no boys spoke of achieving popularity or hegemony through intellectual dominance. However a few considered that they managed to avoid being unpopular because they enjoyed explaining to other boys things they did not understand.

Good at schoolwork, bad at school culture: unpopular boys

The interviews with the boys in the study demonstrated that the phrase 'good at school' is too undifferentiated. For, as we have seen, few boys managed simultaneously to be good at managing relationships and at managing schoolwork. Most, however, managed to steer a course between these two which allowed them to avoid being seen as unpopular. Jim (below) demonstrates what boys in the study typically said about quiet, hardworking boys:

RP   *What about - are there boys, that are quite quiet [inaudible] in school in class?*
Jim   *Some of them are.*
RP   *Yeah, (3) How do you get on with the quiet boys? (3)*
Jim   *We don't. (1)*
RP   *You don't?*
Jim   *We are friends with them - but they don't walk around with us or anything.*
RP   *Ah, don't they? Yeah, why's that?*
Jim   *Don't know. (3)*

RP *Are they not interested in football? (1)*
Jim *Not really. (1)*

It is unusual for people to produce accounts that construct their identities in ways that make them look bad (van Dijk, 1992; Potter and Wetherell, 1987). It is not that people are attempting to dissimulate, but that any account also presents the self to the self and the maintenance of self-esteem requires that the self is presented in positive ways. It is, therefore, difficult for boys to be asked questions that imply their unpopularity, since this immediately places them in a troubled subject position. Perhaps not surprisingly, many boys were reluctant to say that they had been teased or bullied. If they discussed it, they avoided trouble either by presenting themselves as people who could deal with the situation in a reasonable and moral way, or by demeaning the boys who treated them badly. In the following extract, Matthew has already eschewed the notion that he is picked on because he works hard. However, when asked the future oriented, hypothetical question, of whether he would be picked on if he did well in an examination, he explains his strategy for dealing with it:

RP *And you said that you haven't been picked on, because you keep away from them (1), but do you have a (1), if you do well in an exam, would you be picked on?*

Matthew *Um - I may do, but I just ignore them, because I know that it will go away if you just ignore them, but some people don't know that if you ignore them that it will go away, some people sort of retaliate, and this is exactly what these people want - 'cos then they have, sort of. Then they know, that this person get annoyed with what they're saying, and tell other people this boy does this. So in the end they'll sort of end up with everyone doing it, and sometimes you sort of notice that happening, 'cos it's only really if people sort of retaliate, they do it. But if you don't retaliate they get bored pretty quickly, so they change what they are doing and do something else.*

RP *So how's does this sort of happen then, (.) these boys have sort of cussed you, or try to pick on you because you've done well (1) in an exam yeah?*

Matthew *And you just ignore them, you sort of you know, laugh with them, 'Yeah I done well in this exam', but that, you sort of change your attitude and pretend you're like them - you know you pretend you're dangerous as well, but really you don't care*

> *much, s::o suddenly, you're playin, yeah, yeah I'm just like you*
> *and things, and soon they get bored, 'cos they realise, they sort*
> *of think that they're exactly the same as you, so they shouldn't -*
> *sort of cuss you because really their cussing themselves. [**RP**:*
> *Right] So you just, so in the end they just stop =*

RP   *= How do you change your attitude then [inaudible] what =*
Matthew   *= Ohhh, you pretend you're cool and you know you hang out*
                 with the group and things, but the instance they stop, you just
                 leave, and you let them get on with their own thing again - you
                 just ignore them again.
RP   *So is that what you do then. If you're getting picked on, you*
                 actually =
Matthew   *I hang out with the group, I pretend to hang out with the group,*
                 but I don't do anything. - I sort of pretend, all cool, but then I
                 leave again, because I might, I don't like doing that so::rt of,
                 they do these odd things and stuff, and I sort of stay away.

Matthew presents a meta-analytic account of the strategy he uses in that
he recognises that he marshals various tactics, including 'pretend(ing) to
hang out with the group' and to be 'dangerous', in order to be left alone
for a while. By this means, he can both avoid the unpleasantness of being
cussed and feel superior to the group who do not realize he is fooling
them. His way of dealing with being unpopular is, thus, to deny it happens to him, but also to be aware of the strategies he uses to reduce the
opportunities other boys have for cussing him.

We have already seen (in Chapters 3 and 7) how Oliver, a boy who said
he did well at school, liked to work, hated football and spent his time with
girls, was painfully teased by many other boys. While Oliver is unusual
in being fairly separate from most other boys, there were some boys who
were equally unpopular because of their orientation to schoolwork. As
was the case for Oliver, many boys were angry as well as upset that they
were teased for working or for being clever. Charles, below, was vitriolic
against boys who tease him and who do not take their work seriously. To
some extent, he wishes that they will experience retribution through
becoming poor unskilled workers:

Charles   *When they do do homework which is fairly rare - they actually*
                 do, they do one or two lines.
RP   *Yeah (2), are you quite, are you quite, um, critical of them for*
                 not doing homework then?

Charles *I reckon they should do it. [**RP**: Mm] I reckon they should just do homework and that's it…If you don't do any homework then it's just tough for you when you go to college isn't it? (1) I th. I, I reckon, I shouldn't be so critical but, I jus sort of can't help - being like that. I reckon eventually even, if I'm, if nobody's, makes them do homework, tough then an they're not gonna get into a college or anything. [**RP**: Mm] And they'll just be peasants on the street - like road sweepers or bus drivers or something crummy like that. [**RP**: Mm] And their teachers will probably, and their parents will might have a [inaudible] at them or something [**RP**: Mm] for wasting loads of school fees . But other than that there won't be much difference for them.*

RP *You said that you, you shouldn't be so critical, w- what why's that?*

Charles *Well I reckon that I shouldn't be so critical and just let them not get into college. 'Cos if I'm critical then they're sort of like, I'm like saving them sort of.*

Most boys could not aspire to the characteristics of those who were popular and disengaged from schoolwork. Neither did most want to fit into that group since they were concerned about getting qualifications. At the same time, those groups of boys who did get on with their schoolwork without meeting the criteria for masculinity common to the schools they attended were very much derided by other boys. Even boys who agreed that they were unpopular in some ways refuted notions that they fitted into such groups claiming that they were the domain of boys who were even less popular than themselves. The ways in which 'non-hegemonic' boys were treated led most boys to try to avoid being constructed in that way. This was an important motivating factor in many boys' continual efforts to negotiate between the two poles of being too conformingly academic, on the one side, and failing, on the other.

Things change over time

While the picture boys present of how they are positioned and position themselves in relation to schoolwork seems depressing in many ways, it is not static. As we have seen in some of the accounts above, things sometimes changed because boys learned better how to manage this task; boys also said that moving up the school made a difference. However, not everyone gave an account of change being in the same direction in relation to performing masculinity and engaging with schoolwork from a position of choice. For example, the following year-7 boy considered that year-8 boys were more likely to fight than were year-7s:

RP   *Right. So, it's only outside school is it that they, they kind of, group together like that?*

Rob   *Mm and in school.*

RP   *Do they, yeah. Do they 'cause trouble, in school?*

Rob   *Mm (2) they'll get mouthy with the teachers and things. [**RP**: Mm] And (4) just generally being a nuisance. [**RP**: Right] They walk around people, they try and trip them up as they walk past.*

RP   *Do they do that, yeah?*

Rob   *Yeah.*

RP   *Yeah. Are these, these other boys in, in year 7 they try and trip up are they, or?*

Rob   *Boys in year 7 don't usually hang around in groups.*

RP   *Oh right, I, I thought you said, 'cos I was asking about, boys in year 7, if there's anyone like that?*

Rob   *There are some people like that but not many. There's loads in year 8.*

It was, however, more likely that boys would say that fighting became rarer over time and that more boys could get on with schoolwork:

RP   *Right. (3) But I mean the group interview people were saying that, that it's, that it's quite important the tough [inaudible] need to be strong that the most popular boys were the ones who could look after themselves [**Angus**: Um] and so these, but you are saying that, that people can't be bothered doing that.*

Angus   *Mo- most people can they can look after themselves [inaudible] but no-one, one really fights anymore.*

RP   *Don't they? No?*

Angus   *No, they all get along 'cos they all know each other (3), so they all get along and don't really have fights.*

RP   *Right (3), so it's because in the first year the people didn't know each other they used, they used to have fights?*

Angus   *Yeah, fights 'cos they didn't know how people was and didn't know how to take them and that so they had fights.*

RP   *Oh, right. What do you mean by that they didn't know how people =*

Angus   *Most people you know when you joke and have a have a laugh
and cuss each other, most people couldn't take um didn't even
know him that much [**RP**: Right] but [inaudible] and to cuss and
all that stuff so they have fights with them start fights ... Most of
them thought they was a bit too ... harder than any one else they
were thinking, 'Ah, I'll cuss them so they can't do nothing,'
[**RP**: Right] (2) so when someone else reacted to it (4) they didn't
like it*

RP   *What, what don't people think that now then? (9)*

Angus   *I don't know. (5)*

RP   *Is it 'cos people know (3) who, who the hardest ones are now?*

Angus   *Yeah. [**RP**: That's it yeah?] Most people know who's hard and
who's harder than them so they don't bother starting.*

    ...

RP   *Do boys who, who work hard and are clever get teased?*

Julius   *They use to but not anymore ... like in the first year they used to
call them boffins and everything but now we know that working
hard isn't something bad 'cos it's better 'cos then you're gonna
have a good future.*

This perception of change is helpful to concerns about boys and education.
For since boys perceive that change is possible, and that it usually occurs
in a direction that is both less violent and that allows boys to study more,
the outlook for those who have the most difficulty in reconciling masculinity and schooling may be more hopeful. However, it is important to bear in
mind that studies of older boys also report that boys 'muck about' more
than girls when they are older than the boys in this study (see, for example,
Mac an Ghaill, 1994; O'Donnell and Sharpe, 2000). At the same time, most
boys gave accounts which demonstrated that their parents were very keen
that they should do well at school. They reported both inducements and
punishments used by parents to encourage them. This encouragement is
likely to become ever stronger as they move up their schools – particularly
since they and their parents are aware of the debates about boys' relatively
poor educational performance in relation to girls.

The impact of teachers on boys

Boys reported many differences in terms of the learning environment that
was made possible in school by particular teachers, or that became

impossible if some boys perceived that they could wield power over teachers. School differences and teacher differences intersect here in that, for example, the culture of threat and 'bunking off' described by Sadam (below) was not evident at any of the private schools we studied:

RP	*Oh, mucking about, yeah, yeah. Quite a few boys do that actually?*
Sadam	*They're, they're all bunking lessons and, they always do that.*
RP	*Right. 'Cos there were some boys ope-, opening the door, in the last interview, yeah =*
Sadam	*= Yeah, yeah.*
RP	*Do, do teachers, do they, sort of see them, moving around then?*
Sadam	*They see them but they really can't do anything 'cos, they get threatened by the pupils. [laughs] That's the problem, like =*
RP	*= Do they?*
Sadam	*Yeah 'cos after school, yeah, pupils go up to them and go, 'you do that to me ever again I'll smash your face in'. [laughs] You know they =*
RP	*= To teachers?*
Sadam	*Yeah.*
RP	*Really?*
Sadam	*Yeah. They've done it before.*
RP	*Right.*
Sadam	*So, em, and then, sometimes the police get involved and sometimes they don't.*
RP	*So some of the teachers are quite scared then, to?*
Sadam	*They're not that scared, it depends what teacher it is, if it's the, if it's, if the teacher's been here for about - a long time say about five or six years then, then he wouldn't be scared. But if it's a new teacher then, like that, yeah, I think they'd be scared.*

From this account, it seems that new teachers at this school are daunted into being unable to provide an adequate learning environment for boys. This meant that some lessons were not easy to learn in, because particular teachers were seen as 'soft' by boys. Boys reported that they liked teachers who let them talk while working and allowed them to make jokes. In the following group interview, boys were pleased that they were in a single-sex school because one of their teachers made jokes they realised would not be acceptable in a mixed-gender classroom. They very much liked his style:

Dave *But our teachers just wouldn't, like, be the same, 'cos like, our English teacher just makes =*

Angus *= he just makes jokes =*

Dave *= we wouldn't even have the same teacher if it was a co-educational school, it would just, the whole format of the lessons and everything would completely change.*

Angus *The teacher aren't sexist are they, but they know what jokes they would enjoy.*

RP *So what kind of jokes does your English teacher make =*

Angus *= Well he just like, 'How did the cat's tail get cut off in the mince room?' =*

Dave *He likes things like a cat's tail put in a socket and plugged in and switched on.*

Angus *Yeah and [inaudible] and stuff like that. [inaudible] You're in Spain and a women says, 'Oh you like [inaudible], two chicks where did they go on a date?'*

Dave *Yeah and like, he made this joke, we were talking about [inaudible] and if he was talking about birds he would have three cards and on those cards he would was like tits big ones and huge ones, and he wouldn't make that joke if there were girls.*

Teachers against boys: the intersection of gender and 'race'

Boys were very much against teachers they perceived as being unfair. Since boys gain masculine status from 'backchatting' or 'dissing' teachers, engaging with students may well be a frustrating task for many teachers of boys. It is perhaps, then, not surprising that some boys' (and girls') narratives indicate that teachers appear to favour girls. Several boys from mixed schools reported, sometimes angrily, that teachers were unfair because they took girls' sides if there were disputes between girls and boys, or because they dealt more harshly with boys when they did the same things as girls or when a girl hit a boy:

RP *What kind of names do they [girls] call you?*

Chris *Um, well, it's not sort of like cussing names. It's like, oh like 'You're dumb, immature like, and pathetic.' Names like that.*

RP *How do the boys respond to that?*

Chris   *Sometimes we say stuff back and then they go to the teachers and*
the teachers tell us off. And like you can't say to them, 'Oh but
they were saying it to us and like hitting us' and stuff like that.
And like the teacher will go 'Ohhh, just let them get on with it.'
And like if we do hit a girl back, we're gonna get expelled
straight away ...

RP   *How's it different being a boy?*

Chris   *Sometimes it can be harder because all the teachers are like, I'll*
say, I'll, um, always stick up for the girls, always on the girls'
side but sometimes, nine times out of ten it'll be like, 'The girls
go first, oh girls' credits' and all that but boys just like, 'Stay
behind after school.' It's always the boys keeping in behind.

For some boys, this perception of unfairness bolstered their opposition to
teachers and to getting on industriously with their work. It is, of course,
difficult to untangle narratives of fairness. It has, for example, repeatedly
been found in work on racialisation and racism that white people who
produce racist discourses often justify them on the grounds that they have
been treated unfairly by, or because of, black people who, they argue, are
really the ones who are unfair or prejudiced (see, for example, van Dijk,
1993; Cohen, 1997; Hewitt, 1996). There has also long been research
which demonstrates how easy it is for teachers and boys to be convinced
that girls are getting a disproportionate amount of attention if teachers
attend to them as much as they do to the boys (for example, Spender,
1983). It may also be the case that current talk of a 'crisis' in boys' attainment leads some well-motivated teachers to deal more firmly with
boys than they otherwise would. This study is not designed to disentangle these issues; nevertheless, they are integral to considerations of boys
and education since narratives such as those presented above produce an
ethos where it is assumed that gendered inequality is encouraged in the
mixed classroom, particularly by women teachers. These discourses, in
themselves, have consequences which require attention and analysis:

RP   *Right(2) Are girls, do you think girls are treated differently in*
school, than boys?(1)

Jim   *They get told off exactly the same as the boys do.*

RP   *Do they, yeah, yeah, do they get told off as much as boys?*

Jim   *Not as much.*

RP   *Why's that?(1)*

Jim   *'Cos when they do something wrong the teacher just says 'Aah just*
stop it', but when the boys do something wrong, like they just shout.

RP *I thought you said the teacher told girls off just as much as boys?*
Jim *Well they do, but if they do something really wrong, but if they say do their homework they just get talken to, but if boys don't do it they get shouted to.*

In the following group interview with black 11-year-olds, two boys develop this same theme:

Daniel *Sometime if a, if a, if a girl pushes you just for spite, yeah an' you like just say 'Don't push me' an' like the teacher's there, yeah, she'll just get annoyed at you an' like you didn't even do nothing. [**RP**: Right] An' they just pushed you for no reason. And if they do it again some teachers are so strict they'll just give you a detention.*
James *Yeah. They give the boys detention but they don't give girls. If they - it's like equal thing. If they like equal, the same thing bad, if they did the same thing bad [Joseph and Daniel giggling] the boy would stay behind a lit longer than the girl. She would just stay in and get told off and the, the boy would just stay in and get told off and have another - have like the Head of Department invite in, going as well. Get told off by.*

Although the black boys quoted above are talking solely in gender terms, many studies have demonstrated that teachers perceive and treat children from different racialised groups unequally and that gender intersects with 'race' to produce worse treatment for black boys (Ogilvy *et al.*, 1992; Sonuga-Barke *et al.*, 1993; Connolly, 1995; Sewell, 1997). As described in more detail in Chapter 6, some of the black boys in the study reported here had no doubt that black boys are 'picked on' by teachers. That these discourses are further reaching than the boys who produce them is illustrated by the fact that, in some mixed-gender group interviews, girls also said that boys are treated unfairly in comparison with girls and that this is particularly the case for black boys. The group interview from which we quote below is from 13-year-olds attending a mixed private school. The group consisted of two white girls, one black girl, one Asian boy, one black boy and two white boys. In this extract, although the talk is dominated by a black boy and a black girl, one of the white girls supports their claim that black boys are unfairly picked on by teachers.

Black girl   *And then one teacher, I'm not going to say which one, they call all the boys by their second names and all the girls by their first names ...*

Black boy   *My teacher calls everybody else by their first name and he keeps calling me by my second.*

RP   *Right ... does he call all the boys by their second name?*

Black boy   *Some boys whom he doesn't like. He calls them by their second, but all the others, he calls by their first. [RP: Right.] It's so annoying ... Once I got into trouble for talking in class and then the teacher give, gave me a detention and then the girl owned up and said it was her talking, but he never gave her a detention.*

Black girl   *No, but another thing is that does come back into race though, because like you're the only black boy in your class.*

Black boy   *I know yeah! [joint giggling]*

Black girl   *No, no seriously, like, no seriously, like certain things like, there's this black boy in my class and there's this other white boy, they're always, like, like they're always in trouble together. The both of them and one of them was allowed to go on a trip, the other wasn't and this one who wasn't was actually black, you know. [RP: Right] I don't know why that is 'cos that's sexism and racism put together.*

White girl   *There's a group, yeah, in our class and, um, they don't do anything and it's like black boys and white boys and some half castes and there's, um, one black boy in it and, um, like they all do the same things, but he's the one who's been threatened to be expelled and stuff, but no-one else has. He's the one who has been threatened and all the others haven't and, um.*

Black girl   *The mixed race one has though.*

Addressing black masculinities as collective responses in a racist culture, Sewell (1997) found that many of the 15-year-old black boys he studied resented being 'othered' by teachers, being perceived as threatening and being picked upon for no other reason they could see other than because they were black. However, for some, the knowledge that teachers were afraid of them was a source of power and an incentive to perform in ways which signified threat.

It is difficult to disentangle the factors that start the process of what comes to be reported as unequal treatment. Nonetheless, it is clearly unsatisfactory that boys (and black boys in particular) should feel that they are subjected to discriminatory treatment which, in mixed schools, is also sometimes noted by girls. Teachers to a large extent, play important parts in what Connell (1996: 213) calls 'schools as agents in the making of masculinities'. A serious consideration of how boys come to occupy their current positions in education requires both more work on teachers' discourses of sexism and racism and recognition that boys are not passively inscribed in the educational process, but are agents within it.

Masculinities *and* attainment?

As we have seen throughout this book, constructions of popular/hegemonic masculinity are pervasive in 11–14-year-old boys' accounts. This masculinity is characterised by toughness, footballing prowess and resistance to teachers and education. The sanctions against boys who work hard at school include teasing and ostracism. Yet, many of the boys we spoke to wanted to be able to attain good qualifications at school. Few were, therefore, entirely happy to behave along the lines of narrowly 'hegemonic' masculinity: joking about in the classroom, confronting teachers' authority and doing very little schoolwork. Most boys were struggling to negotiate the canonical narrative which opposes popular/hegemonic masculinity and being seen to work hard. Thus, even those who were identified by other boys as 'geeks' or 'boffs' made great efforts to construct themselves as more popular than some other boys or vented their anger against those who bullied them, dismissing them as less worthy in many ways. The majority of boys found ways to position themselves 'in the middle' in terms of popularity and negotiated ways in which they could get on with some schoolwork, but not be constructed as unpopular. Some managed the difficult balancing act of being popular in many ways while also succeeding at school. An important strategy for these boys was to be able to make other boys laugh, to laugh at themselves and to show that they were sometimes disengaged from schoolwork or resisting authority by, for example, skipping lessons. Some appeared to be using a strategy identified by Mac an Ghaill (1994) of doing well without being seen to make an effort at school.

Part of the story of boys' educational performance concerns their construction of girls as opposites to boys (see Chapter 4). Many boys made direct comparisons with girls, who were seen as naturally more compliant and studious, but therefore also preferred by teachers and more likely to go on to make something of themselves. For example, one white 11-year-old boy told us that 'Girls listen more and get down to work and don't give backchat to teachers whereas boys have to be macho', and that 'if boys listened more they could get a good job and earn more money'. Similarly, another white 14-year-old suggested that, 'If someone said would you rather work or play football, I'd say football. But if someone said to girls would you rather play netball or study, they'd say study.' He thought that the girls' attitude was much better as 'this is the time you need to learn to get good marks. When you grow up and get a job you can have fun.' Whilst this is clearly a moralising account which could represent the boy's attempt to impress the adult interviewer, it is also consistent with comments from many boys who seem tired of the effort involved in sustaining the abrasive, 'hard' attitude to life represented by their version of the masculine ideal and cynical about whether any boys actually met the ideal.

Teachers obviously play an important part in what happens in their classrooms. Many boys gave amused accounts of 'soft' teachers who they reported were often threatened or overruled by popular boys so that they could not provide an adequate learning environment. However, in general, they seemed to prefer teachers who could keep order, but also joked with them. They had a keen sense of injustice and many reported that their teachers unfairly treated boys, with some (both black and white) also saying that teachers particularly picked on black boys. While this does not necessarily indicate that most teachers are unfair in these ways – particularly since, from their own accounts boys can make life difficult for teachers – the pervasiveness of this narrative from boys is important to considerations of boys' educational attainment.

The complexity of the negotiations boys make in order to be able to survive at school demonstrates that debates on boys and education have to take note of the difficulties posed by canonical narratives of masculinities within school cultures. Far from being mindless in engaging with 'lads' culture', many boys struggled to manage the contradictions they faced in order to gain some qualifications at school. The fact that some considered change possible as they moved up the school may be a hopeful sign.

9

On the way to adulthood: relationships with parents

But then now, he's, he's like stopped ringing an' he's, he's got his other family now I think he's just, I don't think he just wants to see me any more. (John, 13)

In psychological and social policy discussions, the key relationships for young people are usually thought of as those with their parents. Much of the 'moral panic' over young men concerns the degree to which they are in or out of communication with, and control of, their parents, and government policy is directed substantially towards insisting on parental responsibility for boys' (and, to a lesser extent, girls') behaviour. In the classic psychoanalytic and psychological literature on 'adolescence' (see Waddell, 1998), teenagers are portrayed as necessarily in conflict with their parents as they start to 'individuate' and experiment with styles and identities of their own, and as they refer more strongly to their peer group for guidance on acceptable and fashionable ways of being. On the other hand, psychoanalytic writers in particular have stressed the importance of maintaining good, 'containing' relationships with parents even during this 'storm and stress' period, and there is also evidence from empirical studies of young people that most of them continue to value their parents' guidance and advice, share their attitudes and seek to be on good terms with them (Rutter, 1997).

The literature on boys' relationships with their parents lays particular emphasis on the significance of the link (or lack of it) with fathers. In some hands, this produces a lament for lost initiation processes which supposedly (probably only mythologically and certainly patriarchally) offered young men clear structures of role and identity as they moved into adulthood (Bly, 1990). The contemporary 'crisis of masculinity' can then be constructed as a product of the lost link with strong and confident fathers – a line of argument which fuses conveniently with a post-feminist backlash and which can also be employed to make lone mothers

225

the target for social criticism. In a less caricature form, however, the question of what boys and young men think of, and are seeking for, in their relationships with their parents and other adults is an important one if it is assumed that the quality of developmental experiences is governed significantly by the quality of the relationships in which development is embedded. Whilst the foundational relationships of young childhood might be especially significant in laying down the expectations and unconscious structures out of which people's identities emerge, there is little doubt that the quality of *continuing* relationships is of major importance for psychological and social well-being. In terms of the experiences of young men, this suggests that the way they relate to their parents will be a crucial factor in determining the degree to which they feel supported and encouraged as they explore the various identity positions available to them. Whether relationships with fathers matter more, or in a different way, from those with mothers is something which remains to be seen.

In our interviews, all the boys were asked in some detail about their relationships with their parents, and this chapter describes what they said. What should be noted immediately is that there is a great deal of variety, with most boys describing reasonably positive relationships, some of them very close and rewarding, but a few having disastrous experiences. An example of a particularly negative situation will be looked at in some detail towards the end of the chapter, but what we will focus on first is the nature of relationships with parents, what boys say they do and do not get from them, and the similarities and differences between relationships with fathers and those with mothers.

What do parents offer?

Talking about their parents, boys often expressed a great deal of enjoyment in their relationships. As described later, there were some differentiations to be made here between relationships with fathers, which were often jokey and playful, and with mothers, which tended to be more serious. But there is no doubt that many boys still, at the ages of 11 to 14, have a great deal of fun with their parents:

RP   *So, erm, you said that with your dad then, you can have a laugh with him and share a joke. You can't do that so much with your mum then? You don't?*

Maurice   *I could if my, if my mum had, a sense of humour like my dad has an' me an' dad, me and my dad 'as same sense of humour.*

RP   *How does that differ then from your mum's sense of humour?*

Maurice   *Dunno, she don't find things that funny (1) like dunno, say like 'You've Been Framed'.*

RP   *Mmm.*

Maurice   *We watching that, me and me dad laugh, she think 'Ahh like, aah he might be hurt' [pathetic tone] or something like that.*

RP   *Oh, I see. Yeah, yeah. (1) Do you think your mum hasn't got a sense of humour?*

Maurice   *She has.*

RP   *What does she laugh at?*

Maurice   *Well, uh, real life things like, Well, I got drunk yeah, at this party went to. My Auntie's party an' I got drunk and she thought that was funny. [laugh] =*

RP   *= She thought that was funny? =*

Maurice   *= I couldn't stand up an' she thought that was funny.*

Calvin, in the next example, enjoyed recalling his parents' response to the news that he had a girlfriend, starting with his mother:

RP   *What did she do this time when you told her about it?*

Calvin   *She burnt the carpet.*

RP   *(Laugh) Oh did she, yeah?*

Calvin   *Yeah, she um, she kept on laughing yeah.*

RP   *Yeah.*

Calvin   *She put the iron down, an it fell flat.*

RP   *Yeah.*

Calvin   *Now there's little holes in the carpet.*

RP   *Right - So how did you feel w- when she, did that?*

Calvin   *I kept on laughing as well.*

RP   *Right, yeah.*

Calvin   *But my dad was furious as well.*

RP   *Your dad was furious?*

Calvin   *Yeah, he was the one that bought the carpet.*

RP   *Oh right…*

Calvin   *But he laughed as well.*

RP   *He laughed as well?*

Calvin   *[inaudible] He was furious but he - he knows it was only an accident so…*

RP   *But, but w- w- w- why, why did he laugh?*
Calvin   *Um:: 'cos it was only a little, hole that's all.*

What comes over in these extracts and in many of the other things said by the boys is the energy of their relationships with their parents, the enjoyment they have in it. As will be seen, a great deal of teasing goes on, particularly between fathers and sons (perhaps paralleling the 'cussing' which goes on between boys at school), and at times this can feel harsh and inhibiting to boys. But they still enjoy the jokes and the extravagant aspects of their parents' behaviour.

More dominant in the interview material, however, is an appreciation of the degree to which parents offer emotional support and guidance, which despite its sometimes restrictive and moralistic aspects is usually valued highly by young people. It is as if they see this as their parents' major job. Emotional support is primarily (but not exclusively) the preserve of mothers. Nineteen boys specifically mentioned turning to their mums for this, and four to their dads, when in need of help. Often, in the boys' accounts, it takes the form of being the person to consult when things are going wrong, for instance over being bullied or getting into trouble at school. The following boy lives with a lone mother:

RP   *How d'you get on with your mum?*
George   *Um (2), I think quite well. 'Cos when I got problems I can go to her an' like (1) ask her for help, or. [RP: Right] Um (2), she generally gives me (2) er support, know what I mean?*
RP   *So, so what kind of problems do you go to (3) her about?*
George   *Usually what happens at school, like with teachers an' stuff.*
RP   *Yeah. (3) What, what does she say to you?*
George   *If I got like a problem, like, an' I can't, can't tell my mum what happened, in a lesson, teacher was shouting at me for something that I didn't do, I say to her, 'What did I do wrong?' ... an' I tell my mum that an' mum says if it keeps on happening then you should, you should, um (1), you should just accept it. Even if it happened [inaudible] just accept it. And, um (1), it would get her more annoyed than you, because you will, um (1), 'cos even though she keeps, um (1), like, she's expecting you to be like, angry an' stuff, an' if you don't show it then, (2) um, then you'll generally feel much better an' (1) she'll be the one that's getting angry.*
        ...

RP   *When I asked you if there was anyone you were emotional with*
        you said it was your mum.

Julius *Yeah 'cos my mum's like - I'm like my mum's favourite 'cos I'm*
        *the youngest [**RP**: Right] so like my mum's, my mum sticks up*
        for me, when people pick on me.

Sometimes it is enough just to get reassurance; at other times the parent (again, particularly mothers) might give direct advice or take active steps to sort the problem out. The important thing seemed to be not so much that action would be taken, but that the boy could have confidence that he was liked and valued by his parent/s, that they were interested in him and would take him seriously. When the relationship had that kind of basis, boys seemed to feel respected and reported being quite open and truthful with their parents (especially their mothers), and turning to them with their difficulties:

> *I dunno, I just, if something goes wrong I always just tell my mum I don't know what it is but something inside me just always makes me tell my mum.* (Daniel, 12, lone mother)
>
> *I'd probably say we both, like my dad and mum, um, basically we have got a good relationship [inaudible] 'cos I respect them, they respect me to do what I want but if as long as it is good and everything and they care for me and everything I care for them, and I could talk to them both about things.* (Khalid, 12, two parents)

RP   *Yeah, yeah. D'you find then that there's a lot of things you can*
        talk about with your mum and dad that you can't talk about
        with boys your age or girls your age?

Gerald *Yeah, definite [**RP**: Yeah] yeah. I mean they're the people*
        I trust most so.

RP   *You trust them most?*

Gerald *Yeah, I trust them implicitly.*

RP   *What do you mean by that, trust [**Gerald**: U::m] what sense?*

Gerald *(2) They'll never deliberately embarrass me, they'll never tell*
        anyone anything I don't want them to, yeah they're always on
        my side. (Gerald, 12, two parents)

Whilst there are many examples in our interview material of the kinds of positive relationships described above, there were also boys for whom life with parents was more problematic. Occasionally (in three clear, and one less certain, examples in our group of 78), relationships with one or other parent seemed extremely tense and disturbed, and in at least one of these instances there were mental health problems in the parent ('My mum's got a mental problem, psychotic' – Zac). More often, the difficulty was the unavailability of parents, either generally in the sense of them simply not being there, or emotionally in that they did not respond adequately to the boys' requests for help. Both these things were true particularly for fathers. Twenty-three boys indicated that their fathers were much less available to them than their mothers, and only two that it was the other way round:

Sadam   *I don't know it's just that, that I don't, don't get to talk to my parents like they always busy or something like that, and I am just playing computer or watching telly or something like that so, or I'm out so (2) the only times when I, um, see them round the telly, but then they are telly watching [**RP**: Yeah] yeah, yeah (3)*

RP   *So you don't get to talk to your parents then?*

Sadam   *Um, not really.*

                ...

RP   *Yeah, yeah (1) would you like to see more of your dad?*

Georgi   *Yeah, I would like to see more of my dad but, that's, that's just, that's just the way things are but [**RP**: Yeah] I can't change it. [**RP**: Yeah] That's just, em, work.* (Georgi, 11, two parents)

Sometimes a boy felt very much more strongly about his father's unavailability or absence – especially when there were grounds to see himself as actively rejected by the father. Here are two examples from boys whose fathers have left:

*Um, we'd go, we used to go bowling a lot. I really like bowling, it's really good. An', well apart from all this 'e used to beat me, but I don't care. It was good just to see 'im really. [**RP**: Yeah] Well that's all I really want. [**RP**: Yeah] It's just to see 'im. I don't really care if we stay in his house, watch a video or summink. As long as we just, as long as I see 'im. [**RP**: Mmm] All it is is a phone call but I'm not sure if he can just be bothered [**RP**: Mmm] any more. So. I mean (2), before I always used to call 'im to see if he wanted to do anything. But I mean, I can't be there all the time to call 'im and (1) he might as well call me from time to time. But 'e 'asn't really. So I've just left it. And say if 'e wants to speak to me, 'e can ring me. [**RP**: Right, right.] So.* (John, 13, mother and stepfather)

*Erm, yeah, I get on more with ma mum 'cos I see her more than my dad -
like I see my dad, like once every two three months 'cos he, he lives in Somerset
(1), far to come [**RP**: Hmm] an' he's got a wife up there as well [**RP**: Hmm],
he's remarried so, erm [inaudible], I'm not really, I don't, like if he says stuff
an goes 'Ah, you know like I always think about you an everythin' I go 'Yeah
I'm not bothered', like, I know all this stuff and, and I don't care [**RP**: Hmm],
like he tell [inaudible] my sisters the younger ones an everything but, I can't be
bothered, I just wanna (1) go, go out play with my mates, like not 'cos I don't
care or anything, I just, like I know what he's gonna say. He says it all the time
he goes 'Ah you know I always think about yer' (1) so [**RP**: Hmm] (1) just gets
a bit boring so I always just say 'Oh, alright then' [inaudible], agree, I go
'Yeah, yeah, yeah'.* (Reg, 13, lone mother)*

Some boys seemed simply resigned to the relative absence of their
fathers, saying it made little difference, others were explicitly sad about
it and wished for more contact and availability. In the case of these two
boys whose fathers have left, it is clear that a lot of hurt was involved:
John is explicit on this, and with Reg it is quite apparent that his father's
absence had led him to feel cynical about all the attestations of care he
received from him – these could not mean much when so little effort was
made to sustain contact. It was rare, however, for a boy to be as negative
about his mother, or to complain of a lack of contact with her.

Mothers' seriousness, fathers' immaturity

The boys we interviewed, with exceptions, were relatively consistent in
their presentation of some of the differences between their mothers
and their fathers. Their fathers were seen as more playful and joking
than their mothers, easier to chat to, often more laid back, perhaps more
childish. Fifteen boys described their fathers as jokey and 12 their mothers as serious. For example:

RP   *I suppose that, I mean you did say that you can share certain
             jokes with your dad that…*
Maurice *Mmm.*
RP   *Yeah.*
Maurice *Say it's, erm, rude jokes I wouldn't my dad tells me, I would-
             n't tell my mum or something or, something like that.*
RP   *What that your dad tells you?*

Maurice   *Some rude jokes.*
RP   *Ok, yeah.*
Maurice   *I couldn't go an' say 'Oh mum blah, blah, blah'.*
RP   *Yeah, your dad sometimes does that?*
Maurice   *I could tell 'er but she wouldn't laugh at it, she'd probably*
           *tell me off but [**RP**: Yeah, yeah], have a go at me dad as well*
           to teach me but (1)
RP   *Yeah, your dad sometimes does that does he? Yeah.*
Maurice   *Not rude jokes but just - say like we watch a film he'd make a*
           *joke. [**RP**: Mmm] An' say oh, at the time it'd be funny but if I*
           go an' tell mum it won't be that funny - 'cos, erm, dunno.

The collusion here is noticeably 'masculine': joking seems to be a way
of establishing intimacy between men and, as part of this process,
excluding the woman. With his mum, 'It won't be that funny'; rude
jokes are something the boy preserves as an arena for special father–son
collaboration. Joking as a way of relating can even be seen as something
boys learn from their fathers en route to becoming masculinised: one
aspect of the mother's imagined complaint is that the father should not
be teaching him such things. A language of masculine closeness, inclusion and exclusion at once, is being established here.

   In separated families, it seemed particularly the case that boys looked
to their non-live-in fathers for 'fun', and that this defined closeness and
enjoyment as a way of using the relatively small, precious time they had
together to the full. In the next example, this again takes the form of
something disapproved of by the mother; perhaps for that very reason it
defines a way of being close to the father. This is, one must assume, a
kind of relationship work: quality time is defined as time to 'muck
around', carefully and intensely preserved:

Barry   *Well, when we, when he used to live with us, when he used to*
           like beat us up, muckin' around.
RP   *Yeah.*
Barry   *It was like him and my little brover - me and my brover Alex.*
RP   *Right.*
Barry   *The 11-year-old. And when we used to muck around and play*
           fightin' my mum used to shout and say 'Stop messin' around.'
RP   *Your mum used to say that?*
Barry   *Yeah, yeah. To all of us.*
RP   *Yeah.*

Barry *But when we was at my dad's house we always like have play fights 'cos it's fun, like pillowfights.*

RP *Yeah. You said though that when you were with your dad your dad used to change channels like when you were watching TV and tell you to pick up things. Does he do that now?*

Barry *Well, really, we're like 'cos we only see him once a week, we don't want to do that. We just want to be with him and muck around.*

RP *Yeah.*

Barry *And go football in the park.*

Interestingly, Barry recalls his father as mucking around and play fighting with his sons even when he lived with them (his mother would shout, 'Stop messing around'); it is the interviewer who reminds Barry that he had earlier said that his father was controlling and belligerent, and this is passed over very quickly by Barry as he constructs his account of how important it is to use his time with his father in having fun. The version of fathering being produced in this section of text is one in which 'mucking around' defines closeness, love even; in its anarchic freedom is something of the pure contact the boy needs with his father in order for the relationship to survive. Interestingly, this particular boy is an example of one who not only saw his father as fun, but who also referred to problems with his mother, who he labelled as 'depressed':

RP *Right, yeah. Would you say you have a good relationship with your mum, than you do with your dad?*

Barry *[Slowly] With my dad, [normal pace] I could talk about more things.*

RP *Can you?*

Barry *Like with my mum I can really only talk about school.*

RP *Yeah.*

Barry *But with my dad, I talk about football a lot, a lot about football.*

RP *Right*

Barry *[Inaudible] with my dad, we joke a lot.*

RP *Do you, yeah?*

Barry *My mum, she has to look after the kids and all that and she's also she's a babysitter – a childminder, I mean, not a babysitter.*

RP *Yeah, yeah.*

Barry *She child minds this boy called Chris, so she's got six children in the house.*

RP   *Right.*
Barry *So it's really like hard for her.*
RP   *Yeah.*
Barry *To like talk to us and joke around with us.*
RP   *Ok. So you find your mum a bit that quite often she's telling you off for things, whereas your dad =*
Barry *= She's depressed a lot.*
RP   *Is she?*
Barry *But my dad, he was, he was he's like always jokin' around. Like he'd like cuss us or somethin', like jokin' around.*

This material portrays fathers as fun and as admired for being fun; this marks them out as distinct from mothers, who are more burdened by cares and responsibilities, and is a significant aspect in the enjoyment and promise of masculinity. What constitutes this 'fun' is juvenile behaviour: rude jokes, play-fighting, mucking about, silly noises. 'As long as it's a joke', says the next boy, anything is OK:

> *My dad's really (1) funny at points. When we're right, I bring my friends over to my house, he'll make jokes. (1) Not about us, but he'll just say. Right, 'cos when we play computer, say, we'll make funny noises and he'll just say 'What's the bb', and then just make you laugh. Mean he wouldn't say to us 'Don't make them noises.' He'll let us do what we want as long as it's OK and it's nothing to do with racist or (1) as long as it's a joke he'll take it OK.*
> (Dean, 13, mixed parentage, lone father)

RP   *So do you think, that, that, that adults don't laugh at those kind of things then or as you grow up you?*
Mark   *My dad does 'cos my dad's very much like me.*
RP   *Is he yeah, yeah?*
Mark   *He likes to muck around quite a lot and say all these silly - names, and*
RP   *Yeah, yeah.*
Mark   *We - laugh quite a lot.*
RP   *Right.*
Mark   *Mum, my mum's more, serious than my dad...*
RP   *Yeah, yeah. Is she the most grown up then do you think? Yeah. So, so even, even, adult men, are less grown up than, adult women?*
Mark   *Yeah. Well they all say that wo-, women know best, that women will do the right thing men do the bad thing. (Mark, 15, lone mother)*

Fathers and sons, in these accounts, are much of a muchness: what the boys seem to be learning is the acceptability of a certain kind of humour and the way in which it defines masculine intimacy. In this respect, it is related to the mutual 'cussing' which many of our respondents described as the ordinary way in which teenage boys communicate with one another.

Predictably, fathers also seem to share an all-engrossing interest in the most important topic in many boys and men's lives, football. Seventeen boys explicitly mentioned having this in common with their fathers:

RP   *Yeah. When your dad is there you speak to your dad more than you do your mum, yeah?*

Ferai   *'Cos I talk about football and stuff.*

RP   *I see, yeah. What do you talk about with your mum?*

Ferai   *Mm, stuff about school (2) stuff like that.*

RP   *Yeah. Do you talk to your dad about school?*

Ferai   *Not, not as.*

RP   *Yeah. Do you do different things with your dad than you do with your mum? Like do you go'*

Ferai   *=Like might - might go to a football match, watch a football match with my dad but my mum won't come. She might come but my mum wants to go like shoppin' more than my dad. Dad don't get that much shoppin' to do. (Ferai, 11, two parents)*

There is perhaps no surprise in this particular gender divide: football is a defining feature of masculine cultures in Britain and however hard a mother might try to be part of it, it is assumed that her heart can never be fully in it. Shopping will come first, or at least – however tolerant she is – her imagination will fail when faced with the awesome capacity of boys and fathers to talk forever about the game:

RP   *OK. You said that you go to Chelsea games with your dad. Um (1), is your mum keen on football?*

Tony   *Um, well she. No not really. She wouldn't wanna go to the games or anything. But, but she puts up with it. She, she's alright with it.*

RP   *She puts up with it?*

Tony   *Yeah.*

RP   *Yeah. What, what d'you mean by that?*

Tony   *Well she (1), she doesn't mind us watching it an' stuff. But she's not, she wouldn't sit down an' watch it with us.*

RP   *She wouldn't watch it?*

Tony   *No. But she's alright about us watching an' going an' stuff.*

RP   *Right. Would you talk about football with your mum, or do you (1) talk about?*

Tony   *No. Not really.*

RP   *No.*

Tony   *She, she, she just knows how good the team's getting on, you know. Sometimes she might say something to me but we don't have like (1) big conversations about it.*

RP   *No. But you do with your dad presumably. Go to matches an' that.*

Tony   *Yeah. Always talking about football.* (Tony, 13, two parents)

Jim, below, links this with the more general issue of fun and mothers' versus fathers' characteristics:

RP   *Right(3)D::o, do different things with your dad than you do with your mum?*

Jim   *Yeah, 'cos when I go football, my dad normally comes to watch me an my mum don't, 'cos its normally cold ... Ah, in the holidays he lets me go work with im.*

RP   *Does he?*

Jim   *Yeah.*

RP   *How do you find that?*

Jim   *Its fun, 'cos at the traffic lights he normally, like, punch me.*

RP   *Oh right, yeah.*

Jim   *In the arm.* (Jim, 12, two parents)

Despite the enjoyment many boys get from their fathers, there are difficulties with this masculine socialisation through jokes and football, not just in terms of developing alternative modes of masculine socialisation, but at the very concrete level of what happens when boys want something else. As described in earlier chapters, for a minority of the boys we interviewed, football was a big turn-off, signifying aspects of masculinity which are narrow and negative (for example, because it interferes with school work), perhaps bullying and brash. Occasionally, for boys like this, their fathers' fascination with football came between them; that is, rather than the father focusing on the son's interests and nurturing his development, the son was left behind because his father's interest was elsewhere, in the game. In the following example, this gains added significance as the boy concerned lived with his brother and father.

RP   *You said, you said that your brother and your dad were quite alike and I was wondering how you felt you're different from them.*

Paul   *It's like 'cos, my brother and my dad are always like [inaudible] about football, they'll always joke around about it, talk about players, how much they cost but I'm like, I'm more like my mum. Speak about, - like those two about football like every six seconds. I like speak to my mum about other subjects and that.* (Paul, 11, lone father)

More generally, the very thing that makes fathers sometimes easier to get on with (their jokes and avoidance of serious topics, their mucking about and general playfulness) makes it harder for many boys to confide in them when they have something important to say. Father–son relationships frequently pivot so strongly on the axis of teasing and fun, that when a boy needs help, comfort or emotional release, he cannot trust his father to be able to manage it. When there is emotion around, the mother, generally speaking, has to bear it:

RP   *Do you find that you can express emotions to your mum, like if you're feeling quite sad about something or feeling quite happy about something, can you express those =*

Joey   *= Mm better to my mum than my dad.*

RP   *Better to your mum, yeah?*

Joey   *Yeah. Like if I was like happy for some reason like if I had a girlfriend and that, yeah, I'd tell my dad. I'll say like 'I've got a girlfriend'. And he'll go, 'Yeah, what's she like', that sort of stuff, right? But, um, if like my girlfriend said I'm dumb and she don't wanna go out with me no more I'll tell my mum not my dad.*

RP   *Oh really, yeah?*

Joey   *Yeah. I wouldn't want my dad, I wouldn't want to say that to my dad.*

RP   *Why's that?*

Joey   *'Cos, you know, 'Dad I've been dumped'. 'Oh have you'. It's just...*

RP   *But you'd tell your mum?*

Joey   *I'd tell my mum, yeah.*

RP   *Why would you tell your mum?*

Joey   *Oh just 'cos, um, I dunno, say she'll go yeah and, er, I thought it easier saying it to my mum than my dad.* (Joey, 13, two parents)

It is noticeable here that when Joey imagined getting his girlfriend, he said he would talk to his dad about her; the father is a connoisseur, experienced with women and they can compare notes, man to man. But when he imagined being 'dumped', it is the mother to whom Joey would turn. Similarly for Matthew, when he had something on his mind his father was not much help, even though he was entertaining and Matthew was not complaining about him:

RP   *Yeah. Suppose you got, any worries or anxieties, I mean, who, do you tend to talk to your mum about them or your dad, or (1) both? =*

Matthew   *=I (1) I talk to both. I sort of talk to one, see what their answer is, and then I go off to the, the other and sort of, [**RP**: Oh, right], compare their answers.*

RP   *Is it, is, do you find, do you get different responses from the two, or?*

Matthew   *Yeah. My, my mum's, always sort of, a bit more my, my dad's sort of, jokes about a bit, but my mum's a bit more serious about it.*

RP   *Oh, right*

Matthew   *So, you get, sort of the serious answer and the jokey answer.*

RP   *Really?*

Matthew   *It's quite good to get both, so you sort of get an idea =*

RP   *= Do you think, could you give me an example, say?*

Matthew   *E:rm, like - I was, getting worried about what options I should do for GCSE, [**RP**: Mm], and my, mum was, was, told me what - sort of sat down at the table, we, we thought about it a lot, when I asked my dad he told me to do something like, er, ballet or something, [**RP**: Right], and stuff like that, which, I just knew I didn't want to do, but it was quite funny sort of, one, it's funny to [inaudible] I'll go to my mum, and she's, really serious about it, and I go to my dad he, you know he doesn't mind because, he knows that, I'll sort it out for myself.*

RP   *Mm.*

Matthew   *He let's me sort it out.*

RP   *So when he said ballet he was kind of joking, was he? =*

Matthew   *= He was joking. (Matthew, 14, two parents)*

These boys seem relatively fortunate in that their fathers are interested in them, even if they do not always respond to the challenge of offering them emotional support. Tariq's story, in the next extract, was at least as common: the father is caught up in his own things, his football mainly, and what the boy learns is not to bother him. He has some idea, as it happens, that his father might be able to help him if he is in trouble; but as the extract makes clear, even this is uncertain; it had never been tested and probably never would be:

Tariq *My mum, it's easier to talk to my mum.*
RP *Yeah, why's that?*
Tariq *I dunno. My mum – she ain't exactly got a temper, somefin' like 'at.*
RP *Mmm.*
Tariq *She don't put me under pressure - we just sit down, you know, and have a little chat, where me dad says like, erm, 'Wait, wait, I'm watching this important football game, I'll talk to you later.' Yeah, it's like that.*
RP *Oh, does he? Yeah, yeah? So sometimes you want to talk to your dad about things and =*
Tariq *Well, not always. Erm, I know not to talk to him that much now.*
RP *Right =*
Tariq *But I do talk to him stuff about 'Oh dad, there's this boy, he erm, he's startin' to pick on me.' [inaudible] I could talk to him about stuff like 'at.*
RP *Yeah, have you spoken to him about that?*
Tariq *Nah, 'cos that hasn't happened. [giggles]*
RP *Right, yeah, yeah.*
Tariq *Like nothin' serious has happened.*
RP *'Cos you said your dad sort of puts you under pressure a bit whereas your mum doesn't. Could you =*
Tariq *'Cos my mum's got more time to talk to me.*
RP *Right.*
Tariq *She works an' everyfin' as a nurse, but on her days off she's always sittin' down or just, she does do cookin', but my dad's always watchin' TV or [quietly] he might be havin' a nap or sleepin' or somethin'.* (Tariq, 11, two parents)

Complaints about fathers' emotional unavailability are very common in our data; so consistently was it represented to us by the boys, that it seemed to rank as one of the most solid characteristics of adult men. When their sons turn to them, they get an absence or something almost as bad: simplistic, playground-level advice which reveals an incapacity to listen or to hold onto and manage distress. Here is another poignant example, similar to the previous one, in which the mother's capacity to listen is counterpointed with the father's unavailability; one might even say, using the word to indicate something brutalised, his stupidity:

RP   *When, when you say that your mum listens more than your dad*
        I was just wondering what, what =

Sadam   *Like, um, if I, I asked her, um, mum would just listen and not*
        say anything, yeah, and she would just listen, but if I say,
        'Mum can you give me some advice?' and then I'd tell her and
        she'd give me advice [RP: Yeah] afterwards.

RP   *Do you talk to her, do you talk more about things that go on in*
        school than you do to your dad?

Sadam   *Yeah, like um, there's a load of things that went on in school*
        'cos everyday I come home she'd go 'How was school' and I
        tell her [RP: Right, yeah] and that's it.

RP   *Would you like to talk about school to your dad more?*

Sadam   *(2)Yeah [RP: Right] but the thing is he is busy and he is hard*
        to talk to [RP: Right] 'cos, 'cos like he doesn't listen that
        much.

RP   *Oh doesn't he?*

Sadam   *He does listen but he won't give you good advice he just say,*
        you know, 'Just go and thump him' or something like that
        [RP: Yeah], yeah, you know so. (Sadam, 12, two parents)

Fathers' jokes often mask an incapacity to deal with the important developmental issues their sons are striving to raise with them:

RP   *What about your dad, do you ask him questions?*

Alan   *Not really, no. He's more likely to turn it as a joke and say, er,*
        shout it out and screamin' it all over the place, and say, 'Why
        you asking me questions like this for?'

RP   *Oh really, yeah.*

Alan   *Yeah, turn it into a joke. And you wanna be straight wiv him and*
        be serious, and he turns it into a joke and I wouldn't really ask
        my dad anyway. (Alan, 12, two parents)

Even issues around planning for the future tended to be handled more by mothers than fathers, although some fathers did take considerable responsibility for monitoring their sons' school progress, often within the context of disciplining them if they did not work properly. In the next example, with a boy who lives with his mother but is in solid contact with his father, there is a notion of the father's investment in the child needing to be repaid:

Archie   *I've got a progress report, it was okay but it wasn't very good.*
RP   *What does your mum and dad say to that?*
Archie   *My mum's seen it, my mum said it could've been better. My dad went away on holiday on Friday and he's not back until the 6th March just before my birthday. My birthday's the 8th March. I'm not going to show my dad it straight away I'm going to wait until after my birthday. So he doesn't angry with me. My dad said 'If I give you things, you have to give me something in return.' If he gets me something for my birthday he's going to expect me to do good in school. That's all he wants for us, he just wants me and my brother to do good in school. If he gives me something and I don't give him nothing in return then he gets angry. Like he'll take my bike away from me or a computer.*

To complicate matters, some boys found their fathers' anger easier to deal with than when their fathers were simply disappointed in them. The interpersonal dynamics here can be very complex, even when the father is reasonably available in the son's life:

Joey   *My report. That's the main thing. I just think, 'Oh what is my dad gonna say?' you know, 'cos I just like, most the time I've not been getting bad, bad reports but my dad would look on, like look at all the bad things on a report instead of the good things. 'Cos my dad wants me to do excellent, you know, so I thought to myself, 'Oh no', I'm gonna, my reports and they like, um, good in class but gets on well with work but is a bit chatty... Like last time it said that and I thought 'What's my dad gonna say?' and he says to me 'It's your life, you know, just like I want you to do well and it's up to you. If you do bad of course I'm gonna help you out but I want you to do well and be able to help yourself.' So I just [inaudible] 'Come on have a go at me. Stop saying that.'*
RP   *So you felt quite bad then when he was saying that?*
Joey   *Yeah 'cos he weren't having a go at me, he was just...*

RP   *Oh, you actually wanted him to have a go at you?*
Joey   *Yeah. I'd rather him have a go at me than say that.* (Joey, 13, two parents)

There were boys, however, for whom their fathers were more available, particularly if their mothers were seen as very busy, or depressed. In the following example, an exception but not unique in our data, the mother was working and the father unemployed. This father had not withdrawn into himself, but seemed, from the boy's account, to be present in his son's life and responsive to his concerns:

> *When I'm wiv my mum, (1) you don't tend to say that stuff, you just like, you don't say that stuff. You ask her the questions, but, you wouldn't be as (1) free, with my dad, 'cos my dad's, erm, unemployed [**RP**: Mm], and 'e's always there for me. I mean, my mum's there for me, but, she's got work and, stuff like that, and she's, workin' or she's out, on a business meeting. With my dad, when I come from school, he's there to, make sure I'm alright and, how I'm doing and, make sure I'm, I'm doing well with my homework., [**RP**: Hm] Having a good start.* (Dean, 13, mixed parentage, lone father)

On the whole, however, it is mothers who were available for boys' confidences and not fathers, with the partial exception of talk about girlfriends. Even here, the story is mixed. Some boys preferred to talk to their mothers about girls and sex because they wanted to be taken seriously, and occasionally because they explicitly rejected any notion of talking to men about intimate things, whereas others saw this as an area for 'man to man' discussion with their fathers. Seven boys indicated a preference for telling their mums about girlfriends and sex, and six their dads. Here are some examples of these various points of view:

RP   *So what kind of things then, do you talk to say your, step dad say about, about, growing up?*
Michael   *'bout any [**RP**: That you couldn't talk to your mum about?] But like, but he talks about anything like, even sex or anything.*
RP   *Right. And you couldn't talk to your mum about that?*
Michael   *Nar not really.*
RP   *Why's that?*
Michael   *I can like joke, joke aroun' say in front of my mum, but, is just, she's a lady so it's different.*

RP   *Right (1) Is, would you feel embarrassed then, talking to your mum about it?*

Michael   *Yeah probably.* (Michael, 13, two parents)

RP   *You said, um, that, er, your dad understands you more than your mum (1) um, and you can talk man to man with your dad [**Sol**: Yeah], about things like girls and, and life, I won- der if you could - sort of expand upon that. What do you mean by, by that?*

Sol   *Well (1) 'cos my dad's a man an he's gone through the boy stage an the man stage, so (2), my mum hasn't gone through the boy stage she just has gone through the girl stage an the woman stage [**RP**: Yeah], she wouldn't know [**RP**: Right], well she would probably know but I couldn't talk to her about it, or anything.*

RP   *H-how do you talk about girls with, with your dad then, what sort of things do you talk about?*

Sol   *How good they look, if they look good at all, [**RP**: Yeah], them kinda things but (1) you don't wanna know.*

RP   *Yeah. So it's about girls that you, you fancy is it, that you talk to your dad about?*

Sol   *Yeah.*

RP   *Yeah. And that would be difficult - you couldn't talk to your mum about that?*

Sol   *No.*

RP   *Why's that?*

Sol   *My mum's a woman innit?*

RP   *So what difference does that make?*

Sol   *My dad would know what I'm talking about rather than my mum.* (Sol, 13, two parents)

RP   *Are there things that you can talk about to your mum that you can't talk about to your dad then?*

Paul   *Yeah, like (1) I like had a girlfriend like mm. Every time I see my mum she goes 'You got a girlfriend?' I go like 'I haven't got time an' that'. But my dad, if I say, oh like 'I got a girl- friend' he'll go 'Oh he's got a girlfriend' and start, taking the mickey outta me an' that. [**RP**: Oh I see, yeah] My dad (1) from Liverpool.*

RP   *From Liverpool, yeah, yeah. (2) Do, when your dad - Does that put you off then telling, telling your dad things like if you've got a girlfriend?*

Paul	*Yeah. I won't tell my dad.*
RP	*You won't. Because he'll take the mickey out of you, yeah, yeah.* (Paul, 11, lone father)
RP	*But are there things that, that you can confide in or tell your mother that you couldn't tell your (1), say your (1), your mother's boyfriend, or your father? Are there things that you can talk to your mother about that (1) that you couldn't talk to them about?*
John	*What things that, what sorta things?*
RP	*I dunno. I'm asking you (1) are there, are there things that ... ?*
John	*Um. (4) Problems at school. [**RP**: Right] Um (5) For example puberty. You could ask your mother about than your father because (1) people say it would be easier if you were a boy to speak to about to your father, but I don't find it is. I think (1) for me anyway, I can speak to my mum about it. [**RP**: Mmm] An' say what all the changes are an' that. So I don't feel silly speaking about it. But I feel a bit silly speaking about it with a boy or a man.* (John, 13, mother and step-father)

Some boys have very good experiences with their fathers in the area of sex education:

Keith	*Have I spoke to my dad about sex? [**RP**: Yeah] Well it all started one day when my dad came up to me and he goes like 'Keith you've gone out and, um, I have to have a little chat with you', and, um, we sat in the sitting room and started talking about girls and, um, you know he said that, um, maybe well not maybe but one day I might do something with a girl, and I was asking him, 'What do you mean I might do something with a girl?' and he started talking about sex and that kind of stuff, and he taught me how to use protection and other things and, um, I don't think if, um, although I wanted to ask him about that but I didn't get the chance because he came and talk to me first. Well I wouldn't have dared to ask my mum ...*
RP	*Right. How did you find that?*
Keith	*(3) Um [**RP**: Were you quite pleased or?], well at first I was shocked because, um, I couldn't believe what my dad was saying to me, but after a while, after I was quite pleased that I had a chat with him. At first, although I wanted to ask him the question*

I'm glad because I didn't get any, um, I was thinking of asking the girls to ask him about it, but he came up to me first so thank God I didn't have to say anything and, um, I just thought, you know I was glad that my dad had, um, taught me something. Although I wanted to talk to him about sex but I didn't know anything about sex and all that stuff. (Keith, 11, lives with sister)

The involvement of some fathers in talking to their sons about sex without too much immature joking was highly valued by those boys who experienced it, suggesting that if this was more extended an experience of fathers it would be very beneficial to their sons. In general, however, the material from our sample of boys shows a relative (but by no means absolute) absence of fathers as serious, stable and emotionally supportive; mothers tended to carry much more of the responsibility for monitoring and helping their sons, while fathers were funny at times, harsh at other times, often unavailable and not much good at intimacy and care. However, there were exceptions to this picture and where they occurred – where fathers were really available – the boys seemed to be appreciative.

Separated fathers

All boys whose parents were separated or divorced were asked about the impact this had had on them. A few showed clearly in their responses their regret for the loss of contact with the parent who had left – in all but three cases the father:

RP *Do you think it's - it makes a difference being in a single-parent family than a two-parent family?*

Lance *Yeah, 'cos like, if you got, like a mum and a dad then if your mum says no to something then you can like, like sort of like, try and get your dad to like [inaudible]. Yeah. Or like change her mind. Or if it is the other way around. And you can like, to talk to her, talk to men about men things more than you can talk to a woman but.*

RP *Can you?*

Lance *Mm, and like girls can talk to their mothers more - than they can talk to their fathers properly and everything.*

RP *So what things can you not talk to your, when you say man things like what?*

Lance   *Like sex and stuff and (1) like, like just like growing up, just like.*

RP   *You can't talk about growing up and sex to your mum?*

Lance   *No.* (Lance, 14, lone mother)

Several boys, however, said it made no difference that their parents were separated, mainly because they felt they still saw quite a bit of both of them. However, a relatively common response, from five of the 26 sons of separated parents, was that separation had probably made things easier (although it might still be tinged with sadness, as in the example from Archie, below) because otherwise there would be severe arguments:

RP   *What difference do you think it makes being in a single-parent family as opposed to two-parent family?*

Dean   *Er, well. I'm (1) well, I'm not sure really 'cos it's a different point. 'Cos if you're with um, if my mum and dad were together and I (1) had them, they were arguing with each other, you'd think it's about you and you'd be upset 'cos you think it's all, 'cos your fault and stuff like that. But I find it's alright apart 'cos my mum and dad want, want me to be(1) healthy and they just want me to be the way I wanna be and as long as I'm hav- ing a good life and that I'm alright. But if it was together you'd think it would be different, it's a different point of view 'cos (1) I wasn't - when I (2), when I, my mum and dad were married and then my mum got pregnant, they were getting split up, they were gonna split up. Not 'cos was pregnant, 'cos my mum was pregnant, it's just they was getting split up anyway 'cos they were arguing too much an' they didn't want me in between it. So, then, but I dunno, if they were together then there'd be a lot of arguing an' then I'd get upset, 'cos, if they were arguing I'd think it was about me and then I'd be upset as well. But now they're apart and, it's just the same as long as I'm alright an' that (1) things are going away.* (Dean, 13, lone father)

RP   *Does it make any different do you think living with your mum or your dad, than say a two-parent family?*

Archie   *Yeah 'cos my mum and dad used to argue, my mum and dad used to argue all the time but then they split up because they thought that, not, they used to argue all the time so that's why my mum and dad split up. But they thought that I was taking it well, but really I felt really sad when they split up and I didn't like it.*

RP   *Did you, yeah?*

Archie *Yeah, but I didn't tell nobody except for my brother. 'Cos I thought everyone would go it's nothing really, Archie, it's nothing, don't worry about, it doesn't matter. So I didn't say nothing, except to my brother, they thought Archie's taking it really well. I did find it sad, but I had to put up with it 'cos my mum and dad used to argue a lot. They just used to argue. Everything used to be okay except for that. Something would happen and my mum and dad would just argue about it. They used to say it's a disagreement. I used to go to my mum and dad stop arguing, stop arguing. They used to say, we're just disagreeing about something. It wasn't really a bad, bad argument, they were just arguing about something.* (Archie, 14, lone mother)

As mentioned above, none of this means that boys are happy when their parents split up, but clearly there are conditions under which it can be a relief.

When relationships fail

Three boys described having relationships with parents which were clearly severely disturbed. In one case (Zac, 13, 2 parents), this was with a mother who was described as having 'a mental problem, psychotic' and whose difficulties had, according to Zac, given rise to considerable violence. In the other two cases, Alan (discussed below) and Pete (14, 2 parents) the problem was with the father. In Pete's case, the father was described in demeaning terms but also as someone who has been brutal to his son and from whom nothing could be expected: 'He just thinks I'm just an annoying little kid who is just there just trying to annoy him ... I'm just an excuse just to get annoyed and that's the way it is.'

To conclude this chapter, we want to present in a little more detail some issues raised by a boy who comes across as very unhappy in his relationship with one of his parents – in this case his father. This boy, Alan, was twelve years old, white and working-class. He impressed the interviewer with his capacity to enter into the interview, to show considerable emotion and thoughtfulness, and to be open about himself and his experiences. This is one of several instances where boys seemed to have used their interviews in what might be called 'therapeutic' ways, to take the presence of the sympathetic male interviewer as a cue for exploring issues of emotional significance, complexity and conflict.

Over the course of the two interviews, Alan described with some feeling how he was often picked on and called 'gay' because of his affectionate relationships with other boys, something which angered and distressed him greatly. He portrayed himself as quite gentle, interested in personality rather than looks in girls, attached to his mother and antagonistic both to racism (although he regarded black boys and girls as largely bullies) and to homophobia (his uncle was gay, he saw nothing either good or bad about this and despised the culture of homophobia which was rife in his school, as in most others). He also told a story, which became highly significant for his presentation of himself, of having been called 'wimp' and 'weed' by his father, who put him into karate lessons so that he could learn to stand up for himself. Alan subsequently became a karate black belt but in some ways this caused him more difficulties, because he knew that if he did hit back at the boys who teased or bullied him he might really do some harm. In fact, on one occasion when he let himself go he broke a boy's fingers and nose, producing an ambivalent response in his parents, who were proud of him for standing up for himself but thought he had gone too far. Alan, therefore, had to rein himself in and produced an account of himself to the interviewer along these lines: people thought he was weak for walking away from fights, but if they only knew they would think differently.

Alan became really emotional about two issues: being called gay and his feelings about his father. What he described, in considerable detail, was a 'lost' father who gave him nothing, who bullied and demeaned him, and who he hated. The story of this relationship is given in exceptionally full detail in the long passage quoted directly below. Parenthetically, it is worth noting that this is one of the longest connected narratives produced by any of the boys we interviewed, perhaps reflecting the intensity of Alan's feelings about his situation and the importance of his anger and sorrow:

RP   *So in what way do you not get along with each other?*
Alan   *We get along - we don't along in a sense that he thinks the world revolves around him, and we have friends over every Saturday night and they have drink with my dad and their two daughters stay the night, every Saturday and he called me selfish 'cos they used to share, in my bed, yeah, an' I used to sleep on the floor in a separate room. An' I said, 'Can I have my own bed on a Saturday night?' an' my dad called me selfish without. Everything I do, is selfish or*

ungrateful in many ways, like if I get a bigger bit of an Easter egg,
I'm selfish. If I have too much ice cream, I'm ungrateful an all this.

RP   *Right. Do you get into quite a lot of arguments with your dad?*

Alan *I don't tend to argue wiv my dad 'cos you can't win wiv him.*
He's a big man and he reckons you're never gonna hurt him and
hit him an' all of this. I don't - I wouldn't hit 'im, but I probably
would kick him. I would kick him or I would hit him if he pushed
me into it.

RP   *Would you, yeah?*

Alan *I don't see him as bad and out of order that I would hit my dad,*
but the things he's done, like he moans at my mum all the time,
an' it's like over this last month, every day he's been moanin' at
my mum and I jus go out the back near my shed and just sit down
an' watch the birds.

RP   *Mmmm.*

Alan *Mean, you can still hear it, shout, shout, shout, really, but they -*
married and they're my parents an' they shouldn't be arguin' an'
then, jus shoutin'. (2) An' then he brings us in, sayin' how
ungrateful we are, er, telling us all this rubbish, sayin', 'Why
don't you say thank you after dinners?' when we do, and all of
this. He's goin', 'D'you know what, son, no matter how old you
are, be, you're never gonna hit me or hurt me' [laughs]. And
I goes, 'D'you wanna bet? 'Cos I'm so angry, I would - I really
do feel like hittin' him sometimes, and really layin' into him, but
I know now, if my dad was to hit me and beat me up properly,
but when I'm older, and when I'm capable, if I was provoked,
I would, and I wouldn't stop.

RP   *Why do you think he said that? I mean what kind of occasions*
does he say, 'No matter how old you are, you'll never be able to
hit me and hurt me'? When does he say that?

Alan *He tells 'cos he moans at us an' I roll my eyes and turn my head,*
'cos I don' wanna hear it, and then he goes, 'Yeah, you roll your
eyes', an' all of this, 'act hard an' be a man for once.' I am
growin' up an I'm gonna be a man an' I'm gonna be a good man.
And there's him, 'Yeah, yeah, no matta what', goin' into 'You'll
never beat me up. 'You wan a bet? 'Cos I really want to hit 'im.

RP   *When he says, 'Be a man for once', does he think that you're not*
a man, then, or what?

Alan *I always used to be gettin' bullied 'cos I was soft an' all of this,*
an' so he got me into karate classes.

RP   *Right.*

Alan   *An', now I know I could hurt someone, I don't want to. He says I'm a wimp and a weed, but I don't see the point. He calls me soft an' I know I'm soft, but I wouldn't hit someone if they comin' round an' hit me on the head. I'd probably push 'em away an' 'en wouldn't hit 'em. Probably get 'em out of it, but I wouldn't hit 'em back. But I don't see the point.*

...

Alan   *Now, to think he's my dad, sometimes it makes me feel sick.*

RP   *Mmm.*

Alan   *That a man like that can be my dad, when to think that before he even knew these friends, before I even came to this school, we was a big family and we was happy. And naw, these last four years, we been steadily goin' down hill.*

RP   *Why do you think that is - why has it changed?*

Alan   *I dunno. My dad keeps wantin' to be young again. He's had cancer twice, he's nearly died. Fair enough. I understand him sometimes being a bit grouchy, but all the time? An' he has been on these pills anti-stress somefing or uver.*

RP   *Mmm.*

Alan   *He er, outa work, now he's got a job wiv 'is friends, but that only to help him out an' he gets paid a little bit o' money an' he goes there Monday to Friday, half day, so. An' 'en, ever since he's had this illness, sort of changed him. He can't - he hasn't - my dad's never been the one to play wiv you anyway, no matta if you're on the floor playin' lego, he wouldn't come down an' play wiv you. He'd sit there an' watch you then after a while go outside an' watch TV or somethin'. I know that, but even so, it's nice sometimes, jus to be a dad, to come and sit down wiv you and sometimes play wiv you, but I've never had 'at. I've never had a father that plays wiv me.*

RP   *Mmm. What about your mum. Does she play with you?*

Alan   *My mum really - I suppose she would if she had the time, but 'cos she does ironin' an' washin' 'cos we done so many activities, she 'as to wash this and iron this an the only time she gets to sit down is sometimes really late in the week night when we're in bed or on a weekend when she's sittin' down and relaxin'. My sister, she asked, dad, 'Can you play with me, a ball game?' An' he goes, 'Nah, ask your mum.' An' all this. So my mum says no, she's jus tired an my sister get the 'ump wiv both of them and stomps off and dad goes into an argument again, so, just leave it be.*

RP   *How does your mum feel when you have a bust up with your dad like, you know, do you - are you able to talk to your mum about it, and does she talk to you about it?*

Alan   *No. Me an' my mum - if my mum's in an argument, I will intervene and if I'm in an argument, my mum will stick up for me as well. So we know if there's nothing secret about me and my mum. My mum realises that he's changed and she understands the situation so she keeps sayin' that it's just me and my sister an my mum and my dad's jus there on the side when he feels like it.*

RP   *Mmm.*

Alan   *So. She understand what I'm feelin', and I understand what she's feelin'. Sometimes he comes out wiv really nasty things, like, 'I don't know why I married you' and all of this. And it really hurts my mum and I can see that. There's me sayin' - I'll get [inaudible] and really get aggressive and start shoutin' at 'im and the next thing throws me the chair and 'at's it, jus shutup an' I jus go out the back.*

The trajectory of this depressing account is reasonably clear. Alan begins with his father's selfishness and the way the father projects this onto him: the father 'thinks the world revolves around him', but it is Alan who gets called selfish for wanting his own bed to sleep in, or for getting small amounts too much of chocolate or ice cream. That this is not just another description of a father's ordinary immaturity rapidly becomes obvious: the father is a bully, relying on his size ('He's a big man and he reckons you're never gonna hurt him'); but Alan establishes right at the start that he is not frightened, just disgusted. He will at some point fight back, because of what his father does. This portrayal of the father as a teasing, provocative bully is unusually powerful here: 'He's goin', "D'you know what, son, no matta how old you are, be, you're never gonna hit me or hurt me"'; the father demeans Alan, 'be a man for once', calls him wimp and weed, verbally abuses his sister and – worst of all, it seems – his mother.

Alan's response to all this is to produce a discourse of his own comparative maturity which enables him to survive his father's attacks in the knowledge that he is better than his father makes him out to be. Part of this is that there is no alternative, but it is also because Alan judges him as a no-hoper, pathetic, not to be bothered with. Sometimes his anger gets on top of him, for instance when his father 'comes out wiv really nasty things, like, "I don't know why I married you" and all of this' towards his mother, but even then he just takes himself away in the end. Mostly, as with the bullies at school, Alan just gets out of the situation, sometimes seething, sometimes with sadness ('I just go out the back near my shed and just sit down an' watch the birds'). He takes refuge in the idea that one day he might fight back against his father, but this is part of something else, a more secure awareness of himself that is impervious to the father's assaults: 'I am growin' up an I'm gonna be a man an' I'm gonna be a good man.'

How Alan maintains this image of himself is a bit of a mystery: perhaps through his success at karate (though this is a mixed blessing), more likely because of the strength of his bond with his mother: 'She understand what I'm feelin', and I understand what she's feelin'.' Certainly Alan does not think he has ever had a good relationship with his father – he has never been involved, never interested enough to play with the children. This has got worse in the last few years in that the father's illness, introduced as 'He's had cancer twice' is seen as one cause of his decline, something which has changed the father's personality: 'An' 'en, ever since he's had this illness, sort of changed him'. However, it is not the illness as such which has damaged their life together, but the father's lack of ability to deal with it. In his own mind, Alan can make a distinction between what might be legitimate worry or depression in the face of life-threatening illness, and what is illegitimate, part of the general inadequacy of his father as a man: 'My dad keeps wantin' to be young again. He's had cancer twice, he's nearly died. Fair enough. I understand him sometimes being a bit grouchy, but all the time?' And this, says, Alan, makes him 'sick' to think that this man is his dad.

Surprisingly, given this extraordinarily negative portrayal of his father, Alan feels not that he has never had a father, but somehow that he has lost one. This becomes clearer in a slightly later passage which, in terms of its version of what life was like before the father's illness, is at odds with the material just quoted: quite nostalgic and grateful. The interviewer asks Alan about 'a time when [he] felt quite sad about something':

Alan   *(2) Yeah. When my dad was ill.*
RP   *Right.*
Alan   *I was so frightened I'd lose 'im 'cos we'd never really had an argument and I hadn't been that old to realise what an argument was, fully, 'an there I was - I was like, six, and my dad jus lyin' there in a hopital bed, with a line goin' fru his skin. An' I'm like, 'Whas that dad?'*
RP   *Mmm.*

Alan *There I am, lookin' at my dad layin' there, practically dead, that hurt.*

RP *Right.*

Alan *An' I think that me and my mum and sister had been worryin' for 'im and now all he wants to do is argue wiv us - it's not a dad, is it?*

The sad memory is of the lost, longed-for father with whom he had 'never really had an argument'; Alan and his sister and mother all worried for him and in a sense he died, returning only as 'and now all he wants to do is argue wiv us – it's not a dad, is it?' Oddly, though, even this might be better than nothing: Alan goes on to comment that when he talks to his girl friends about his troubles with his father:

> *they say, try, try be nice to him. Try and play his game and all of this, 'cos most of 'em have lost dads fru uver fings and it makes me realise that I'm quite lucky, although he is arguing, and he's really quite out of order, that I'm still lucky to have a dad And that's the sort of thing still makes me care for him in a way. To realise I'm so lucky to have a dad.*

Given what has gone before, it seems unlikely that the memory here is of a 'real' loving father, although probably he was more available pre- than post-illness. But what Alan seems to be working on is a notion of fathering which might have once been available to him – might, in some debased way, still be of use. Possibly there is some responsiveness to the interviewer in this, which encourages the fantasy of the nurturing father. In any event, it does not last long. Shortly afterwards in the interview there is the following exchange:

RP *Right. Do you look forward to the future, do you have any anxieties or worries?*

Alan *I have worries in the fact that one day I know I'm gonna die and one day I'm gonna have children - hopefully - and a wife an' I worry that I won't turn, I'll turn out like my dad.*

RP *Do you, yeah?*

Alan *Yeah, an' that's what I don't wanna do.*

RP *Right.*

Alan *All my friends have dads that build tree houses wiv them and play wiv 'em. I can't build nothing. 'Can I borrow your hammer dad?', 'As long as you put it back afterwards', 'Do you wanna*

> *come an' help me dad?', 'No, I'm cooking'. Other dads would just, 'Yeah, come on I'll help you hammer that in' or somefin. 'Okay then'. You be pleased for your dad to help you. Like me - my friends say, 'Why isn't your dad helpin' you?' Like my friend, Lewis, 'Why ain't you dad helpin' you?', 'Oh, er, he's cookin'. You make up excuses 'cos you know your dad wouldn't, he's probably layin' on the sofa.*

RP   *Mmm.*

Alan   *It upsets me when I go round my friend Lewis's house, 'cos he's had trees, and his dad's bought a tree all the way from Epping Forest that was on sale, and put it in and it's taken well, and he's built a tree house in it and it's really upsettin' for me that his dad helped him build a tree house and my dad won't even help me put a radio together. Or, even play wiv me. It hurts.*

RP   *Right.*

Alan   *To know that - really, I don't think I've got a dad.*

RP   *Mmm.*

Alan   *I know it sounds cruel, but to me, all a dad is, to make me - and put food on our plate. I mean, that's all a dad seems to me.*

RP   *Mmm*

Alan   *I mean, I know you're meant to love your dad, but [quietly] I haven't found a reason to love my dad.*

RP   *Right.*

Alan   *I mean he hasn't done nothing wiv me, has he?*

There are many compelling things about this interchange, which draws again on a very concrete fantasy of the father doing something with his son, a kind of generational transfer or masculine rite of building, as well as a symbolic set of connections with making a home. But for Alan it is not just that his father fails in the traditional masculine tasks, that he cooks instead of hammers. It is rather that he hasn't 'found a reason to love [his] dad', his dad does nothing with him, is nothing to him. What this produces, it seems, interspersed with the anger, is despair.

Conclusion

In this chapter, we have drawn attention to the use that boys made of the interview to describe aspects of their experiences of their parents, and of the significance of the image of 'fathering' to them. We have stressed the theme of fathers' immaturity, which often makes them fun to be with, especially in separated families where mothers are worn down by the pressures of keeping things going. But this same immaturity makes the fathers unavailable, physically sometimes, emotionally very often, to help their sons with issues of importance: worries, hopes, ways of dealing with the world. Notwithstanding this, many boys have positive experiences of their fathers which they cherish and seem clearly to benefit from. Many more confide in their mothers and seem to respect them, despite often seeing them as having different interests and attitudes of mind.

Some material from one boy, Alan, was presented at length because of the intensity and poignancy with which he describes the breakdown in his relationship with his father. Amongst the many interesting things in this interview, Alan's maintenance of an alternative vision of fathering in opposition to his deeply dismal experience of his own father is of great interest. His account displays considerable anger and unhappiness, but also holds onto an idea, partly nostalgic, partly aspirational, that there might be something else on offer, that caught up with Alan's determination to become a 'good man' there could be a 'good father' somewhere. What Alan fears is turning out like his father; what he wants is a father who is involved with him, interested in him, available. Alan seems to have derived protection from his closeness to his mother who, he says elsewhere, can do no wrong; this has given him some inner confidence that he is basically all right himself, whatever anyone might say. But his bitterness remains: faced with our interviewer, an adult male who is interested in him and encourages him to speak, he offers a lament for a damaged and now psychologically lost father who has been evacuated from the space symbolised by the 'fathering' which so many boys imagine and desire.

Conclusion

Throughout this book, we have emphasised how rich and full of expression the accounts boys give of their lives can be. The image of the angrily grunting and inarticulate teenager is not one which stands up to scrutiny when one looks at what can happen when boys are given the opportunity to reflect on their experiences and are encouraged to talk. It is worthy of note that almost all the boys who were interviewed individually became engaged in very thoughtful and rich discussions with the interviewer, often entrusting him with deeply felt material which they seemingly did not speak about elsewhere. Material of this kind included uncertainties over friendships, disappointments with parents, anger with absent or unavailable fathers, feelings of rejection and 'stuckness' in relationships, ideas about girls and fears and aspirations for the future. All this suggests that, given the right circumstances, boys can be very thoughtful about themselves and their predicament. Even at age 11, they are often capable of reflecting in a complex way on how their actual lives are at odds with what they would wish them to be, and even about how constraining certain aspects of masculine identity might be for them. They often spoke particularly poignantly about losses in their lives and also about how much value they placed upon parents who attended to them sensitively and seriously – and how disappointed they were by parents who did not.

What it is that produces such a contradiction between the everyday assumptions about boys and the reality of their capacity to show psychological depth and sophistication is a question of some complexity. As Hollway and Jefferson (2000) suggest in their description of a project interviewing working-class people about crime, perhaps it is simply that most individuals – boys, in our case – have very limited encounters with people who really listen to them in an active, sympathetic and thoughtful way. Hollway and Jefferson link this with the idea of 'recognition', which they gloss as follows:

> Recognition is not about reassurance, if that is based on the avoidance of
> distress and therefore unreliable in telling the truth. It depends on the feeling
> that the other can be relied upon to be independent, to reflect back a reality
> which is not compromised by dependence or avoidance. To strive after this as
> the basis for an ethical relationship in research is to pursue the values of
> honesty, sympathy and respect. (p. 99)

This kind of recognition is thought within some psychoanalytic theories
to be a basic necessity for the emergence of psychological well-being
(see for example Benjamin, 1998); that is, seriously acknowledging the
existence of others *as subjects* is a crucial element in producing people
who have confidence in their worth and their own capacity for thoughtfulness and positive relationships. Perhaps it is no accident that 'respect'
and 'dissing' (disrespecting) are a powerful opposition in the life and language of contemporary British young people, sometimes as a joke but
often as an indication of their perceived positions as undervalued and dismissed. As we described in the Introduction, young men in particular are
most commonly regarded as social problems, a responsibility for 'society'(that is, adults) who have to take steps to manage them and constrain
them so that the turbulence of their developmental demands are properly
controlled. The boys we interviewed had a strong consciousness of this
and often internalised and reproduced it themselves, in their discussions,
for example, of boys' immaturity and the wildness of some difficult boys.
However, they also showed great strength of feeling about the struggle
they have to make themselves heard by adults; more to the point, when
faced with an adult who did work hard in order to listen to them, they
showed great life and fun, and considerable emotional as well as intellectual intelligence. A lesson we draw from this, perhaps generalisable, is
that part of the 'problem' of young masculinities is the construction of
young masculinities as a problem – that is, that this 'problem' is discursively produced and reproduced as a cultural phenomenon. This embod-
ies a major lack of recognition, experienced daily by many boys and
young men in British society.

Throughout this book, we have mainly allowed boys to 'speak for
themselves' and seen our primary task as representing their views, and
those of girls. This has not meant that we have completely neglected an
analytic or interpretive stance, however. For one thing, we have structured
the material given us by our participants to draw out views on issues of

particular theoretical and social interest. In addition, by the juxtaposition of different views, sometimes held by the same boys at different points in their interviews, we have tried to articulate the range and diversity of viewpoints and to show how these are structured in relation to class and 'race' differences. A great deal has come from this; for example, one compelling finding which we have dwelt upon at length is the impossibility of understanding masculinities in isolation from other constituting features of boys' lives. At least in our London sample, it is clear that masculinities are constructed out of a complex network of identity factors, including 'race', ethnicity, social class and sexuality. This means, for example, that young masculinities are routinely 'racialised'; that is, they are experienced as marked by fantasies of 'race' plus features of cultural life. Being positioned as a young man within, for instance, Muslim culture in London is different from growing up white; both these kinds of masculinity are also experienced in the context of ideas (fantasies) of African Carribean black masculinity with its associations (to the boys) of certain kinds of attractive style and physical 'hardness'. Both class and sexuality are also entwined with this process of generating masculine identities, a process visible in assumptions about physical prowess and about heterosexuality. Indeed, the construction of hegemonic masculinity as a contrast with a repudiated 'gay' identity is a major feature of young men's talk. Homophobia is one clear marker of much emergent masculinity in this age group, suggesting that the struggle to establish oneself as 'normatively heterosexual' is a very significant feature of identity formation for these boys.

In addition to this, however, we have tried to hold onto the possibility of analysing the identity constructions of boys as performances generated in the context of tensions between social structures and individual anxieties. We have begun to demonstrate that social 'discourses' are immensely powerful in making available specific masculinities which boys can inhabit, but that not only the 'choice' of (or, better, positioning within) any specific set of masculine identities, but also the feelings aroused by this positioning, are entwined with complex and often unconscious emotional states. For example, in our analysis of racism we have described how white masculinity is produced in discursive tension with racist ideology, and how the adoption of racist positions by boys can be related to unconscious feelings of loss and anxiety about 'otherness'. We believe that this combination of discursive and psychoanalytically informed psychology can move forward debates about what can be 'read into' and 'read out of' personal narratives.

It is worth considering here the sense that we make of what the boys and girls in our study said. We have summarised some general findings in the Introduction and given more details throughout the book, but there is also a place for a more interpretive, perhaps speculative, formulation based on these. In our view, some major elements in the identity constructions of young men in contemporary London are as follows:

1. Boys struggle to find a forum in which they can try out masculine identities which can be differentiated from the 'hegemonic' codes of macho masculinity. The ways in which masculinities are 'policed' by peers and adults (for instance, teachers) communicate to boys a message that alternative, what are conventionally thought of as 'softer', ways of being are abnormal for males – that they are girlish and hence subject to opprobrium and exclusion. This narrows the possibilities as boys constrict their identities to a polarity in which they are either 'properly masculine' or feminine, with the feminine pole also being linked to homosexuality. For all boys, not just those who do not experience themselves as 'hegemonic', this is problematic, in that the danger of wandering from the path of 'true masculinity' has to be continuously monitored and guarded against. For those boys who do not fit the hegemonic ideal, a great deal of work has to be done in creating accounts of how 'in fact' they are really masculine, despite appearances; but even 'hard' boys suffer from the isolation imposed on them through fear of intimacy or expressing their vulnerabilities. As a consequence, they become more extreme in their repudiation of these possible other masculinities, because recognising them evokes a void in their lives.

2. Boys often have considerable fun together and on the whole have good relationships with parents, albeit usually differentiated by gender, with more serious and intimate contact with their mothers and more joking interactions with their fathers. However, many boys communicate a strong sense of loss when talking about their relationships, particularly with fathers, and sometimes idealise the ways in which girls interact or other boys' fathers engage with their sons. In some cases, this is because fathers are physically absent; quite often, however, it seems to reflect a broader sense of something missing emotionally in the lives of boys and young men – perhaps of men in general. This is linked with the first point above, about the narrowness of acceptable masculinities, but it is also a more specific assertion: despite bravado and claims to the contrary on the part of boys

themselves, they very frequently communicate a lack at the centre of their masculine identities. This lack relates to the impoverished emotional contact they so often have with fathers and with other boys, and it is experienced by them as more deeply enervating than they can consciously acknowledge.

3. Boys are very well aware of their standing as socially and educationally problematic and resent this too. Sometimes this feeds into a vicious cycle in which they enact delinquencies as a way of expressing the anger which they feel; very frequently, it is visible in an attitude of antagonism towards adults, who are seen as disparaging boys and favouring girls all the time. It is not that boys necessarily disagree with the discourse of girls' greater 'maturity', but the possibility that they too regard girls as more mature in their attitudes to work and relationships does not prevent them seeing the discourse itself as an indication of how society as a whole (represented particularly by the adults they know) writes them off. The refuge boys take in the hardness of hegemonic masculinity, in sharp and aggressive styles and attitudes, is partly a response to this perception. The frequent reference to 'fairness', especially in relation to being treated *unfairly* by teachers, is also part of this phenomenon.

4. Some boys suffer especially badly from the narrowness of conventional masculinities: for example boys who are not physically hard, who are bookish, who find teasing and 'cussing' difficult to manage, who are dependent and emotionally vulnerable. Some of these boys might find relationships difficult under any circumstances, but the construction of masculinities on the basis of a forceful rejection of non-hegemonic alternatives contributes strikingly to these boys often being friendless, the butt of jokes, bullying and homophobic insults, and unable to share their experiences and anxieties with others. It takes considerable sensitivity, but under the right circumstances – which sometimes includes the presence of girls in a group – very painful stories can be evoked and these can have an unsettling impact on even other 'hard' boys.

5. As described at the start of this Conclusion and in Chapter 1, boys can be emotionally and intellectually articulate, thoughtful and insightful. It is as if they need permission to be so in a non-moralistic context, and that when they are like this it highlights both their neediness and their promise. While 'hardness' is high status, most boys have a firm appreciation of moral codes and of the importance of close and supportive relationships; they just do not have enough of the latter, and have to get by with cussing and comradeship at best, alienation at

worst. Many boys want to become good fathers and have succeeded in preserving an image of what this might mean, sometimes against the odds. The fantasy space which allows this is both impressive and at times upsetting, as they hold onto an image of a possible future which might be better than their present situation.

What to do about boys

We have not intended, in this book, to test out alternative ways of doing 'boys work', but we nevertheless have some suggestions built out of our primary impression of the need to validate a wider range of ways of being as attributes of acceptable masculine identities. First, the experience we had interviewing boys in groups, both single sex and mixed, made it clear that the open discussion format – perhaps particularly with an adult other than a teacher – could very productively allow the basis for thoughtful discussion. Boys did joke and tease and at times mess around, but it was not difficult either to manage them (adults' perennial fear) or to get them to talk in focused ways about their perceptions and experiences. Moreover, at times and especially in the mixed sex groups, the discussions seemed to open out new avenues for boys to think about redressing the distortions produced by the constraining hand of hegemonic masculinity. We cannot really say if the fact of our interviewer being a man was helpful, but it is possible that this was the case, especially given so many boys' complaints about the men in their lives and their wish for better contact with them. We would certainly advocate the active creation of discussion spaces of this kind, using small groups which can tackle issues and sustained by adults patient enough to get past the teasing and cussing surface. Schools are the obvious places in which to do this as children are present there willy-nilly; our experience is that such groups can thrive in the school environment.

Secondly, the tendency of many intervention projects to focus on boys on their own and to offer mainly conventional 'male' activities such as sports, has an obvious rationale in building group solidarity and indeed making the projects acceptable to boys, but our view is that too much emphasis on what are taken to be 'natural' boys' activities feeds into the discourse of a narrowly exclusionary 'hegemonic' masculinity and thus makes the construction of alternatives more difficult. For example, what seemed to provoke some boys to rethink their attitudes to football in our study was the presence of girls who could challenge the way boys acted towards one another when playing, and indeed could offer a model in which football was less abrasive and all-consuming, and more fun. At times, this led boys to acknowledge the difficulties involved for some of them in managing the oppressively competitive and homophobic policing of masculinity through football, and to recognise the difficulties experienced more generally by 'soft' boys. Even without girls present, our interviews showed that boys responded positively to relatively gentle challenges about the effects of narrowly constructed masculinities on themselves and others and, as described above, gave evidence that many boys wish for something different, broad enough to allow for greater intimacy with, and tolerance of, others. Our suggestion here is not that the importation of girls into boys' activities will in itself solve the problems (although more flexible mixed-sex groups and events in schools and youth-work settings would probably be of benefit, at least to boys), but rather that the idea that boys' 'excess energy' should be channelled into boyish things like sport and military or outward-bound schemes misses the point that, on their own, these are exactly the kind of 'hard' activities which support the construction of the narrow mode of masculinity which is itself a large part of the 'problem' of boys. This is not to oppose football and other sports – as we have noted, girls' *enjoyment* of football, played differently, was part of the challenge to the boys we interviewed. It is rather to argue for a broadening of boys work (in line with some contemporary projects) to confront the assumption that real boys only do hard things.

While we are critical of the emphasis placed on boys-only activities as ways of 'taming' their supposedly wild nature, equally we are concerned about the tendency to problematise boys in boys-only groups. Boys were constructed by almost all the girls we interviewed, as well as some of the teachers we spoke to, as troublesome and immature when they were with other boys, and, in striking contrast, as sensitive and thoughtful when they were not. As we have reported, boys were much louder and funnier in the single-sex groups than they were when interviewed individually, and many of them were much more misogynistic. But the view that boys are basically thoughtful, reflective and sociable so long as they are not with other boys serves to reproduce boys' problematic behaviour as a feature of what they are like together. As we argued above, the boys we interviewed were aware of being seen as troublesome; importantly, however, their stories about being picked upon by teachers or other adults were usually when they were with other boys – in the class, the playground, assembly or on the buses. It was this problematisation of boys in groups which made them resentful and may have contributed to their behaving badly when with other boys.

To complicate this, however, most boys themselves drew a radical distinction between what it was like being with a group of boys than when they were on their own with an adult or with girls. Some of these boys, when interviewed individually, were critical of the insensitivity and competitiveness of boys in groups. In opposition to this, they idealised girls and their (potential) relations with them and/or constructed themselves as autonomous individuals who stood out from their male peers, were not obsessed with football, knew how to be mature and how to be civil to girls, and were, at least in part, concerned about their work. While these boys may have been engaging in critique of popular, 'hegemonic' forms of masculinity, they often sounded quite elitist, and like the girls and the teachers who condemned boys' collective behaviour, appeared to preclude the possibility of boys being 'soft,' caring, sensitive, thoughtful and reflective with their male peers.

In encouraging boys to be critical of hegemonic masculinities, we would stress that it is important not to idealise and align with boys on their own in opposition to boys in groups, but instead to highlight the contradictory ways boys position themselves and are positioned by others in groups of boys and 'on their own'. That is, we need to think of these contradictions as key features characterising contemporary young masculinities, which boys should be encouraged to reflect upon and explore. This, we suggest, can best be done working with boys in *combinations* of single-sex and mixed groups. As noted above, boys could become very thoughtful when faced with girls' criticism; however, if we confine 'working with boys' to boys in mixed groups, one danger is that this might reinforce the assumption that with girls (so long as there are not too many boys present) boys can be sensitive, but as soon as they are with their mates they revert to their true, troublesome selves. We suggest, in contrast, that by encouraging boys to talk about themselves and their relations in single-sex groups, close and supportive relations with other boys can be forged. (This was certainly possible, as we saw among some of the boys we interviewed in single-sex groups.) One way of encouraging boys to reflect upon their different and contradictory identities would be to remind them when they were in the single-sex group of what they were like and what they said when they were in the mixed group, and vice versa. This needs to be done in a sensitive way, for it may easily be interpreted by the boys, especially in the light of the contemporary moral panic and their awareness of this, as an accusation of inconsistency.

An area which stood out for us in our interview material was that of the strong sense of loss so many boys communicated when talking about their relationships with parents (especially fathers), and more broadly when they acknowledged the difficulty of speaking intimately to others. There really does seem to be an embargo on close, dependent contact between young men and between them and their fathers, which feeds into an idealisation of girls and women that itself is stereotyped and alternates with overt misogyny. Hard though it obviously is for most fathers to respond in ways boys want, presumably because they are themselves the product of a culture which constructs masculinity as alien to dependence, this is an area of fundamental importance, and many boys seem to be asking for change. The 11 to 14-year-olds we interviewed enjoyed their fathers' jokes and teasing, but even those with good relationships were explicit in wishing for more emotional access to their fathers, and appreciative of it when it occurred. Perhaps one small idea here, arising from our observation of the richness of the boys' talk in groups and in individual interviews, is to get parents actively involved in such discussions – in schools, in clubs or anywhere else where boys and men might be.

In this section, we have been laying stress on what might be done for boys, but of course there are very broad implications with regard to gender, 'race' and class relationships. British masculinities (as others) are socially constructed from within a culture in which sexual, racial and class inequalities are still deeply embedded, and these are reflected in the ways in which boys make sense of themselves, in what they take to be acceptable and what they oppose. For most boys, femininity is disparaged even when girls are desired and at times idealised; social class is an axis around which different masculinities form (for example, physical hardness versus academic elitism); and ethnicity is a focus for contestation and (through racism) abuse. Homophobia is rife in schools, both as part of boys' general distancing from femininity and as a set of specifically oppressive practices aimed at boys who do not meet the hegemonic 'ideal', or who might actually be gay. The result of all this, for girls as well as for boys, is to sustain discourses of gender identity which are narrow and constraining and which reproduce inequalities and suffering from generation to generation.

Tackling all this is obviously mostly a task at the general social policy and cultural level, and as such beyond the scope of what we can deal with in this book. However, facing boys and men, teachers and youth workers, educationalists and the like with the ways in which these social factors structure the possibilities of masculine identities is one way in to challenging their power. We found that boys could be sophisticated and thoughtful about all these things – about what they could learn from relationships with girls (though they tended to idealise and disparage them), about how social class is divisive (though they usually reiterated class assumptions in their talk), about the destructive power of homo-phobia on their relationships with each other (though they continued to mock and pillory boys thought to be gay) and about the injustices of racism (though they drew on discourses of 'race' continually). Building on this thoughtfulness without moralising but by simply questioning boys' experiences – and also without embodying sexism, racism and homophobia in teaching and other adult practices – will never be enough on its own, but at least is something which could be done, and could make a difference to boys.

Appendices

1 Details of individual and group interviews conducted with boys and girls

mc = middle class
wc = working class
? = class indeterminate
age is given in brackets immediately after the name.

School 1 (state mixed)

Boys

Archie (14) mixed parentage mc, lone mother, half brother aged 15
Greg (11) black African mc, lone mother, 3 sisters aged 15, 18 and 20
James (12) white English wc, 2-parent family, sister aged 7, brother aged 13
Kim (13) Asian Chinese wc, 2-parent family, 4 sisters aged 9, 15, 16 and 23 and
    3 brothers aged 17, 20 and 22
Sol (13) black African Caribbean mc, 2-parent family, 7 older brothers
Vandad (12) white Turkish wc, 2-parent family, 1 sister aged 8

Girls

Christina (11) Vietnamese, 2-parent family, 3 sisters aged 6, 7 and 14
Christine (14) black African, dad lives and works in Africa, lives with mum and
    3 sisters aged 10, 5 and 1
Emma (14) white English, lone father, 1 brother, aged 11 and 3 sisters, aged 2, 7
    and a twin sister,
Lisa (11) white English, mother and stepfather, sister aged 14
Nasha (14) black African Caribbean, lone mother, 2 brothers aged 9 and 10
Susan (11) black African Caribbean wc, lone mother, 2 sisters aged 22 and 26

School 2 (private mixed)

Boys

Arthur (12) white English mc, 2-parent family, younger brother
Keith (11) black African mc, living with sister in UK, 5 sisters, 3 of whom live
    in UK, aged 24, 26 and 28, lives with 24-year-old
Han (11) Asian mc, lives with aunt and uncle and cousins, girl aged 13 and boy
    aged 6 in UK

Mark (15) white English mc, lone mother, no siblings
Praful (14) Asian mc, 2-parent family (only one interview), plenty of cousins –
 mainly girls, no siblings
Terry (14) white English mc, 2-parent family, sister aged 16, brother aged 19

School 3 (state mixed)

Boys

Benny (14) white English wc, 2-parent family (only one interview), 2 sisters
 aged 5 and 15, brother aged 18
Chris (11) white English wc, mother and stepfather, no siblings
Don (14) black wc, lone mother (only one interview)
Ferai (11) black mc, 2-parent family, brother aged 16, sister aged 19
Harry (12) white English wc, mother and stepfather, sister aged 8
Joey (13) white English wc, 2-parent family, brother aged 9
Maurice (14) white English mc, 2-parent family, no siblings

School 4 (private mixed)

Boys

Joe (12) black African Caribbean mc, 2-parent family, brother aged 5 and sister
 aged 18
Lance (14) black African Caribbean mc, lone mother, brother aged 13
Pete (14) white English mc, 2-parent family, brother aged 16
Raymond (12) mixed parentage mc, 2-parent family, 3 brothers aged 3, 4 and 8
 and 2 sisters aged 6 and 9
Sam (14) Asian mc, 2-parent family, 2 sisters aged 11 and 12
Scott (12) white English mc 2-parent family, brother aged 9

Girls

Jane (13) white English mc, 2-parent family, brother aged 13
Janice (14) white English mc, 2-parent family, sister aged 9
Judy (11) white English mc, 2-parent family, sister aged 13
Petra (13) black African Caribbean, lone mother, sisters aged 26 (lives with
 them) and 24
Sarah (11) mixed parentage mc, 2-parent family, sister aged 8
Yasmine (14) Turkish, aged 13, 2-parent family, sister aged 16 and brother aged 17

School 5 (state mixed)

Boys

Andy (13) white English wc, 2-parent family, sister aged 5
Donald (12) white English wc, lone mother, half-brother aged 11, 2 half-sisters
 aged 13 and 15
Julius (13) black African class?, lone mother, sister aged 19, brother aged 17
Oliver (12) white English wc, 2-parent family, 2 brothers aged 19 and 23 and
 step-sister (rarely see) about 20

Reg (13) white English wc, 2-parent family (only one interview), 4 sisters aged 4, 6, 10 and 13

Simon (12) white Turkish wc, 2-parent family, 2 sisters aged 2 and 11

School 6 (state mixed)

Boys

Calvin (12) black African mc, 2-parent family, 2 brothers, 1 aged 18, hasn't seen the other one

Daniel (12) black African Caribbean mc, lone mother, 3 sisters, 1 aged 17 doesn't live with him and 2 younger sisters

Gerald (12) white English Jewish mc, 2-parent family, 2 half-sisters in their 30s

Georgi (11) white half-Italian, half-English mc, 2-parent family, 2 brothers aged 7 and 18 and 1 sister aged 14

Olu (11) black African wc, lone mother, 2 sisters aged 2 and 6, and 3 brothers aged 14, 18, and 20

Pervaiz (12) Asian class?, lone mother, no siblings

Girls

Andrea (11) white English, lives with mum and her boyfriend, brother aged 17

Alison (12) black African Caribbean, lone mother, 2 sisters aged 4 and 5 (one lives with her father)

Angie (14) black African, 2-parent family, 2 sisters aged 2 and 18, and 1 brother aged 10

Dawn (13) white English wc, 2-parent family, 2 sisters aged 7 and 12

Diana (14) white Kosovo, 2-parent family, 2 sisters

Yemi (13) black African wc, lives with mother and stepfather, 4 brothers, aged 0, 1, 6, 9 and 1 sister aged 13

School 7 (state single sex)

Boys

Carl (13) black African Caribbean class?, 2-parent family (only one interview) brother aged 17

Charles (11) white English mc, 2-parent family, no siblings

David (11) white (half-English/Italian) mc, 2-parent family, 1 brother aged 11

George (14) black African mc, lone mother, 3 brothers aged 8, 12 and 20, 1 sister aged 17

John (13) white English wc, mum and stepdad, no siblings

Mo (14) Asian (Afghan) mc, 2-parent family, 1 sister aged 19

Norman (13) white English mc, 2-parent family, 2 sisters aged 16 and 18

Paul (11) white English wc, lone father, 2 brothers aged 2 and 5 live with mum and he and his older brother aged 14 live with their dad

Sean (11) mixed parentage wc, lone mother, 1 brother aged 7

Tony (13) white English mc, 2-parent family, 1 brother aged 10 and 1 sister aged 16

School 8 (private single sex)

Boys

Albert (13) white English mc, 2-parent family, one interview
Angus (12) white English mc, 2-parent family, no siblings
Charles (12) white English mc, 2-parent family, 2 sisters aged 11 and 7
Crispin (13) white English mc, 2-parent family, brother and 2 sisters all in their 20s
Dave (11) white English mc, lone mother, brother aged 8 and sister aged 14, one interview
Thomas (13) white English mc, 2-parent family, 1 sister aged 15

School 9 (state mixed)

Boys

Jerry (12) white English wc, 2-parent family, brother aged 17
Derek (14) white English wc, lives for a week with mum and a week with dad, 2 brothers aged 9 and 12
Zac (13) Asian mc, 2-parent family, 2 brothers aged 8 and 14 and 1 sister aged 17
Barry (12) white Greek class?, lone mother, 3 brothers aged 3, 8 and 11, 1 sister aged 15
Tariq (11) Asian mc, 2-parent family, 1 sister aged 15
Alan (12) white English wc, 2-parent family, sister aged 9

School 10 (state mixed)

Boys

Rob (12) white English wc, 2-parent family, 2 sisters aged 8 and 11
Craig (11) black African Caribbean mc?, lone mother, brother aged 20 lives in Jamaica, 3 sisters aged 11, 15 and 19
Jed (14) white English mc, 2-parent family (only one interview), 2 brothers aged 22 and 24
Jim (12) white half-Greek, half-English wc, 2-parent family, brother aged 9
Michael (13) white half-Greek, half-English mc, mother and stepfather, 1 sister aged 16 and 2 half sisters aged 5 and 12, not living with him.
Mustafa (13) white Iranian mc, lone mother, brother aged 18 lives in Iran

Girls

Claire (11) Africa Caribbean, lone mother, 3 brothers aged 14, 10 and 5, and 1 sister aged 13
Ethel (14) English white, lone mother, 2 brothers aged 16 and 18
Felicity (11) English white wc, 2-parent family, 1 brother aged 13
Iona (12) Turkish, 2-parent family, 2 sisters aged 3 and <1 year
Pauline (13) African Caribbean, 2-parent family, 2 sisters aged 11 and 15
Rosa (14) Turkish Cypriot, 2-parent family, 2 younger sisters

School 11 (private single sex)

Boys

Colin (14) mixed parentage mc, lone father (only one interview), sister aged 8
Graham (12) white English mc, 2-parent family, sister aged 14
Ibrahim (12) Asian class? 2-parent family, 3 sisters aged 6, 9 and 14
Leroy (14) black African mc, 2-parent family, brother aged 13, 2 sisters aged 10 and 11
Matthew (14) white English mc, 2-parent family, brother aged 21, sister aged 8
Ranjiv (12) Asian mc, 2-parent family, brother aged 16

School 12 (state single sex)

Billy (14) white English wc, 2-parent family, 2 sisters aged 10 and 17
Bob (14) mixed parentage mc, lone mother, brother aged 17
Christos (11) white Greek wc, 2-parent family, 1 brother aged 10, 2 sisters aged 10 and 13
Jack (13) black African mc, 2-parent family, 2 brothers aged 10 and 17
Khalid (12) Asian wc, 2-parent family, 3 brothers aged 14, 18 and 19
Sadam (12) Asian wc, 2-parent family, no siblings

2   Characteristics of the participants

Table 1   Boys interviewed individually (78) by age and ethnicity

Ethnicity	*Age*					*Total*
	11	*12*	*13*	*14*	*15*	
Asian	2	5	2	3		12
Black	5	3	4	4		16
Mixed parentage	1	1	1	3		6
White	7	17	11	8	1	44
Total	15	26	18	18	1	78

Table 2   Boys interviewed individually (78) by ethnicity and social class

Class	*Ethnicity*				*Total*
	Asian	*Black*	*Mixed*	*White*	
Working	3	2	1	20	26
Middle	7	11	4	23	45
Unsure	2	3	1	1	7
Total	12	16	6	46	78

Table 3   Boys interviewed individually by family structure

Family structure	2-parent	Mother and step-father	Lone father	Lone mother	1/2 mother and 1/2 father	Relatives
Frequency	51	4	3	17	1	2

Table 4   Group interviews (45) by gender and ethnicity

Mixed gender	Single sex	Multi-ethnic	Monoethnic black	Monoethnic white English	Monoethnic Asian	Monoethnic Turkish
9	36	34	3[1]	5[2]	2	1

Notes: [1] Of the monoethnic group interviews with black children, one of these was with middle-class children only. [2] Of the monoethnic group interviews with white children, one of these was with working class children only, and two with middle-class children only.

Table 5   Girls interviewed individually (24) by age and ethnicity

School year	Ethnicity				Total
	Asian	Black	White	Mixed	
7	1	4	6	1	12
9	0	5	7	0	12
Total	1	9	13	1	24

Table 6   Girls interviewed individually by family structure

Type of family	2-parent	Mother and step father	Lone father	Lone mother
Frequency	14	3	1	6

3   Protocol for group interviews

These are more loosely structured than the individual interviews. The following is a list of some of themes, and questions around these, which were raised in the group interviews. It should be stressed, though, that what themes were covered and the direction the interview took depended on the interests and dynamics of the particular group. Though similar sorts of topics were addressed in the group than the individual interviews, in the group interviews there was much more variation on which topics were covered and the amount of time spent on these. For example, issues around ethnicity dominated the conversation in some of the monoethnic interviews, and relations between boys and girls were highlighted in most of the mixed-gender interviews.

Introductions
Could each of you tell me a bit about yourselves, your name, age, what your parents/guardians do, where they come from, and also could you tell me something about your interests.

The group
Do you all know each other? Do you mix much with each other? Who do you go around with? Why? Do boys go around in groups or on their own? What's it like being with other boys? What do you do with other boys?

Development
What was it like when you first came to the school? How do you get on with older/younger boys in the school? Have you changed much in the last two or three years? If so, how? Do you think much about the future? What do you imagine you will be doing? Do you think you might change? If so how? Do you look forward to the future? Have you any worries?

School
What do you like, dislike about school? What kind of teachers do you like/dislike? Are some boys popular at school? What makes them popular? Are some boys unpopular? Why? Are any boys here popular? How does this school compare with your last school? Is it different or much the same here? How do you get on with boys from other schools? Are you glad you go to this school or would you prefer to be in another? Do you have any worries about schoolwork and homework or is it OK?

Relations with girls
Do you mix much with girls? If not why not? If so when do you mix with them and what do you do with them? Is it similar or different being with girls as it is with boys? Do you mix more or less with girls than you did in primary school? Would you like to be in a mixed or a single-sex school? Do boys have girls as friends? Do you? Do you? What's it like having girls as friends? Is it different having girlfriends than girls as friends? Do boys in your year have girlfriends? Do you? Do you imagine having a girlfriend? Would you want to have a girlfriend?

Comparing girls and boys
Do you think boys and girls are similar or different? If different how? Are there different kinds of girls? Do some girls do things boys usually do? If so what do you think of them? Do some boys do things girls usually do? If so what do you think of them? Do girls and boys get treated the same or differently at school?

Family

Have you got brothers/sisters? How do you get on with them? Is it different or similar having a brother/sister? Do you do different or similar things with them? How do you get on with your mum/dad? Do you do similar or different things with them? Do you talk about different or similar things with them? Do your parents treat you in the same way as your brothers/sisters?

Interests

What do you like doing at home? Do you have any hobbies? Do you watch much TV? What programmes do you like and why? Do you watch films? What do you like and why? Do you play computer games? What games do you like? Who do you play with? Do you play on your own, with other boys, with girls? Is it different or similar playing with boys and girls?

Ethnicity

Do you think of yourself as having a 'race'? If so what? Do all the boys at the school mix a lot with boys from other 'races' or do they tend to go around in separate 'race' groups? What about you? What about your best friends? Do they tend to be from a particular 'race' or are they mixed? Do you think there are differences between boys from different 'races' or are they much the same? Have you come across or experienced racism at all? If so where, and what happened? Is there any racism in school? Are there differences between girls from different ethnic backgrounds. If so what?

Reflections

How did you find the interview? Was it what you expected it to be like? Would it have been different if there had been girls present/Would it have been different if it had been all boys/all girls? Would it have been different if it had been a woman interviewer? Would it have been different if it had been a black interviewer?

4   Protocol for individual interviews

Rationale for the interview

The aim of the interview is to develop an understanding of the ways young men (aged 11–14) conceptualise and experience themselves and others and the world around them by encouraging them to provide narrative style accounts of their lives. In developing a list of categories and questions our intention was not to standardise each interview by prescribing the exact questions and the order in which we would ask them. How the interview proceeds will depend very much on the sorts of responses that the particular interviewee/s give. We would hope to cover the categories or fields we have identified, but the links between these are open, and the order in which they are addressed, as well as the time spent on each one, will be specific to each interview. In one interview, for example, the interviewee/s may introduce issues around ethnicity and in another issues around the media when discussing relations with other boys. The questions for each category are ones which we might ask, but which ones we ask, whether we modify them or ask different and related questions again depends on the responses of particular interviewee/s. The following list of categories and questions, then, should be seen as an aide memoire for us reminding us of the areas we want to cover and the sorts of questions we want to put to our interviewees, not a list of all the questions which we will ask all the boys in the same order. A key aim of the project is to be boy centred, and this, we hope is exemplified in the interview procedure which allows boys to influence the direction and pace of the interviews.

Aide-mémoire

Details
Do you live with parent/s, guardian/s?
Do you have brother/s or sister/s? If so, how old are they? Are you like them? Your age?
What jobs do your parent/s, guardian/s do?
Which school do you go to?
Where do you live? Do you live near school? What kind of house do you live in?

General self-description
Could you tell me three things you think are important about yourself?

Media
What are your favourite TV programmes? What do you like about them? Do you talk about them? With whom? If you were making a TV programme for boys of your age, what would you include in it?
Do you watch films/videos? What do you like? Why?
Do you play computer games? What kinds?
What do you like about them?
Do you read comics or magazines? What stories or articles do you like most? If you could design a comic or magazine for boys of your age what things would you put in it? Do you read magazines specifically for men? Do you ever read magazines or comics for young women or girls? Do you enjoy these?
Do you read books? What do you read and why?

Identificatory figures
Are there some people you admire? Are there some people you wouldn't like to be like?

Relationships and attitudes to girls
Do you tend to spend most of your time with boys or girls?
What difference does it make being with girls?
Do you have friends who are girls? Do you do the same things with girls as with boys who are friends? Is there a difference between girls who are friends and girl friends?

Do you think girls are more emotional than boys? How do they show it?

Are there tough girls?

Do you think everyone is treated fairly at school? Do teachers prefer girls? How do you know? Have you ever thought girls have it easier than boys?

What kinds of names do boys and girls get called? For what?

Defining characteristics of a boy

If you were to describe boys to someone from another planet who had never experienced boys before, what would you say?

What difference does it make being a boy?

Ethnicity

What ethnic group do you think you belong to?

Do you see some boys as belonging to a different ethnic group to you? How would you describe their background? Do you go around with boys from this/these backgrounds? Why/why not? Do you do the same things with them as boys from your 'own' ethnic background?

Can you imagine having a girlfriend from a different group?

Do you think boys are treated differently because of where their parents come from? Is your ethnic background important to you? What difference does it make being a boy from this background? Are you pleased you are from this background? Have you ever thought you'd not like to be?

Are there things you dislike about boys from other ethnic and cultural backgrounds? Are there things you admire about boys from other ethnic and cultural backgrounds?

Relations with boys

I wonder if you could tell me how you get on with other boys, for instance at school or with friends you see outside?

What do you and your friends like doing together?

What kinds of things do you talk about?

Are there different kinds of boys?

What kinds of boys do you mix with?

Are some boys popular? How do they get to be popular?

Do teachers prefer some boys to other boys? What makes you think so?

Do some boys get picked on by other boys? For doing what?

Does anyone have a girlfriend/boyfriend yet in your class? What difference does it make having a girlfriend?

Are you happy about the class you're in at school? Would you like to be in another class?

Tell me the kind of things you and your friends find funny? (Do boys and girls laugh at the same things?)

Are there things you talk about only with boy friends?

Social class

Do you feel you belong to a particular social class?

Do you see some boys as belonging to a different social class than you?

What makes you recognise someone as belonging to the same social class as yourself?

What difference does it make being a boy of your class?

Would you say your friends are mainly from the same class as you? Do you have friends from other social classes?

What are the good/bad things about being in your class? Ever felt you'd like to be in aother class? What difference would it make?

Relations with adults

Generally speaking, how do you get on with adults?

Are there adult men/women who are important in your life?

Do you talk about and do some things with your mother/stepmother and not with your father/stepfather? What?

Do you talk about and do some things with your father/stepfather and not with your mother/stepmother? What?

Are there things you talk about with your friends and not with your parent/s or stepparent/s?

Are there things you talk about with your parent/s or stepparent/ and not with your friends?

Emotions

Can you think back to a time when you felt really happy? Did you talk to anyone about how you felt? Who?

Can you think of a time when you felt worried or under pressure? Did you talk to anyone about how you felt? Who?

Do other people sometimes tell you about their worries? If so, who?

What do you think are some of the things which boys get most anxious about?

Do you think it's alright for boys to talk about their worries or do they have to keep quiet about them? If so, why?

Do some boys you know ever get violent? Why? What about you? Do you ever get violent? If so, about what? What do you do?

Change and future orientation

What are the things you're most looking forward to when you get older? What are the things you're least looking forward to when you get older?

What do you imagine you'll be doing when you get to your parents/step-parents' age? What kind of person do you think you'll be? What job/s do you want/expect to get?

Do you want to be single, married live with another person/people? Would you like to have children? (Sons/daughters)

How do you think you have changed in the last few years?

How do you imagine you'll change in the next few years?

Photo exercise

The interviewee/s are asked to select from 20 different large photographs of boys and/or men in various situations (a) 2 which show someone who is most like them, (b) 2 which show someone who is least like them, and (c) 2 which show someone they would most like to be like. They are asked to give reasons for their choices.

5   Protocol for individual interviews with girls

As with the questions for boys this is not prescriptive. Rather it is an aide memoire, identifying the topics which need to be covered and kinds of questions which might be put to the girls. Again the pace and direction of the interview is dependent on the responses of the particular girl being interviewed.

Family
Do you live with parents/guardians? What do they do? Do you have brothers/sisters? How do you get on with them? How do you and your brothers'/sisters get on with your parents? Is your mum/dad the same or different with you and your brothers/sisters? Would you have liked to have had a brother/sister? Do your brothers/sisters do more or less work around the house than you? Do you play games with your brothers/sisters? If so what? Do you do similar or different things with your mum and dad?

Definition of a boy
I wonder if you could define a boy or say what a boy is to someone who had never experienced boys before, say to someone from another planet.

Relations with boys
Do you mix much with boys? If not why not? If so when do you mix? What sorts of things do you do with boys and girls – similar or different? What's it like being with boys – is it similar to or different from being with girls? Are you different or similar with boys and girls? Are there things you can say to a girl that you can't say to a boy, or things you can say to a boy that you can't say to a girl? Do you like being in a mixed school or would you prefer to be in a single-sex school? Do you have boys as friends? If not why not? If so how did you get friendly with them. What do you like about them? Are the boys you're friendly with like other boys or different?

Differences between boys
Are all boys much the same or can you say there are different kinds of boys? If so how do boys differ? What kinds of boys do you like or dislike?

Ethnicity
Are boys from different 'races' different or much the same? Are there any things you like or dislike about boys from particular 'races'? With boys you mix with, what 'race' are they?

Comparing boys and girls
Some people say boys and girls are similar, and some that they're different. What do you think? If they're different, how? Some people say boys are more

mature than girls and some that girls are more mature. What do you think? Do you do things which boys or girls tend to do?

Development
Have boys of your age changed much from what they were like a few years ago or are they much the same? If they've changed how? What about girls? Have they changed? Have you changed? Do girls now relate to boys differently than they used to in primary or just the same? Do they mix more or less or the same?

Boyfriends
Do you have a boyfriend? If so what's he like? What's it like having a boyfriend? Do you imagine having a boyfriend in the future? Why/why not? What would you like him to be like? (Looks, aged, ethnicity, character.)

Boys relations with teachers
Do teachers treat boys and girls the same or differently? Are teachers easier on girls than on boys or boys than on girls.

Good and bad things about being a boy
What are the good or bad things (if any) about being a boy.

Identity as a girl
I was wondering whether you preferred being a girl than a boy or if ever you'd like to be a boy.

Photo exercise
Describing what was going on in photos featuring boys and men and whether they liked or didn't like the boys/men.

Reflections on the interview
How did you find the interview? Was it what you expected it to be like? Do you think this interview would have been much the same or different if I had been a man.

References

Anthias, F. and Yuval-Davis, N. (1992) *Racialised Boundaries: Race, Gender, Colour and Class and the Anti-Racist Struggle*. London: Routledge.

Arnot, M., David, M. and Weiner, G. (1999) *Closing the Gender Gap: Postwar Education and Social Change*. Cambridge: Polity Press.

Askew, S. and Ross, C. (1988) *Boys Don't Cry: Boys and Sexism in Education*. Milton Keynes: Open University Press.

Back, L. (1990) 'Racist Name Calling and Developing Anti-Racist Initiatives in Youth Work', Research paper in ethnic relations, no. 14, University of Warwick.

Back, L. (1994) 'The "White Negro" revisited', in A. Cornwall and N. Lindisfarne (eds), *Dislocating Masculinity*. London: Routledge.

Back, L. (1996) *New Ethnicities and Urban Culture*. London: UCL Press.

Benjamin, J. (1995) 'Sameness and Difference: Toward an "Over-Inclusive" Theory of Gender Development', in A. Elliot and S. Frosh (eds) *Psychoanalysis in Contexts*. London: Routledge.

Benjamin, J. (1998) *Shadow of the Other: Intersubjectivity and Gender in Psychoanalysis*. New York: Routledge.

Berlotti, E. (1975) *Little Girls*. London: Writers and Readers.

Billig, M. (1991) *Ideology and Opinions*. London: Sage.

Billig, M. (1992) *Talking of the Royal Family*. London: Routledge.

Blatchford, P. (1998) *Social Life in a School*. London: Falmer Press.

Bleach, K. (1999) 'Why the Likely Lads Lag Behind', in K. Bleach (ed.), *Raising Boys' Achievement in Schools*. Stoke-on-Trent: Trentham.

Bly, R. (1990) *Iron John*. Brisbane: Element.

Bohan, J. (1997) 'Regarding Gender: Essentialism, Constructionism, and Feminist Psychology', in M. Gergen and S. Davis (eds), *Toward a New Psychology of Gender*. London: Routledge.

Boulton, M. and Smith, P. (1992) 'Ethnic Preferences and Perceptions among Asian and White British School Children', *Social Development*, 1: 55–66.

Brown, H. (1995) *Expectations for the Future: An Investigation into the Self Esteem of 13 and 14 Year Old Girls and Boys*. London: Health Education Authority.

Bruner, J. (1990) *Acts of Meaning*. Cambridge, MA: Harvard University Press.

Butler, J. (1990) *Gender Trouble*. Cambridge: Polity Press.

Butler, J. (1993) *Bodies that Matter*. New York: Routledge.

Butler, J (1997) 'Gender as Performance: An Interview with Judith Butler for *Radical Philosophy*, by Osborne, P. and Segal, L.', in K. Woodward (ed.), *Identity and Difference*. Milton Keynes: Open University Press.

Canaan, J. (1991) 'Is "Doing Nothing" Just Boys' Play? Integrating Feminist and Cultural Studies Perspectives on Working Class Masculinities', in S. Franklin,

C. Lury and J. Stacey (eds), *Off-Centre: Feminism and Cultural Studies*. London: Routledge.

Chodorow, N. (1978) *The Reproduction of Mothering: Psychoanalysis and the Sociology of Gender*. London: University of California Press.

Cohen, M. (1998) ' "A Habit of Healthy Idleness": Boys' Underachievement in Historical Perspective', in D. Epstein, J. Elwood, V. Hey and J. Maw (eds), *Failing Boys?, Issues in Gender and Achievement*. Buckingham: Open University Press.

Cohen, P. (1997) *Rethinking the Youth Question*. Basingstoke: Macmillan – now Palgrave.

Collison, M. (1996) 'In Search of the High Life: Drugs, Crime Masculinities and Consumption', *British Journal of Criminology*, **36**: 428–44.

Connell, R. (1987) *Gender and Power: Society, the Person and Sexual Politics*. Stanford, CA: Stanford University Press.

Connell, R. (1989) 'Cool Guys, Swots and Wimps: the Interplay of Masculinity and Education', *Oxford Review of Education*, **15**: 291–303.

Connell, R. (1995) *Masculinities*. Cambridge: Polity Press.

Connell, R. (1996) 'Teaching the Boys: New Research on Masculinity, and Gender Strategies for Schools', *Teachers College Record*, **98**: 206–35.

Connolly, P. (1994) 'All Lads Together?: Racism, Masculinity and Multicultural/ Anti Racist Strategies in a Primary School', *International Studies in Sociology of Education*, **4**(2).

Connolly, P. (1995) 'Boys will be Boys?: Racism, Sexuality and the Construction of Masculine Identities among Infant Boys', in J. Holland and M. Blair (eds), *Equality and Difference: Debates and Issues in Feminist Research and Pedagogy*. Clevedon: Multilingual Matters.

Connolly, P. (1998) *Racism, Gender Identities and Young Children*. London: Routledge.

Cornwall, A. and Lindisfarne, N. (eds) (1995) *Dislocating Masculinity*. London: Routledge.

Davies, B. (1997) Constructing and Deconstructing Masculinities through Critical Literacy', in C. Griffin and S. Lees (eds) Special Issue 'Masculinities in Education', *Gender and Education*, **9**: 9–30.

Dijk, T. van (1992) 'Discourse and the Denial of Racism', *Discourse and Society*, **3**: 87–118.

Duncan, N. (1999) *Sexual Bullying*. London: Routledge.

Eder, D., Evans, C. and Parker, S. (1995) *School Talk*. New Brunswick: Rutgers University Press.

Edley, N. and Wetherell, M. (1995) *Men in Perspective – Practice, Power and Identity*. London: Harvester Wheatsheaf.

Edley, N. and Wetherell M. (1997) 'Jockeying for Position: The Construction of Masculine Identities', *Discourse and Society*, **8**: 203–17.

Epstein, D. (1997) 'Boyz Own Stories: Masculinities and Sexualities in Schools', in C. Griffin and S. Lees (eds), Special Issue 'Masculinities in Education', *Gender and Education*, **9**: 105–14.

Epstein, D., Elwood, J., Hey, V. and Maw, J. (eds) (1998) *Failing Boys?, Issues in Gender and Achievement*. Buckingham: Open University Press.

Epstein, D., Kehily, M., Mac an Ghaill, M. and Redman, P. (forthcoming) 'Boys and Girls Come Out to Play: Constructions of Gender in School Playgrounds', *Men and Masculinities.*

Farrington, D. (1995) 'The Development of Offending and Antisocial Behaviour', *Journal of Child Psychology and Psychiatry*, **36**: 929–64.

Francis, B. (1998) 'Oppositional Positions: Children's Construction of Gender in Talk and Role Plays Based on Adult Occupation', *Educational Research*, **40**: 31–43.

Francis, B. (1999) 'Lads, Lasses and (New) Labour: 14–16 Year Old Students' Responses to the "Laddish" Behaviour and Boys' Underachievement Debate', *British Journal of Sociology of Education*, **20**: 357–73.

Frosh, S. (1994) *Sexual Difference, Masculinity and Psychoanalysis.* London and New York: Routledge.

Frosh, S. (1997) 'Screaming under the Bridge: Masculinity, Rationality and Psychotherapy', in J. Ussher (ed.), *Body Talk.* London: Routledge.

Frosh, S. (2000) Intimacy, Gender and Abuse: The Construction of Masculinities', in U. McCluskey and C. Hooper (eds), *Psychodynamic Perspectives on Abuse: The Cost of Fear.* London: Jessica Kingsley.

Frosh, S., Phoenix, A. and Pattman, R. (2000) ' "But it's Racism I Really Hate": Young Masculinities, Racism and Psychoanalysis'. *Psychoanalytic Psychology*, **17**: 225–42.

Gilbert, R. and Gilbert, P. (1998) *Masculinity goes to School.* London: Routledge.

Gillborn, D. (1990) *'Race', Ethnicity and Education: Teaching and Learning in Multi-Ethnic Schools.* London: Unwin-Hyman/Routledge.

Gilligan, C. (1995) 'The Centrality of Relationship in Psychological Development: A Puzzle, some Evidence and a Theory', in M. Blair and J. Holland with S. Sheldon (eds), *Identity and Diversity: Gender and the Experience.* Clevedon: Multilingual Matters.

Griffin, C. (1985) *Typical Girls? Young Women from School to the Job Market.* London: Routledge and Kegan Paul.

Griffin, C. (1997) 'Troubled Teens: Managing Disorders of Transition and Consumption', *Feminist Review*, **55**: 4–21.

Griffin, C. (2000) 'Discourses of Crisis and Loss: Analysing the "Underachieving Boys" Debate', *Journal of Youth Studies*, **3**(2).

Hall, S. (1992) 'The Question of Cultural Identity', in S. Hall, D. Held and T. MacGrew, *Modernity and its Futures.* Cambridge: Polity Press.

Hall, S. and Jefferson, T. (eds) (1975) *Resistance through Rituals.* London: Hutchinson.

Haywood, C. and Mac an Ghaill, M. (1997) ' "A man in the Making": Sexual Masculinities within Changing Training Cultures', *The Sociological Review*, 576–90.

Hebdige, R. (1979) *Subculture: The Meaning of Style.* London: Methuen.

Hewitt, R. (1986) *White Talk Black Talk: Inter-Racial Friendships and Communication amongst Adolescents.* Cambridge: Cambridge University Press.

Hewitt, R. (1996) *Routes of Racism: The Social Basis of Racist Action.* Stoke on Trent: Trentham Books.

Holland, J., Ramazanoglu, C. and Sharpe, S. (1993) *Wimp or Gladiator: Contradictions in Acquiring Masculine Sexuality*. London: Tufnell Press.

Holland, J., Ramazanoglu, C., Sharpe, S. and Thomson, R. (1998) *The Male in the Head; Young People, Heterosexuality and Power*. London: Tufnell Press.

Hollway, W. (1984) 'Gender Difference and the Production of Subjectivity', in J. Henriques, W. Hollway, C. Unwin, C. Venn and V. Walkerdine, *Changing the Subject*. London: Methuen.

Hollway, W. (1989) *Subjectivity and Method in Psychology*. London: Sage.

Hollway, W. and Jefferson, T. (1995) 'The Risk Society in an Age of Anxiety', Paper presented to the 1995 British Criminological Conference, Loughborough University.

Hollway, W. and Jefferson, T. (2000) *Doing Qualitative Research Differently*. London: Sage.

Jackson, D. (1990) *Unmasking Masculinity: A Critical Autobiography*. London: Unwin Hyman.

Jackson, D. (1998) 'Breaking out of the Binary Trap: Boys' Underachievement, Schooling and Gender Relations', in D. Epstein, J. Elwood, V. Hey and J. Maw (eds), *Failing Boys?, Issues in Gender and Achievement*. Buckingham: Open University Press.

Jackson, D. (2000) 'The Fear of Being Seen as White Losers: White, Working Class Masculinities and the Killing of Stephen Lawrence', unpublished paper.

Johnson, R. (1997a) 'Contested Borders, Contingent Lives: An Introduction', in D. Steinberg, D. Epstein and R. Johnson (eds), *Border Patrols: Policing the Boundaries of Heterosexuality*. London: Cassell.

Johnson, R. (1997b) 'Scandalous Oppositions: Cultural Criticism and Sexual Regulation in Contemporary Britain', Inaugural Lecture, Nottingham Trent University, 25 June.

Jukes, A. (1993) *Why Men Hate Women*. London: Free Association Books.

Katz, A. and Buchanan, A. (1999) *Leading Lads*. London: Topman.

Kehily, M. (1999) 'Understanding Heterosexualities: Masculinities, Embodiment and Schooling', unpublished paper presented at Voices in Gender and Education Conference, University of Warwick.

Kehily, M. and Nyak, A. (1997) ' "Lads and Laughter": Humour and the Production of Heterosexual Hierarchies', *Gender and Education*, **9**: 69–87.

Kenway, J. and Willis, S. with Blackmore, J. and Rennie, L. (1998) *Answering Back: Girls, Boys and Feminism in Schools*. London: Routledge.

Kessler, S., Ashenden, D., Connell, R. and Dowsett, G. (1985) 'Gender Relations in Secondary Schooling', *Sociology of Education*, **58**: 34–48.

Kitzinger, C. and Wilkinson, S. (1996) 'Theorising Representing the Other', in S. Wilkinson and C. Kitzinger (eds), *Representing the Other*. London: Sage.

Kryger, N. (1998) 'Teachers' Understanding and Emotions in Relation to the Creation of Boys' Masculine Identity', in Y. Katz and I. Menezes (eds), *Affective Education: A comparative view*. London: Cassell.

Laberge, S. and Albert, M. (1999) 'Conceptions of Masculinity and of Gender Transgressions in Sport among Adolescent Boys: Hegemony, Contestation and Social Class Dynamic', *Men and Masculinities*, **1**: 253–67.

Lees, S. (1986) *Losing Out: Sexuality and Adolescent Girls*. London: Hutchinson.

Lloyd, T. (1990) *Work with Boys*. Leicester: National Youth Bureau.

Mac an Ghaill, M. (1988) *Young, Gifted and Black: Student Teacher Relations in the Schooling of Black Youth*. Milton Keynes: Open University Press.

Mac an Ghaill, M. (1994) *The Making of Men: Masculinities, Sexualities and Schooling*. Buckingham: Open University Press.

Mahony, P. (1985) *Schools for Boys? Co-Education Reassessed*. London: Hutchinson.

Majors, R. (1990) 'Cool Pose: Black Masculinity and Sports', in M. Messner and D. Sabo (eds), *Sport, Men and the Gender Order*. Illinois: Human Kinetics Books.

Majors, R. and Billson, J. (1992) *Cool Pose: The Dilemmas of Black Manhood in America*. New York: Lexington.

Messerschmidt, J. (1994) 'Schooling, Masculinities and Youth Crime', in T. Newburn and E. Stanko (eds), *Just Boys Doing Business?* London: Routledge.

Messner, M. and Sabo, D. (eds) (1990) *Sport, Men and the Gender Order*. Illinois: Human Kinetics Books.

Miles, S. (1998) *Consumerism – As a Way of Life*. London: Sage.

Morgan, D. (1996) 'Learning to Be a Man: Dilemmas and Contradictions of Masculine Experience', in C. Luke (ed.), *Feminisms and Pedagogies of Everyday Life*. New York: SUNY.

Murphy, P. and Elwood, J. (1998) 'Gendered Learning Outside School: Influences on Achievement', in D. Epstein, J. Elwood, V. Hey, and J. Maw (eds), *Failing Boys?, Issues in Gender and Achievement*. Buckingham: Open University Press.

Nayak, A. (1999) ' "Pale Warriors": Skinhead Culture and the Embodiment of White Masculinities', in A. Brah, M. Hickman and M. Mac an Ghaill (eds) *Thinking Identities, Ethnicity, Racism and Culture*. Basingstoke: Macmillan – now Palgrave.

Nayak, A. and Kehily, M. (1996) 'Playing it Straight: Masculinities, Homophobias and Schooling', *Journal of Gender Studies* 5(2): 211–30.

Noble, C. and Bradford, W. (2000) *Getting it Right for Boys... and Girls*. London: Routledge.

O'Donnell, M. and Sharpe, S. (2000) *Uncertain Masculinities: Youth, Ethnicity and Class in Contemporary Britain*. London: Routledge.

Ofsted/EOC (1996) *The Gender Divide: Performance Differences between Boys and Girls at School*. London: HMSO.

Ogilvy, C., Boath, E., Cheyne W., Jahoda, G. and Schaffer, H.R. (1992) 'Staff–Child Interaction Styles in Multi-Ethnic Nursery Schools', *British Journal of Developmental Psychology*, 10: 85–97.

Pattman, R. (1991) 'Sex Education and the Liberal Paradigm', unpublished PhD thesis, Birmingham University.

Pattman, R., Frosh, S. and Phoenix, A. (1998) 'Lads Machos and Others', *Journal of Youth Studies*, 1: 125–42.

Phillips, A. (1998) 'How Boys Create Barriers to Learning: Challenging the Anti-Learning Culture in School: An Action Research Project', unpublished paper. Goldsmiths College.

Pollack, W. (1998) *Real Boys: Rescuing our Sons from the Myths of Boyhood*. New York: Henry Holt.

Potter, J. and Wetherell, M. (1987) *Discourse and Social Psychology: Beyond Attitudes and Behaviour*. London: Sage.

Prendergast, S. and Forrest, S. (1997) 'Hieroglyphs of the Heterosexual: Learning about Gender in School', in L. Segal (ed.) *New Sexual Agendas*. Basingstoke: Macmillan – now Palgrave.

Raphael Reed, L. (1999) 'Troubling Boys and Disturbing Discourses on Masculinity and Schooling: A Feminist Exploration of Current Debates and Interventions Concerning Boys in School', *Gender and Education*, **11**: 93–110.

Rattansi, A. and Phoenix, A. (1997) 'Rethinking Youth Identities: Modernist and Postmodernist Frameworks', in J. Bynner, L. Chisholm and A. Furlong (eds), *Youth, Citizenship and Social Change in a European Context*. Aldershot: Avebury.

Reay, D. (1999) 'Sugar and Spice and All Things Nice?: Gender Discourses and Girls' Cultures in the Primary Classroom', Paper presented at conference on Gender and Education, University of Warwick.

Redman, P. (1998) 'Romantic Heroes: Schooling, the Unconscious and the Narrative Production of Heterosexual Maculinities', Paper presented at Gendering the Millennium, International Conference, University of Dundee.

Redman, P. and Mac an Ghaill, M. (1997) 'Educating Peter: The Making of a History Man', in L. Steinberg, D. Epstein and R. Johnson (eds), *Border Patrols: Policing the Boundaries of Heterosexuality*. London: Cassell.

Renold, E. (2000) ' "Coming Out": Gender, (Hetero) Sexuality and the Primary School', *Gender and Education*, **12**: 309–26.

Rodkin, P., Farmer, T., Pearl, R. and van Acker, R. (2000) 'Heterogeneity of Popular Boys: Antisocial and Prosocial Configurations', *Development Psychology*, **36**: 14–24.

Rudberg, M. (1999) 'Boy Bodies – The Question of Intimacy', Paper presented at a seminar on Masculinity and Boyhood Studies, The Royal Danish School of Educational Studies, Copenhagen, 19 December.

Rutter, M. (1997) *Psychosocial Disturbance in Young People*. Cambridge: Cambridge University Press.

Salmon, P. (1998) *Life at School: Education and Psychology*. London: Constable.

Scott, J. (1992) 'Experience', in J. Butler and J. Scott (eds), *Feminists Theorize the Political*. New York: Routledge.

Segal, L. (1990) *Slow Motion: Changing Masculinities, Changing Men*. London: Virago.

Segal, L. (1993) 'Changing Men: Masculinities in Context', *Theory and Society*, **22**: 625–41.

Seidler, V. (1989) *Rediscovering Masculinity: Reason, Language and Sexuality*. London: Routledge.

Seidler, V. (1994) *Unreasonable Men*. London: Routledge.

Sewell, T. (1997) *Black Masculinities and Schooling: How Black Boys Survive Modern Schooling*. Stoke on Trent: Trentham Books.

Skeggs, B. (1992) 'Paul Willis, Learning to Labour', in M. Barker and A. Breezer (eds), *Reading into Cultural Studies*. London: Routledge.

Skelton, C. (1998) 'Feminism and Research into Masculinities and Schooling', *Gender and Education*, **10**: 217–27.

Sonuga-Barke, E., Minocha, K., Taylor, E. and Sandberg, S. (1993) 'Inter-Ethnic Bias in teachers' ratings of Childhood Hyperactivity', *British Journal of Developmental Psychology*, **11**: 187–200.

Spender, D. (1983) *Invisible Women*. London: Writers and Readers.

Storm-Mathisen, A. (1998) *Buying Pressure... What is That? A Preliminary Project on the Meaning of Clothing among 13 Year olds*. Lysaker: SIFO.

Talonen, T. (1998) ' "Everyone at School Thinks I am a Nerd..." – Schoolboys' Fights and Ambivalence about Masculinities', *Young*, **6**: 4–18.

Thomson, R. (1996) 'First Sex: Gendered Experience, Expression and Explanation', Paper presented at the New Psychologies conference, Scotland, June.

Thomson, R., McGrellis, S., Holland, J., Henderson, S. and Sharpe, S. (1998) 'From "Peter André's Six Pack" to "I do knees" – the Body in Young People's Moral Discourse', Paper presented at the British Sociological Association Conference, University of Edinburgh.

Thorne, B. (1993) *Gender Play: Girls and Boys in School*. Buckingham: Open University Press.

Tizard, B. and Phoenix, A. (1993) *Black, White or Mixed Race*. London: Routledge.

Troyna, B. and Hatcher, R. (1992) *Racism in Children's Lives'*. London: Routledge.

Vizard, E., Monck, E. and Misch, P. (1995) 'Child and Adolescent Sex Abuse Perpetrators', *Journal of Child Psychology and Psychiatry*, **36**: 731–56.

Waddell, M. (1998) *Inside Lives*. London: Duckworth.

Walker, B. (1997) ' "You Learn from your Mates, Don't You?": Young People's Conversations about Sex as a Basis for Informal Peer Education', *Youth and Social Policy Issue*, no. 57.

Walker, B. and Kushner, S. (1997) 'Understanding Boys' Sexual Health Education and its Implications for Attitude Change', Final report of research funded by E.S.R.C., Centre for Applied Research in Education, University of East Anglia.

Walker, B. and Kushner, S. (1999) 'The Building Site: An Educational Approach to Masculine Identity', *Journal of Youth Studies*, **2**.

Walkerdine, V. (1981) 'Sex, Power and Pedagogy', *Screen Education*, **38**: 14–25.

Walkerdine, V. (1988) *The Mastery of Reason*. London: Routledge.

Walkerdine, V. (1990) *Schoolgirl Fictions*. London: Verso.

Walkerdine, V. (1997) *Daddy's Girl: Young Girls and Popular Culture*. Basingstoke: Macmillan – now Palgrave.

Wetherell, M. and Edley, N. (1998) 'Gender Practices: Steps in the Analysis of Men and Masculinities', in K. Henwood, C. Griffin and A. Phoenix (eds), *Standpoints and Differences: Essays in the Practice of Feminist Psychology*. London: Sage.

Wetherell, M. and Edley, N. (1999) 'Negotiating Hegemonic Masculinity: Imaginary and Psycho-Discursive Practices', *Feminism and Psychology*, **9**: 335–56.

Whitson, D. (1990) 'Sport in the Social Construction of Masculinity', in M. Messner and D. Sabo (eds), *Sport, Men and the Gender Order*. Illinois: Human Kinetics Books.

Widdicombe, S. and Wooffitt, S. (1995) *The Language of Youth Subcultures: Social Identity in Action*. London: Harvester Wheatsheaf.

Wight, D. (1994) 'Boys' Thoughts and Talk about Sex in a Working Class Locality of Glasgow', *The Sociological Review*, **42**.

Willis, P. (1977) *Learning to Labour*. Aldershot: Gower.

Willis, P., Jones, S., Canaan, J. and Hurd, G. (1990) *Common Culture: Symbolic Work at Play in the Everyday Cultures of the Young*. Milton Keynes: Open University Press.

Wood, J. (1984) 'Groping Towards Sexism: Boys' Sex Talk', in A. McRobbie and M. Nava (eds), *Gender and Generation*. London: Macmillan – now Palgrave.

Woodward, K. (1997) 'Concepts of identity and difference', in K. Woodward (ed.), *Identity and Difference*. London: Sage/Open University.

Yates, L. (1997) 'Gender Equity and the Boys' Debate: What Sort of Challenge Is It?, *British Journal of Sociology of Education*, **18**: 337–47.

Index